W9-BLD-916

MY GIRLS

YEADON PUBLIC LIBRARY
809 LONGACRE BLVD.
YEADON, PA 19050

MY GIRLS

A LIFETIME *with*
CARRIE AND DEBBIE

TODD FISHER
WITH LINDSAY HARRISON

WM
WILLIAM MORROW
An Imprint of HarperCollins*Publishers*

791.43
FIS

Passages from *Wishful Drinking* and *Shockaholic* by Carrie Fisher are reprinted here with permission from the Estate of Carrie Fisher and Simon & Schuster.

The names and identifying characteristics of some of the individuals featured throughout this book have been changed to protect their privacy.

All photos courtesy of the author and the Estate of Debbie Reynolds unless otherwise noted.

MY GIRLS. Copyright © 2018 by TD Productions LLC. All rights reserved. Printed in the United States of America. No part of this book may be used or reproduced in any manner whatsoever without written permission except in the case of brief quotations embodied in critical articles and reviews. For information, address HarperCollins Publishers, 195 Broadway, New York, NY 10007.

HarperCollins books may be purchased for educational, business, or sales promotional use. For information, please email the Special Markets Department at SPsales@harpercollins.com.

FIRST EDITION

Library of Congress Cataloging-in-Publication Data has been applied for.

ISBN 978-0-06-279231-0

18 19 20 21 22   DIX/LSC   10 9 8 7 6 5 4 3 2 1

To all of you

who loved my girls

as much as I did

CONTENTS

INTRODUCTION

For as long as I can remember, people have asked me what it's like to be the child of famous parents. And for as long as I can remember, I've wondered how I could possibly know what it's like *not* to. After all, I have nothing to compare it to. It just was and is my reality, my "normal," a circumstance I didn't create or question or analyze. I watched *Father Knows Best* and *Leave It to Beaver* as a child, and I knew things weren't like that at my house. But I never thought they were normal and we weren't.

Another popular question is "What's it like growing up in your mom's shadow?" A time came when my sister Carrie would bristle at that question. Not me. I happen to think that growing up in the shadow of Debbie Reynolds was a safe, beautiful, privileged place to be, and I thrived in it. According to her, I came into this world smiling. I'm not surprised. I'm sure I knew what a fortunate life I had ahead of me—not an entitled life, certainly not a perfect, pain-free life, just a fortunate one. My family, my life, and my experiences are gifts as far as I'm concerned, gifts that could be taken away if I stop being grateful for them and start taking them for granted.

I've started writing this memoir several times, over a lot of years, but it took on a new urgency in December of 2016, when my sister and my mother suddenly died a day apart. Now it's not just a memoir anymore. It's a long love letter and thank-you note to the two most pivotal, extraordinary women I've ever known. It was hard-wired in me from the day I was born that they were "my girls," and they always will be. As the family archivist by default,

I owe my girls a thorough, honest, unapologetic account of the life I've lived with them and without them, because neither of them would have tolerated anything less from me.

And so in their honor, here, through my eyes, is the true, no-holds-barred story of Debbie, Carrie, and me.

813 GREENWAY DRIVE

Me and My Girls.

On September 26, 1955, twenty-three-year-old movie star Debbie Reynolds married twenty-seven-year-old teen-idol crooner Eddie Fisher. The couple instantly became America's Sweethearts, mobbed by the press and hordes of screaming, swooning, adoring fans wherever they went. The birth of their daughter, Carrie Frances Fisher, on October 21, 1956, made headlines around the world. They were darling. They were envied. They seemed almost too good to be true.

Which, of course, they were.

In the late spring of 1957 Eddie gave a concert at the Palladium in London. Debbie flew there to meet him. It speaks volumes about the state of their marriage by then that Debbie brought along her best friend from childhood, Jeanette Johnson, so she'd have someone to talk to.

From London, Eddie, Debbie, and Jeanette headed on to Europe to meet super-producer Mike Todd and his impossibly gorgeous movie-star bride Elizabeth Taylor, who were on an extended honeymoon. Mike was Eddie's closest friend, and Debbie and Elizabeth had gone to school together as teenagers on the MGM Studios lot. Eddie was Mike's best man at their wedding. Debbie was Elizabeth's matron of honor.

The five of them spent a few days together at a magnificent villa in the South of France. Debbie and Jeanette had made plans to head on to Spain and leave Eddie with Mike and Elizabeth, to give Eddie the space Debbie had learned he needed and apparently preferred. Debbie described her last night at the villa in her 1988 book, *Debbie: My Life*:

> Neither Eddie or I drank in those days, but at dinner I asked the butler to bring him a beer. Eddie was in a great mood whenever he was with the Todds, and the beer loosened him up more. He was acting as if I were actually his wife, even showing affection. After dinner, Jeanette went up to bed. The rest of us moved from the dinner table to the library. I ordered Eddie a second bottle of beer. The ice melted entirely.
>
> He got drunk on two beers that night. Not only that, but he became very amorous. Elizabeth and Mike had put him in the mood, or he forgot whom he was with. It was a happy time with all of us entertaining each other with stories and jokes. Eventually they went

off to make love and I turned to Eddie and said: "Why don't we do the same?" And so we did.

I had wanted another child as soon after Carrie as possible. I'd hoped she would have a brother who would be as close in age to her as I am to my brother Bill. Bill was always my strength and my ally when I was growing up. He still is to this day. I wanted Carrie to have that too.

At that stage of my marriage to Eddie, he wasn't interested in sleeping with me. There was less and less opportunity for me to get pregnant.

I just remember praying to God that night that I would be pregnant. We had a good time and there weren't many of those. . . .

I just knew when I left that I was pregnant. I couldn't have known, but I knew.

Nine months later, Debbie Reynolds gave birth to me. They named me Todd Emanuel—Todd for Mike Todd and Emanuel after Manny Sacks, the recording executive who started Eddie on his record career. Mike and Elizabeth came to see me, and Mike was thrilled to have his best friend's son named after him.

"For the first time in our marriage, I finally felt very happy and secure," my mother would later write.

Unfortunately, it didn't last. On March 22, 1958, when I wasn't quite four weeks old, Mike Todd was killed in a plane crash in New Mexico. About a month later, my father left my mother for his best friend's widow, Elizabeth Taylor. As my sister Carrie described it decades later, in a book called *Wishful Drinking*, "My father flew to Elizabeth's side, gradually making his way slowly to her front."

Debbie was devastated. "Numb," as she described it. "Blank . . . as if I were alone on the top of a mountain, like floating in space."

It was one of Hollywood's biggest, most notorious scandals. The world was stunned. Eddie and Elizabeth were vilified. Eddie was declared a philandering, opportunistic loser, and Elizabeth was labeled a bad-girl, home-wrecking slut. Debbie, the good girl, the innocent, unsuspecting victim and single mom, was globally embraced with love and sympathy.

Carrie and I were too young to remember the insane tabloid feeding frenzy. But I do have one flash of a visual and emotional memory in the aftermath of our parents' breakup that's as vivid to me today as it was the morning it happened. Mom and Carrie and I were still in the Conway Drive house we'd lived in with Eddie before he left. I was maybe two years old, sitting on the floor, happily playing with my toys. Carrie, age four, was standing on the couch, staring out the window at the street, watching for our father, who was supposed to pick us up for a visitation. He never came.

I couldn't have cared less—you can't miss what you've never had, after all, and our father was a virtual stranger to me. But I knew Carrie was upset, and I didn't like it that this "Eddie" person, this "Dad," had made my sister cry.

My childhood memories don't really come into sharp focus until we were living at 813 Greenway Drive in Beverly Hills. When you're a child, your home is your universe, and my universe on Greenway Drive was heaven on earth.

My mom was fun and funny and playful and smart and beautiful. It was one of the core facts of my life that she and I adored each other, that we'd had a rare connection from the moment I started growing in her belly. She went off to work every day to make movies, whatever that meant. The man of the house was Mom's husband Harry Karl. Tall, mellow, grand, and well dressed, he was the epitome of American aristocracy, with big black-rimmed glasses and perfect hair. He loved us and was kind to us, but Carrie and I knew he wasn't our real father. He was eighteen years older than Mom, but he called her "Mother." She wanted us to call him "Daddy Harry." We liked the guy, but calling him Daddy Harry felt as awkward as if she'd asked us to call him "Snugglebunny." I was relieved when Carrie finally told Mom that we just weren't feeling the Daddy Harry thing, but as a gesture of compromise, Carrie and I created our own nickname for him by softening the *r*'s in his name so that it sounded like a hybrid of "Hawwy" and "Howie."

Mom's parents and older brother, our grandfather Ray and grandmother Maxene Reynolds and our uncle Bill, lived a half hour away on Evergreen Street in Burbank. Maxene's widowed mother, our great-grandmother Maxine Harman, lived in their converted garage. Grandpaw, as I called him, was a mechanic and carpenter who'd moved his family from Texas for a steady job with the Southern Pacific railroad when Mom was a seven-year-old aspiring gym teacher. He was a good, no-nonsense, undemonstrative man of few words, who never responded to "I love you" with anything more than a simple "Ditto." He raised his children and grandchildren on the edict "There's no such word as *can't* in this family," and I loved being with him and learning from him.

Grandma was an outspoken, emotional woman who held anything involving Hollywood in nothing short of contempt, especially when her beloved Baptist Nazarene church kicked her out for having a daughter who'd become an actress. Uncle Bill was a classic man's man, solid as a rock, a talented athlete in his youth and never one to back down from a challenge or a chance to protect and defend his little sister, Mary Frances, better known as Debbie Reynolds. And Grandma Harman was warm, round, and affectionate, a devout Baptist Nazarene who adored her granddaughter in spite of, rather than because of, her stardom.

We loved them and they loved us. We were essential parts of one another's lives, and it was always fun to spend time on Evergreen Street in Burbank. But nothing compared to what Carrie came to call her and my "shared experience of privilege and our shared experience of weirdness" at 813 Greenway Drive.

I was aware that, thanks to Mom's uncanny instinct for real estate investing, we had a house in Palm Springs, a house on Carbon Beach in Malibu, a condo in Spain, and a cabin in the mountains of Colorado, but Greenway Drive was home. Pulling up the wide, steep driveway that circled the front of the house was like pulling up to a museum. There was landscaping between the road and the sidewalk, but no gates or security fencing. In those days, stalkers were rare. In fact, the term was generally unknown. Our home was very accessible, and there was no shortage of cars and people coming and going at all hours of the day and night.

The modern architecture was softened by plush landscaping, yard sculptures, and an elevated marble walkway that led through a terrarium full of monkey ferns to our green twelve-foot-tall front doors with overscale brass knobs. The doors opened to a traditional foyer with a grand staircase (Mom always believed in making a great entrance and a great exit). Visitors waited in the sitting area to the right of that staircase to be escorted to whomever was expecting them. A row of tall windows behind the sitting area allowed a view through the terrarium to the outside of the front doors, which came in handy as a lookout when the doorbell rang—Carrie and our friends and I always checked to see who was standing there, particularly when we'd done something we thought might have triggered a neighborhood or police response. It never hurt to know in advance if we'd gotten away with it or if we needed to take evasive action.

To the left of the grand staircase was a large bar area that led to a music room and den, with a living room positioned between the staircase and the bar area. If you stood at the spot where the bar area and the living room connected, you could see an indoor living

The house at 813 Greenway Drive.

area about a hundred feet long. If you counted the outdoor patio area, visible through the tall windows at the far end, you were looking at about three hundred feet of living space that included the formal dining room and an outdoor informal dining area—all of which, added together, created the almost daunting illusion of an elegantly furnished football field. Floor-to-ceiling pocket panels, covered in tapestries, were installed to partition off the rooms if the occasion demanded, but the default position was wide open for large-scale entertaining.

A replica of the Rodin sculpture *The Kiss* stood sentinel at the entrance to the living room. Two-thirds of that room's perimeter was comprised of twenty-foot-high glass walls with sliding doors that opened to the patios. One wall opened up to a secret storage area filled with a treasure trove of items I loved exploring while I hid during hide-and-seek games with Carrie, although sometimes, to throw her off, I'd hide inside the massive walk-in fireplace.

The music room housed a glistening grand piano and rehearsal areas, and the formal dining room featured a twenty-foot-long dining table beneath a gigantic crystal chandelier. A mirrored terrarium bordered the room, home to twenty-foot-tall indoor trees that thrived under a huge, electronically controlled skylight. And everywhere you looked—on walls, on tables, in cubbies, *everywhere*—you'd find masterpiece-quality paintings, statues, and sculptures, placed so perfectly that, rather than being ostentatious, they simply seemed to belong there.

The breakfast nook was adjacent to the large-scale kitchen and its wall of eight commercial-sized refrigerators, each of which had its own designated purpose and temperature. The insane freezer area was crowded with huge quantities of meat and themed pastries for parties and holidays, and the adjacent rooms of cabinets held dishes, glasses, flatware, cookware, and a pantry that could have passed for the receiving bay of a small grocery store. There was rarely a day when delivery trucks weren't pulling into the driveway, bringing everything from party food and alcohol to staples like bread and cereal. I was probably in my teens before I ever set foot in an actual grocery store, or even had a clue what the inside of one looked like.

Carrie's and my bedrooms were down the hall from the den—hers first, then mine. We each had our own marble bathroom with a Roman bathtub, our own sitting room, and our own giant dressing room with floor-to-ceiling cabinets, dressers, and sliding racks for shoes and accessories.

Mom and Harry's private quarters were up the grand staircase in the foyer. Beyond the sitting area at the top of the stairs was my mother's fully furnished hair salon, stocked with everything her personal stylist—sometimes her friend and hairdresser-to-the-stars Sydney Guilaroff—might need. The highlight of the salon as far as I was concerned was the endless supply of different-sized curlers, which I found to be much more useful as soldiers who could be lined up in formation, could ambush one another, and might even be impaled with white plastic picks during particularly fierce battles.

The master bedroom had wall-to-wall windows with remote-controlled drapes that opened to a wraparound balcony overlooking the Los Angeles Country Club. Because Harry was over six feet tall, the bed was custom made to be even larger than a California king.

Mom's mirrored dressing room and palatial bathroom were rose-colored, with marble accents. Harry's were furnished with gleaming mahogany, designed to accommodate his apparent belief that It's All About the Facade. He had literally dozens of suits, and rather than be caught dead in the same shirt twice, he'd wear his nonstop supply of monogrammed shirts once and then throw them away. None of his shirts had buttons. He much preferred his platinum-and-jeweled shirt studs, with matching cuff links for his requisite French cuffs. His collection of custom ties was so vast it required an eight-foot-wide cabinet. Hidden drawers in another cabinet in the back of the room held his gold sovereigns, jewelry, and a stash of any tabloid articles that particularly caught his eye.

A smaller bedroom and office Harry used when he didn't want to disturb his wife led to his-and-hers exercise rooms. Hers was a ballet barre installed in an expanse of mirrored walls, where Mom toned, rehearsed, and did her stretches. His was devoted to exercise equipment, a steam room, and a barber chair, sink, supplies, and traditional barbershop pole. Harry's barber came every day to shave him and to wash, color, and style his hair, and at least once a week the barber was accompanied by a revolving cadre of manicurists with what turned out to be a wide variety of skills.

A stairway from there opened into a screening room the size of an art-house theater, filled with lush custom seating, beer taps, a soda fountain, a popcorn maker, and a huge drape to hide the floor-to-ceiling screen. The equipment in the projection room was state-of-the-art at the time—35 mm and 70 mm projectors, multichannel optical and magnetic sound, and both CinemaScope and Todd-AO lenses. Once or twice a week we'd have MGM screenings at our house. An MGM projectionist brought whatever movies we wanted, and he'd thread them up and run them for us. As a result, I hardly ever missed a movie, and there were many I watched again and again. They fueled my imagination and filled my head with countless movie references, derivations, and trivia still at my ready command to this day. In other words, at a very young age, I become an incurable film junkie.

And then came the backyard, where a waterfall splashed nonstop into the L-shaped swimming pool. The waters kept right on cascading down to a second pool and then a third one, our favorite because it looked the coolest. Grandpaw built Carrie a playhouse about the size of a one-bedroom condo. The tree house he built for me was so big that Grandma Harman had a thirty-foot Monterey pine craned in to support it.

The five-car garage adjacent to the screening room was home to our fleet of cars. Mom usually drove her Silver Cloud "Chinese Eye" Rolls-Royce with mink carpets and a custom paint job of dark emerald green, so transparent and three-dimensional it looked as if you could go swimming in it. Harry bought himself a shiny new Lincoln Continental every year, and a new Rolls-Royce every year or two that always sported his personalized *HK* license plates.

And what family of four doesn't need a steady stream of the latest top-of-the-line Chrysler station wagons? Mr. Greenberg tended to the general fleet, while Harry's personal driver Phil Kaplan was in charge of driving and maintaining the requisite family limousine.

Obviously, between the cars, the house(s), and the occupants, 813 Greenway Drive required a whole lot of maintenance, and it took a full-time and/or live-in staff to accomplish it. They were a fascinating assortment of people, a part of our lives. Our laundress, Leetha, was an albino black woman who commuted from the poorest parts of East Los Angeles. She stood about four-foot-eight, had a squeaky voice, and was funny as hell, and everyone knew you didn't mess with Leetha or her impeccably kept laundry. She was also extremely protective of Carrie and me, despite her occasional empty threat, in her thick southern drawl, "I'm gonna tan yo' hide, you don't behave."

Mr. and Mrs. Yang lived in one of the downstairs apartments. Mr. Yang, our head cook, was a world-class chef. He had a Fu Manchu mustache and, harmless as he was, seemed angry most of the time, which made him an irresistible target for Carrie and me. Mr. Yang had a collection of kitchen knives. They were so precious to him that no one else was allowed to touch them. One of us would casually grab one of those sacred knives to cut a piece of cheese or something, and he'd go nuts and chase us with a meat cleaver, shouting, "Getty outta my kitchen!" He never did understand why two small children found being chased by an enraged Asian man with a meat cleaver was so endlessly hilarious.

Mrs. Yang, who couldn't have been sweeter, was in charge of the housekeeping and support staff. She also declared herself in charge of polishing the brass inlays in the floors, convinced that no one else could do it properly. Her voice was invariably the first one Carrie and I heard on school mornings. She'd gently knock on Carrie's door and call out, "Callie-fish! Time to getty up fo' schoo'! I love-ally you, bay-bay!" Then there would be a pause, and the soft sound of Mrs. Yang's Chinese slippers scuffing up the hall to my door, followed by another gentle knock and "Ta-fish!

Time to getty up fo' schoo'! I love-ally you, bay-bay!" It became such a distinctive private, iconic detail of our childhood that my current license plate reads *Tafish*, and Carrie and I ended every phone call and text to each other with Mrs. Yang's good-morning greeting: "I love-ally you, bay-bay!"

Our Japanese gardener, Elmer, was a survivor of the World War II internment camps. He was incredible, as talented a landscaper as he was hardworking. Thanks to Elmer, our vast property was always thriving and flawless. Somehow there was never a single dead branch or a single leaf on the ground, and Elmer accomplished it without a word of complaint. He just did his job, did it well, and did it gratefully. Even as a child I noticed this and respected it.

Leonard Zincovich, aka Zinc, was a Polish ex–police officer and our head of security. He was a strong, imposing body builder who was a huge fan of Shaklee vitamins before anyone else had ever heard of them. Zinc was in charge of our intensely unfriendly German shepherd guard dogs, Senator and Mark, who understood only German-language commands. He was assisted by a retired FBI agent named Mr. Jackson, and the two of them, with the help of Senator and Mark and plenty of reinforcements when situations demanded, took great care of us.

Mary Douglas, our African American housekeeper, never lived with us, but for many years she was as much a part of 813 Greenway Drive as we were, and a part of the family. Mary's sister Gloria Clayton eventually worked for Carrie while Mary went right on working for Mom; and Carrie and Gloria were so close that, several lifetimes later, Carrie honored her by recruiting her for a small part in her film *Postcards from the Edge*.

Given that backdrop, you may find it hard to believe, but Mom tried her best to keep us from being obnoxiously spoiled. While we were given pretty much everything we asked for, and permitted, even encouraged, to exercise our imaginations to the fullest, we couldn't just say, for example, "I want a pony," snap our fingers, and have a pony, stable, and ranch hand appear in the backyard. Similarly, we would never have been allowed to run up and down the aisles of toy stores emptying shelves into our shopping cart. It's not as if every day was a Christmas-present bonanza at our house, and when Christmas did roll around, Mom moved heaven and earth to make it special, especially the year that Carrie almost blew her cover.

Carrie and I were conducting our usual inventory of the mountain of presents under the tree when she noticed that somehow, suspiciously, the handwriting on the tags from "Eddie" and from "Santa" was identical to Mom's. It was too horrible to contemplate that the three of them might be the same person. Eddie? Whatever. But Santa? If Mom and Santa were the same person, and Mom was obviously real, that led to the unthinkable conclusion that there was no such thing as Santa Claus. Deeply shaken, we demanded an explanation from Mom. And Mom, who couldn't bear to see her children disappointed, promptly hired one of her actor friends from MGM to surprise us at our house in full Santa mode—red suit, white beard, big round belly, and all. Problem solved. We never questioned Santa Claus's existence again until we finally got over him on our own.

It was thanks to another close friend of Mom's, the much-beloved actor/comedian/writer Harold Lloyd, that Mom and Carrie adopted a Christmas tradition they embraced all their lives. Harold had a room built at his amazing home to house a living, growing thirty-foot Douglas fir pine tree, and all year around he kept it beautifully, densely decorated with ornaments he collected from around the world. It really was always Christmas at Harold Lloyd's house, and Mom and Carrie were so enchanted by the spirit of that thought that for as long as they lived, both of their homes eventually featured fully decorated Christmas trees in their living rooms three hundred and sixty-five days a year.

Especially around the holidays, but for the rest of the year as well, the media couldn't seem to get enough of Debbie Reynolds with her two adorable moppets, so on a fairly regular basis Carrie and I would be dressed up in pristine little matching outfits and paraded around with our mother in front of throngs of still cam-

Our family Christmas card photo, 1961.

Carrie, Mom, Grandma, and me, 1961.

eras and 8 mm movie cameras. We didn't mind doing it, and we were marginally well behaved in front of the press, but it was kind of boring until one day when Grandma Harman showed up, saw what was going on, pulled Mom aside, and let her have it.

"You're ruining these kids!" she scolded her. "You want them growing up thinking life is just a nonstop photo shoot? It's not normal! Let them play! Let them get dirty! Let them be children and have some fun!"

Mom, who always valued her family's down-to-earth, no-nonsense advice, immediately took it to heart. She led Carrie and me straight to the curb in front of the house and set us down in the small stream of water in the gutter at the edge of the street. I still have the footage and still marvel at how perfectly it foreshadowed Carrie's and my distinctly different personalities. I was into it with no coaxing whatsoever, wet and muddy in the blink of an eye, splashing around, making a mess and loving every second of it. And there sat Carrie right beside me, still pristine except for the seat of her dress and intending to stay that way, a bit distant from the whole thing, the sweetest look on her face as she picked up a leaf and daintily dipped it into the water.

Until we were old enough to invite friends over, Carrie and I

BFFs from the very beginning.

were each other's playmates and confidants. We even took baths
together. She was tough and adventurous and intensely inquisitive,
always pointing at things, always asking "Why?" about anything
and everything, even when she could barely talk. Very uncoordi-
nated and terrible at sports, she was always hurting herself, and I
was always getting in trouble for not watching her closely enough
to prevent it. She enjoyed hitting me with a plastic baseball bat and
knocking me over. When Mom caught her at it, she looked inno-
cently up at her and explained, "Baby fall down." I was Carrie's
Smurf, her live doll, and she was my girl.

No one ever claimed with a straight face that Carrie and I had a
lot of supervision when we were growing up, but Mom really did
take the best shot a workingwoman could at being there for us and
giving us some structure in our lives. A proud Girl Scout when she
was growing up, she insisted that her shooting schedule allow her
time to attend Carrie's Girl Scout meetings on Friday afternoons.
Whenever it was humanly possible, the family sat down to dinner
together at precisely 7:00 P.M., and Mom was there every night at
bedtime to tuck us in. Thanks to another difference between Carrie and me, it wasn't easy.

I've always been a championship sleeper. Mom would come into
my room, sit on the edge of my bed, and begin quietly singing "A
Home in the Meadow" from *How the West Was Won* in that angelic
"Tammy" voice of hers, and I'd be out cold within the first three
or four bars.

Then, probably with a long sigh, she'd proceed back up the
hall to do battle with Carrie's chronic insomnia. Even as a very
small child, Carrie was nocturnal. She couldn't sleep no matter
how tired she was or how hard our mother tried to help her. Mom
would rub her back, rub her feet, sing to her, read to her, stroke
her hair, anything she could think of, but Carrie's mind wouldn't
and couldn't slow down enough to give her enough peace to doze
off. When all else failed, as it usually did, Mom, according to Carrie, gave her over-the-counter sleeping pills. I have no reason to
believe or disbelieve this, nor am I knowledgeable enough to as-

sume that it led to some of Carrie's future problems. All I know without a doubt is that if it's true, Mom had no idea, in the late 1950s or early 1960s, that she might be doing her daughter harm, as if she would ever deliberately harm one of her children or any child, for that matter.

In fact, in 1957, our mother was elected president of the Thalians, which was one of her lifelong passions. The Thalians was founded in 1955 by a group of actors who were determined to prove that contrary to popular belief, people in the entertainment industry weren't just a bunch of shallow, irresponsible, self-absorbed partyers, and they began by devoting their considerable energy and money to children with mental health problems. Debbie Reynolds never made a commitment without throwing her heart and soul into it, and this organization was no exception. She loved her fellow members of the Thalians almost as much as she loved the children they were devoted to helping, and she saw to it that Carrie and I spent time with some of them at fundraisers.

I was old enough to understand that the children at those fundraisers were "different," but I was too young to understand why. I remember asking Mom, "How come Carrie and I are like this, and they're like that?" Her reply was "That's not the point. The point is, What can we do for each other?"

A valuable lesson from one particularly memorable Thalians fundraiser at our house has served me well throughout my life and, I really believe, has helped me through some rough times. It was a typical star-studded event, and everyone was thoroughly enjoying themselves—so much so, in fact, that for several minutes, no one noticed that one of their officers, Mr. Gold, had suddenly turned gray, slumped in his chair, and died from a massive heart attack. It obviously wasn't anyone's fault, and it's not as if a quick response would have saved Mr. Gold's life. But it really bothered me that people could be so preoccupied with themselves, with entertaining and being entertained, that it could take a while for anyone to catch on that a friend of theirs had dropped dead right in front of them. I made a promise to myself that night that I've kept ever since, to never so completely lose myself in any moment that I fail to pay attention to what might be going on around me. I'm a little more cautious and a lot more vigilant than I was before, and I've never regretted it.

To the best of my knowledge, poor Mr. Gold was the only casualty in the history of parties at 813 Greenway Drive, and when I look back, it seems as if there were hundreds of them. Mom and Harry loved to entertain. They did it often, and they did it well. That their guest lists were like a Who's Who of Hollywood was something that never registered at the time. They were just family friends hanging out at our house, and the fact that their names happened to be Jimmy Stewart or Frank Capra or Judy Garland or Cary Grant or Eva Gabor meant nothing more than that. My only yardsticks were whether I liked them and whether other people seemed to like them as well.

It was impossible not to notice, for example, that the life of almost every party was Groucho Marx. Groucho didn't just attend parties, he held court. All he had to do was open his mouth and a circle of celebrities would gather around him, tuned into him, not wanting to miss a single word, a single joke, a single one-liner you knew they were going to be quoting later and laughing about for days. I was too young to get most of his double entendres, but I wasn't too young to understand that he was rare and genuinely admired by the best and the brightest in the Golden Age of Show Business.

There were only two guest bathrooms downstairs in the house, which made for a lot of wandering by the usually hundred or so guests in search of relief. I wasn't interested enough to keep track of any of them, and one night I was the one who had to go. I headed to my room as always, through my dressing room and on to the door to my toilet. The door was open, and I stepped over the threshold to find none other than Bette Davis sitting on the stool.

I was absolutely horrified. I would rather have cut off an appendage than walk in on any woman sitting on the toilet, but Bette Davis? My mom's idol? A woman who'd always been one of Mom's biggest fans and supporters and, from the movies I'd seen her in, one crazy powerful actress?

Bette Davis, in the meantime, simply looked up at me with a pleasant, unembarrassed smile, almost as if she'd been expecting me.

I leapt far enough back to get her out of my line of vision, muttering something that was supposed to be an apology but was probably a few strung-together nonsense syllables, to which she cheerfully replied, "Todd, it's okay."

Then, to my incredulity, as I was about to sprint back to the party until the coast was clear, she started chatting with me through the still-open door.

"So, tell me, Todd, what do you want to be when you grow up? Do you like sports? What's your favorite one? You know, your mother is very special to me. Has she ever told you about the first time she and I met?"

She went on and on, really pretty cute under the circumstances, while I stood there outside the door wondering what the hell a well-mannered boy was supposed to do in this ridiculous situation. It seemed rude to keep standing there, but even more rude not to hold up my end of the conversation, so I ended up staying, sliding down the wall to sit on the floor and chat with Bette Davis until she finished her business on my toilet. When that finally happened, she emerged from the bathroom, patted me on the head with an endearing "You're a doll," and went right back to the party.

For the most part, my friends and I found those grown-up parties exactly as interesting as you found your parents' parties when you were a child—that is to say, not even a little. We'd kind of drift in and out to check out the food and then disappear into my room to play. One night we were intensely involved in a slot car race when who should come strolling into the room but James Garner.

James Garner had been to several of Mom's parties. He'd always seemed nice enough, pleasant but not really into the whole Hollywood scene, and I hadn't paid much attention to him or his movies until he was elevated to icon status in my eyes by starring in *Grand*

Jimmy Stewart and Lucille Ball at a typical
legendary party on Greenway Drive.

Prix, which I'd watched in our screening room approximately a
million times. So now it wasn't just James Garner who had come
strolling in and sat down on the floor to play slot cars with my
friends and me—it was THE James Garner. It was *Grand Prix*
James Garner.

He hung out with us for an hour, and we even had a friendly little argument. All the slot cars had their corresponding Formula 1
names printed on them, and to show off that I knew my way
around race cars, I held one up to him and announced, "Here's
an Indy Eagle." To which he replied, "No, that's a Brabham." We
debated back and forth for a couple of minutes, and of course I
eventually found out that the manufacturer had mislabeled some
of the cars. He was right, I was wrong, and when Mom had him
autograph an eight-by-ten-inch photo for me a few weeks later,
the inscription read, "Next time we're together, don't try to tell
me an Indy Eagle is a Brabham." I still have that photo, as well as
the *Grand Prix* helmet he gave me, my first helmet, and last but
certainly not least, a tendency to smile very fondly every time I
think of James Garner.

But with the possible exception of poor Mr. Gold, the award
for Most Dramatic Behavior at a Greenway Party goes to (pause

for drama) Richard Burton and his beautiful, eerily familiar wife Elizabeth Taylor.

Yes, in 1964, Elizabeth Taylor divorced Eddie Fisher and, nine days later, married Richard Burton, with whom she'd been having a highly publicized affair for two years.

And yes, my mom and Elizabeth Taylor had buried the hatchet. It seems that, by pure coincidence, Mom and Harry had found themselves on the same cruise ship (ironically, the *Queen Elizabeth*) as Richard and Elizabeth. The four of them had dinner together on the ship, to the hysterical glee of the tabloids, and Elizabeth and Richard were welcome on Greenway Drive from that night on.

No one ever knew why or what started it, but at the memorable party I was referring to, Elizabeth and Richard got into a fight. A yelling, screaming, top-of-their-lungs, mutual bitch-slapping fight, and they were oblivious to the discomfort of a houseful of other guests. I remember Carrie and me gaping at them with identical incredulity. We'd never seen a couple behave like this before, let alone in public. We'd never even heard Mom and Harry so much as raise their voices at each other. This was insane, like a train wreck happening right there in our own living room, and we couldn't take our eyes off them. Within moments Mom pulled them aside and sent them upstairs so they could continue this ugliness in private, where it belonged in the first place.

What was almost even more bizarre was that after several more minutes of loud, profane yelling behind the closed door of the master suite, there was a sudden, almost deafening silence from behind that same closed door. Finally, after about another twenty minutes, Richard and Elizabeth emerged from the master suite, happy and in love again as they descended the grand stairway and rejoined the party as if nothing had happened.

That night was the first time I had ever heard the phrase *makeup sex*. I was just too young to know or care what it meant.

Parenthetically, I was at a party at Carrie's many, many years later when someone led me over to Elizabeth, who was sitting on a sofa by herself. She immediately took my hand and pulled me down to sit beside her, and for the next hour she talked, in extreme detail, about nothing but how much she'd loved Mike Todd and how, no matter how many other loves might come along, she was sure no one could ever measure up to him. I sat there and listened, not especially interested but a little fascinated that this woman, who'd technically been my stepmother for about ten minutes (okay, to be accurate, more like five years) and who, along with my father, had dealt my mother one of the most devastating betrayals of her life, seemed to feel connected to me, maybe because I was named after the greatest love of her life.

Family history aside, Elizabeth Taylor, arguably the most beautiful, most recognized face in the world, cared what I thought of her, which, come to think of it, was kind of a microcosm of the paradox of my early childhood on Greenway Drive: the extraordinary ordinary, the unusual usual, the common privilege—not right or wrong, just different, and in case I forgot to mention it, a glorious amount of fun.

It was impossible to believe it would ever go away.

2

THE GOOD LIFE

"Ta-fish" and "Callie-fish" when the world was our playground.

If any one room was the hub of 813 Greenway Drive, it was the den. The den was our TV room, cozy, comfortable, not over-scale like the rest of the house and filled with enough overstuffed furniture for the whole family and plenty of friends. The den was where Carrie and I would meet first thing every morning, fresh out of bed, our comforters (predictably, hers was pink, mine was blue) wrapped around our shoulders while we sat on the floor vents where the heat came out and finished waking up together.

The den was where Carrie and I watched Saturday morning car-
toons, *Father Knows Best*, *Leave It to Beaver*, *Bonanza*, and *Green
Acres*.

The den was where Grandpaw taught me to play chess when I
was about seven years old. He wasn't one of those teachers who'd
offer gentle encouragement and let me win every once in a while.
Instead, when he'd make some smart strategic move and take my
queen or something, he'd let out the most glorious laugh, slam his
hand on the card table, and yell, "Bam! Didn't see that coming, did
you?" Whether child psychologists would have approved of this
approach, I have no idea, and he wouldn't have cared. All I know
is, it worked for me—I was a rated chess player by the time I was
in my early teens.

And the den was where Mom routinely tried to firm up the bond
between Carrie and me and our stepfather.

Harry had a very regimented schedule. He left the house at the
exact same time every day, and he got home from wherever it was
he went at the exact same time every afternoon. He'd then head
into the den and settle into his overstuffed chair to read the paper,
carrying his ever-present jigger and a half of J&B and soda on
the rocks in a short leaded crystal tumbler. Laid out and waiting
for him on the end table beside his chair would be a crystal bowl
of redskin peanuts, a crystal cigarette holder that held exactly one
pack of his Kent cigarettes, and a heavy crystal ashtray. At exactly
6:30, half an hour before our family dinner at exactly 7:00, Mom
would usher Carrie and me into the den. Harry would put down
his paper, summon a refill of his J&B and soda, and have us tell
him about our day. It wasn't a very fulfilling ritual for Carrie and
me, or probably for Harry either, but we knew it meant a lot to our
mother to see us go through the motions of spending Quality Time
with our stepfather, so none of us ever complained.

Even as a child I was well aware that his beautiful movie star
wife and her children, his ready-made family, were a dream come
true for Harry, and he seemed to have the best intentions. He was

just hopelessly inept when it came to knowing what to do with us now that he had us.

Take, for example, the father-son Little League game. I loved playing Little League baseball. Mom came to every game her schedule would allow, and she was the best, most enthusiastic cheerleader any kid could ask for. So when the father-son game came along, she saw it as a perfect opportunity for Harry to be a dad and participate in a fun activity with his stepson. And as an added "dad" thing to do, she insisted that Harry drive us to the game, rather than have the Karl-Fisher father-and-son team roll up in the family limo with Harry's chauffeur Phil Kaplan at the wheel.

Harry was all for it, and it was fine with me.

Harry immediately dispatched Phil Kaplan to go out and buy him a baseball glove. Phil came home with what was undoubtedly the most expensive glove in the store. It also had "brand new" written all over it, so spotless and unbroken-in that it might as well have still had the price tag dangling from it. But hey, it wasn't as if my biological dad was pushing and shoving to go with me instead of Harry, so as far as I was concerned, some effort was better than no effort at all.

The day of the game Harry and I loaded our equipment—that is to say, my batting helmet, cleats, etc., and his pristine stiff-as-a-board glove—into the back of his latest Rolls-Royce and headed off to the park. I noticed that he was definitely not dressed to play baseball, but I assumed he was planning to take care of that once we got there, or whatever a seven-year-old tells himself in situations like that.

We'd traveled only a few blocks when Harry came to a stop sign on Whittier Drive and blew right through it, oblivious to the cop car that was sitting right there on the relatively quiet street. Within seconds there were flashing lights and a siren behind us. Harry pulled over, rolled down the driver's window, and pleasantly complied with the officer's request for his license and registration. After a quick glance at them, the cop walked back to his squad car and spent what seemed like quite a long time on his police radio before returning to Harry's window.

"Mr. Karl," he said, a little apprehensive, "uh, you know, this, uh, driver's license expired twenty-six years ago."

I swear I tried to stifle my laughter.

Harry didn't so much as flinch. "Yeah," he replied, "I've been meaning to take care of that."

Forget stifling. I was in hysterics. It was such classic Harry.

The cop handed back Harry's license and registration with a dismissive "Don't run any more stop signs," and on we went to the game. I was still laughing and Harry wasn't giving the momentary delay another thought.

The park was crowded with fathers, Little League sons, and lots of spectators. The players were given their position assignments, and the dads, some of them celebrities, trotted out onto the field in their sweats, jeans, sneakers, cleats, beaten-up gloves, and baseball caps. And there in their midst came Harry, in a slow, elegant walk en route to his designated shortstop position, still in the clothes he'd worn to the game—silk pants, a silk shirt with platinum-and-emerald studs and matching cuff links, a sport coat, a Piaget watch, monogrammed gold crushed velvet slip-ons, perfect hair, and of course, his spanking new glove. Except for the glove, he looked as if he'd wandered by on his way to drinks at the Polo Lounge. I was embarrassed, more for him than for me, and I kept my eyes focused on the ground to avoid seeing my teammates and their dads gaping at him.

One moment during the game itself has stayed with me. I was at bat, and I connected with a drive to center field, right over Harry's head. He leapt up to try to catch it and missed. In the process, he messed up his perfect hair, his feet slipped around all over the place in his traction-free velvet footwear, and his Rolls-Royce keys on their heavy platinum and diamond fob flew out of his pocket. I stood there, safe on first base, torn between wondering if it was too late to pretend I'd never seen this shortstop before in my life and thinking, "At least he tried."

We joined Mom in the den for a debriefing when we got home. She couldn't wait to hear how it went. She really had her heart set on creating a happy family for us, with Harry at its helm. I knew that. I could see it in her face. So I told her it went great and left it at that. Like I said, at least he tried, and at least he was *there*.

I wasn't nearly as willing to give points for "at least he tried" when it came to the saga of my pet alligator. Back then, it wasn't illegal to keep alligators as pets—or if it was, we didn't know about it—and I'd gotten him as a present from a former nanny who'd moved to Florida. I fell in love with him on the day he arrived. I named him Stanley, got him a nice big aquarium to live in, and kept him well fed with raw meats and insects. When he outgrew his aquarium, I moved him and some nice big rocks into my Roman bathtub, and he was happy there, assuming it's possible for a boy to know when his alligator's happy. He'd sit so contentedly on his rocks in that tub when I took showers with him, and my friends and I took him on regular swims to make sure he got plenty of exercise.

Carrie and her friends might not have thought he was as cool as we did, but they were kind of fascinated with him. One day Carrie decided to show off and let them watch her hand-feed him. In the process of offering him some raw chicken, she got too close to his mouth and he bit her. Why she didn't just toss his food to him from a safe distance as she'd seen me do a thousand times, I never did understand. But the bottom line was, my alligator bit my sister and made her bleed, and Mom immediately declared that Stanley had to go.

I declared just as immediately that no, he didn't. It was hardly Stanley's fault or mine that Carrie didn't know enough not to feed an alligator by hand, so why should he and I be punished for her carelessness? Carrie had a sparrow named Benny we'd rescued in Palm Springs when he fell out of his nest. Was Carrie being

Greenway Drive pets—Carrie with her sparrow, Benny,
me with my alligator, Stanley.

ordered to get rid of Benny? No. If she didn't have to give up her pet, why should I have to give up mine?

Mom's lame excuse was that it wasn't safe for Stanley to live with us anymore. Between Carrie's friends and mine, there were always a lot of children around our house, and Stanley was, after all, a full-grown alligator. Of *course* he was a full-grown alligator. He was a baby alligator when I got him. What did she think he was going to grow up to be, a Shetland pony? If it wasn't safe to have an alligator around the house, she should never have let me keep him in the first place.

Finally, when she and I were thoroughly frustrated with each other, she left the room. Good, I thought. Case closed. I won.

A few minutes later I was in the den, watching TV, when Harry walked in, J&B and soda in one hand, Kent cigarette in the other. He turned off the television and sat down close to me, closer than he'd ever sat before.

"You know, Todd, Mother thinks it would be better if you found a different pet, so let's talk about finding you another one."

Maybe I should have seen it coming, but I hadn't—Mom had obviously recruited Harry for the fatherly chore of convincing me that Stanley had to go. I couldn't believe it. He saw that I was getting upset and my eyes were welling up, and it completely threw him. He'd never seen me like this before. So, with the look of a man who knew exactly how to handle this, he reached into his pocket, pulled out his platinum-and-diamond money clip, peeled off a couple of hundred-dollar bills, and extended them to me. (Harry considered any bills smaller than hundreds to be nothing more than pocket change and usually left them on various counters around town. He even had a ten-thousand-dollar bill he loved to flash, just to see the look on people's faces.)

I immediately burst into tears and ran out of the room. I was horrified that this man had actually tried to bribe me into giving up my pet, and Harry was horrified to have run across a problem that money couldn't solve.

A few days later I came home from school or wherever to discover that Stanley was gone. It seems that at Mom's insistence, with Harry's usual support, Zinc, our head security guard, had been recruited to get rid of Stanley. I was heartbroken and furious.

But as luck would have it, that wasn't the end of the story.

A year or so went by. The Los Angeles Country Club, which abutted our property, was having its annual pro-am tournament, not televised but covered by a lot of local media. So there we all were one evening, watching the news together in the den, when the big headline from that day's golf at the L.A. Country Club appeared, with footage. It seems the tournament had come to a screeching halt as the officials tried to figure out what to do about the full-grown alligator that was hanging out on the twelfth green, eating everyone's golf balls.

Yes, there was Stanley, stealing the show at a celebrity-studded pro-am, looking healthy and complacent, while animal handlers were summoned to remove him from the golf course and on-air newscasters scratched their heads, wondering what on earth a live alligator was doing there in the first place.

Zinc quickly solved the mystery. He confessed that when he left the house with Stanley a year earlier to "get rid of him," he couldn't bring himself to do it by killing him. Instead, right or wrong, without a word to anyone, he'd simply turned him loose on the adjacent country club grounds and wished him godspeed. How Stanley survived for a year on his own was anyone's guess, but he made it, and I was thrilled.

Phone calls were made from Greenway Drive to the proper authorities, and Stanley was taken to his new home at a local zoo, where he lived a long, safe, well-fed life, with the help of monthly support checks from Debbie Reynolds.

If only all the news on TV had been that comforting.

Our den was also the place where Carrie and I learned that the world wasn't such an idyllic place after all. Besides letting us know that Stanley's story had a happy ending, the news told scary stories about the Cuban Missile Crisis, and the assassination of our president in Dallas, and Frank Sinatra's son being kidnapped.

Mom and Frank Sinatra had done a movie together called *The Tender Trap*, and they were friends. We were sorry for Mom's friend, but frankly, we didn't give it any more thought than that. After all, it had nothing to do with us.

Carrie and I rode our bikes to school every morning—down the steep driveway, a right on Greenway, another right on Whittier a block later, a few more short blocks, and we were there in a matter of minutes. Very soon after the Frank Sinatra Jr. kidnapping, we discovered that we were being followed by no less than the FBI. And they didn't just see us safely into the school building and drive away in their black sedans. The agent assigned to Carrie and the other agent assigned to me would actually sit in the partitioned cloakroom in the back of our classrooms, accompany us to the playground for recess, and return to their cloakrooms until school was out. Then they'd follow us home again and not drive away until we were inside the house and back under the safe, watchful eyes of Zinc, Mr. Jackson, and their two fearless, potentially lethal German shepherds. Carrie and I started closing our drapes at night to cover the bedroom windows in our rooms that looked out over the back-yard. Even with the drapes closed, we were both still frightened. What if, on the other side of those drapes, there was a dark, shad-owy figure wearing a mask lurking around behind the glass, ready to kidnap us, maybe even kill us? My room had the added bonus of a French door that led to the patio, and I'd lie awake long after bed-time, watching to make sure that latch didn't start silently moving, listening for that door to suddenly creak open or one of the panes to come crashing in. It was a fear I didn't conquer for many more years and many more houses.

It turned out that a few of our classmates who were also celebri-ties' kids were getting the same FBI bodyguard treatment we were in the wake of the Frank Sinatra Jr. kidnapping, but that didn't make it any less embarrassing, unnerving, and paranoia-inducing. I don't remember exactly how long it went on, I just remember that it seemed like forever. I'm sure the FBI was exactly appropri-ate in their response to that kidnapping, and I'm sure our parents were right and responsible to cooperate with the FBI's efforts to protect us. For us, though, it was a loss of innocence and a per-sistent reminder that there might be targets on our backs because we had a famous mom and dad. Then again, if the president of the United States could be shot and killed with the whole Secret Ser-vice trained to take care of him, what hope was there for the rest of us, celebrities' kids or not?

Around the same time all this was going on, some guy snuck onto our property from an adjacent Los Angeles Country Club fairway. All I remember about it is that he was trying to get to Mom. He made it all the way to the house and her second-floor balcony; he broke her bathroom window; and he was shot as he was climbing in through the broken window. Infrared beams and added motion detectors were immediately installed to set off wail-ing alarms the instant they detected any movement at all—which unfortunately included any harmless critters who wandered by, but none of us complained.

Carrie and I confided in each other more times than I can count about this nebulous fear that had invaded our lives, this subtle, perpetual sense of unease that seemed to diminish only when we kept ourselves too busy to notice it. We didn't talk to Mom about it. For one thing, there was nothing more she could do about it than she'd already done; and for another thing, we were afraid she'd blame herself for the targets on our backs her celebrity created. This subtext of fear made Carrie more fragile and edgy, while it made me more vigilant and even more protective of my mother and my sister, "my girls."

In fact, it was protecting one of my girls that led to my first fight. I was in fifth grade, and I saw some guy named Willie Bretton picking on Carrie. I'm not a fighter, but I wasn't having it. The guy was older and bigger, and a wrestler. I didn't care. I flew at him and started hitting him with everything I had, yelling, "Leave my sister alone!" It didn't take him long to pin me, and he held me down for several minutes while I fought as hard as I could to get him to let me go, not so I could walk away but so that I could hit him some more.

I ran into Willie Bretton about twenty years later while I was visiting Israel, where he'd become a Hasidic rabbi. We both re-membered that fight and chuckled about it, and he admitted he'd been afraid to let me go because he could tell I wasn't even close to giving up. He was right. I take after my mother—if you get us started and want us to stop, you'd better just kill us. In our family we called it "redlining"—pushing our engines past their maxi-mum RPMs until they blow.

I saw Mom redline only a handful of times. On three of those occasions she couldn't hold it in, and she punched three different men in the face. On the first occasion, when she did hold it in, I had no idea what was happening, and she terrified me.

We were in Las Vegas. She was headlining at the Desert Inn, and the band was getting ready to start. I was in the sound booth, looking down onto the stage, when Mom walked into view with a look I'd never seen before—I'd seen *the look,* as in anger, as in "Finish your homework OR ELSE," or "I'm not telling you again to brush your teeth." But this was red-hot rage, and I was startled by it, watching her like a hawk, when suddenly, several steps on-stage, she passed out. I don't think my feet touched the ground as I flew from the sound booth through the maze of catwalks to get to her. I had her in my arms, with my heart pounding like crazy, when she came to and immediately tore into one of the horn play-ers. I never did find out why she was so enraged at him, but I did learn that on those rare occasions when Mom was pushed past an-ger to redlining, one of two things was going to happen—either she'd contain it and faint or she'd start swinging.

I'm sure Eddie saw her redline a few times during their brief marriage, which would be at least part of the reason that, even though years had passed since their divorce, and even though they'd both long since moved on, Eddie Fisher was still afraid of Debbie Reynolds, whether or not he would have admitted it.

After Elizabeth Taylor tossed Eddie to the curb for Richard Burton, Eddie married the lovely actress and singer Connie Ste-vens, who gave birth to daughters Joely and Tricia before their divorce two years later. His recording career was on a serious, ir-reversible decline from its massive success in the 1950s. It was as if the public had never forgiven him, and never would, for betraying their beloved Debbie Reynolds with that harlot Elizabeth Taylor. (For decades I had strange men stopping me on the street to ask if I'd like them to "take care of that son-of-a-bitch father of yours.") But Eddie wasn't broke, and he most definitely wasn't lonely. There were always women around. *Always*.

Sadly, he was also a drug addict, dating back to the height of his recording and touring days in the mid-1950s, thanks to regular visits from Dr. Max Jacobson, aka "Dr. Feelgood," aka "Dr. Nee-dles." Dr. Needles dispensed his suspiciously popular "vitamin" shots to a massive celebrity clientele that over the years included everyone from President John F. Kennedy Jr. to Judy Garland to Humphrey Bogart to Marilyn Monroe. That these "vitamins" turned out to be mixed with generous doses of amphetamines probably explains why Dr. Needles's patients were so instantly energized by them, and why many of those patients, including Eddie, became so addicted.

While all that was going on and not going on in Eddie's life, Mom was obviously thriving. Her career was solid, and she was married to a multimillionaire who played a whole lot of cards with a whole lot of very influential show business friends at the very exclusive Friars Club. Between Mom's healthy temper and her and Harry's endless list of contacts, it wasn't in Eddie Fisher's best personal or professional interest to piss off Debbie Reynolds . . . again.

I'm sure it was some combination of fear and whatever guilt he could muster that led to my first clear-ish memory of Eddie. One of Mom's great passions was throwing birthday parties. Birthday parties were almost an obsession with her, whether you wanted one or not, and every party had to be an upgrade from the year before, not excluding the probability of some giraffes and elephants on hand to mingle among the guests. I don't remember which of my birthdays it was, but Mom rented a party bus and took a busload of my friends and me to a puppet show. She not only "invited" Eddie to join us, she also had us wear matching pullover velour shirts, as if our dressing alike would magically bridge the wide father-son gap that had always existed between us.

When I thought back on that day years later, I realized it was kind of a dangerous move on her part to even imply that Eddie might become a presence in my life. She risked setting me up for all the disappointments I'd seen Carrie go through because of his empty promises, and cutting us off from him altogether would probably have been much simpler and much safer. On the other hand, it wasn't in Mom's emotional arsenal to keep us from getting to know our father. I'm sure in her mind she'd provided us with the security and stability she'd grown up with by marrying Harry, while Eddie was her first love and her first lover, the husband who'd given her the children she lived for. Banishing him from our lives completely just wasn't a part of her chemical makeup.

Not that Mom was turning handsprings around the yard when

Thanks to Mom, every birthday was a big deal.

Eddie invited me to bring a friend for a sleepover at his house for the first time, but she clenched her jaw and shouldered through it. And if I had any expectations of this man I barely knew, I have to admit, he exceeded them.

He had a spectacular house, a modern rustic masterpiece designed by architect George MacLean. It was on Beverly Estates Drive, off Mulholland, with remote-controlled moving walls, amazing textures, and giant windows that looked out past the pool all the way across Los Angeles to the ocean and Catalina Island. If I hadn't been too young to know what a bachelor pad was, I would have thought this was what they're supposed to look like.

He seemed as if he was happy to have us there and was really trying to be a dad, so what better (and more Eddie) thing to do than to take us shopping? We bought ten G.I. Joes, with every possible accessory, and took them back to the house to play with them. It was then I discovered that Eddie might have been a poor excuse for a father, but he was a great playmate. He was as into those G.I. Joes as we were, not just going through the motions of having fun but actually having it, like a big, happy kid. (And in case it's not already obvious, there would have been zero chance of Harry's playing with G.I. Joes.) Then he suggested the three of us go swimming, and next thing we knew, while we were splashing around, he turned the pool into a giant bubble bath. The bubbles must have been two feet thick in that pool. It was fun and silly, and I never had a clue what brought it on or what kind of damage it did to the filtration system.

I was taking a shower one day after another play session in Eddie's pool when the shower door swung open and a very pretty, very naked Scandinavian woman stepped in to join me. She wasn't alarmed to find me in there. She was just taking a shower. That a little boy happened to be taking one in the same shower at the same time was either pure coincidence or a spontaneous effort at water conservation, but whichever it was, it was so not a big deal to her that she didn't give it a second thought. I, on the other hand, had never seen a naked woman before, let alone been in a shower with one, and I was embarrassed and immediately scooted out of there. I'm convinced that Eddie would have stopped it if he'd known about it, not because he wouldn't have gotten a huge kick out of it but because he knew that if Mom found out, he would have been dead. I wasn't sure she would have killed him, but I was sure she would have put an end to my trips to Eddie's, so I kept my mouth shut.

And then there was Carrie's and my first sleepover at Eddie's together. Some woman, I think maybe a *Playboy* model or something, happened to be living with him. She seemed nice enough, and the four of us went to a movie. Somehow between the time she dropped us off and the time the movie was over, Mom learned that Eddie and his girlfriend du jour were "living in sin," and we arrived back at Eddie's to find Mom waiting for us in the driveway, leaning against her Rolls-Royce, her face locked into *the look*. I don't remember a single word's being said. I just remember that Carrie and I scuffed into the house, gathered our stuff, scuffed outside again, climbed into Mom's car, and were driven back home. No explanation was given. No explanation was necessary.

The more time I spent with Eddie, the more I caught on that he hadn't attracted my mom and all those other women by being a celebrity with the personality of a flounder. He was adorable. He was charismatic. He was totally engaging when he was engaged. When you had his focus, you were special, essential, the most important person in his world.

The trick was remembering not to get fooled into believing it meant something. I had a great time with Eddie when I visited him at his house. I'm sure he had a great time with me too. It just didn't change a thing. It didn't mean we were any closer or better connected, or that I would see him more often. He'd be as absent as ever until some distant next time, when he would be fun and adorable and engaged and engaging—and if you weren't careful, would almost fool you all over again.

A classic Eddie story, from several years later:

I was twenty, living in a little house in Coldwater Canyon, when I was surprised by a call from a rehab facility where Eddie had been making yet another attempt to get clean and sober.

"We're ready to release your father," the woman said, "but he has nowhere to go."

I took a breath and finally said, "Okay, I'll take him."

I picked him up at the facility, brought him home, and set him up in my guest room. And for the next three months, he stayed with me. Needless to say, I'd never spent that much time with him in my life, and I have to admit I enjoyed it, especially considering how small that house was.

He was initially very overweight, and I was a vegetarian health nut at the time, so I decided to get him in shape. We went on lots of walks and took many rides on my motorcycle. We ate baked potatoes and popcorn and watched war movies together. I hired his arranger/conductor Eddie Samuels to come over and rehearse with him on the upright piano Mom had given me, and there was no doubt about it, Eddie Fisher hadn't lost that amazing voice. One day an attractive young woman around my age stopped by to check on him. She turned out to be Terry Richard, a former Miss Louisiana who was divorced from Eddie after a six-month marriage. I'd never met her or even heard of her before, but she occasionally took walks with us and seemed to still care about him. I never asked him for a dime, he never offered one, and I honestly didn't mind a bit.

Then one day I came home from work and he was gone. Just like that. Gone. No note, no thank-you voice mail, no nothing. It was months, maybe even years, before I heard from him again. Oh, well.

Mom had given me a beautiful old Indian belt. I loved that belt. So did Eddie. I let him borrow it a couple of times while he was staying with me. That was gone too. A long, long time later I found out that he gave it away. Oh, well.

A few days after he left, on a Sunday afternoon, I got a call from a place called David Able's Storage, asking if I was Eddie Fisher's son. When I confirmed that I was, the man on the phone said, "We're having an auction down here today, and we have a lot of your dad's stuff, in case you're interested."

I told him I'd be there ASAP and jumped in my car. There were no ATMs in the late 1970s, and banks weren't open on Sundays, so I had to pull some strings to convince them to take a check. But I came home from that storage place with Eddie's plaques from Vietnam and Korea; a framed, autographed picture of him with President Truman; his Golden Globe Award; his Emmy nominations; and armloads of other treasures, all of which I still have. The only missing items were his seven gold records, which I haven't seen since he lived on Beverly Estates Drive. To this day I have no idea where they are.

Eddie never asked about any of the things I brought home from storage that day. I never showed them to him or even told him I had them. I shouldn't have been surprised. That's just who Eddie was.

I lucked out—I could have a good time with him when he was around and go right on with my life when he wasn't. Carrie wasn't that lucky. Despite all the times he disappointed her and hurt her, despite all his prolonged absences from her life, she never stopped yearning for him to love her back, and I'll never doubt that as best he could, he really did. That little girl was still inside her, standing on the sofa, staring out the window watching for her daddy to come pick her up, and believing that somehow if she'd been more interesting, more compelling, more lovable, more worth it, he wouldn't have left in the first place. Mom couldn't convince her it wasn't true. I couldn't convince her it wasn't true. There wasn't a therapist or a drug or a bottle of alcohol that could convince her it wasn't true. No one but Eddie could have convinced her it wasn't true, and it was one of her greatest joys that she got to help take care of him at the end of his life.

After he died in 2010, Carrie wrote a beautiful passage about their relationship in her book *Shockaholic*:

> There is something in me that is joyous, that's joyful . . . and when I love, I love for miles and miles. A love so big it should either be outlawed or it should have a capital and its own currency.
>
> And that, along with an unfortunate affinity for illegal substances and a diagnosis of manic depression, are among the many gifts bequeathed genetically by my father. . . .
>
> So this is what we shared in addition to brown eyes, good singing voices, and kidney stones. This is what we shared instead of a wealth of common experience and history. . . . And for a long while, that was enough, perhaps because it had to be and partly because I finally realized that the way to have a satisfying, even fulfilling, certainly reliable and predictable relationship with my dad was for me to take care of him. To make him feel loved, appreciated and understood. To parent my parent was the pathway to my rela-

tionship with Eddie Fisher. . . . Enough of a relationship to where I miss him now. A lot. And I miss him in a very different way than how I missed him throughout my childhood.

Then I missed the idea of him. Now I miss the man—my dad.

That my sister, my girl, finally got to experience the peaceful, connected, uninterrupted love she'd always longed for from him is the greatest gift he could have given me.

3

IGNORANCE IS BLISS

At home with Carrie.

They say ignorance is bliss. I guess that explains why I had such a blissful childhood.

There were a lot of guys from the executive suites of show business, the shadows of Las Vegas, prestigious business management offices, the Friars Club, the FBI, even much closer to

With Mom and Carrie on the set of *The Mating Game*, 1958.

home, who were holding one end of a great big rug, ready to pull it out from under us. For a long time Mom was as blissfully ignorant as Carrie and I were. When she started finding out that we were in free fall, she tried her damnedest to keep us from knowing. And I was too busy being a curious, industrious, happy boy to notice anyway.

Though my favorite place on earth was 813 Greenway Drive, a close second was MGM Studios, where my mom had been making movies since she was sixteen years old, from *Singin' in the Rain* to *The Unsinkable Molly Brown*, *How the West Was Won*, *Tammy and the Bachelor*, *The Tender Trap*, and the list goes on. Some of Hollywood's greatest films had been made there—*Gone with the Wind* and *The Wizard of Oz* and *Ben-Hur*, to name just a few. Stars like Clark Gable, Fred Astaire, Greta Garbo, Lana Turner, Paul Newman, Spencer Tracy, Katharine Hepburn, Elizabeth Taylor, Lucille Ball, Esther Williams, Laurel and Hardy, Frank Sinatra, the Marx Brothers, Gene Kelly, Jimmy Durante, Donald O'Connor, and Judy Garland had inhabited those back lots and sound stages and dressing rooms, and eaten in that commissary.

Mom had been taking me to MGM Studios since I was a toddler. I got haircuts there. I hung out with her castmates and crews. I played with Carrie and our friends on the *Showboat* boat, on the pirate ship, on the man-made rock formations and lagoons, in the European village, in the Western town (my favorite), and in all the other fantasy worlds on that back lot. MGM was a magical

Playing, making our movies, and growing up on the MGM back lot.

place to me, almost hallowed, better than Disneyland any day. Between trips to the studio and the hundreds of films we screened on demand in our projection room, I developed a healthy fascination with making movies.

I had exactly zero interest in following in my parents' footsteps and becoming a performer. I loved watching Clark Gable and Cary Grant and Jimmy Stewart and Paul Newman and all those other great actors. But I didn't want to be them. I wanted to be David Lean and make movies like *Lawrence of Arabia* and *Doctor Zhivago*, or George Roy Hill, and make a movie like *Butch Cassidy and the Sundance Kid*. I wanted to know everything there was to know about sets, sound, props, lighting, projectors, cameras—all those elements that went into transforming a script into those amazing images on the screen. My fascination evolved so gradually and so naturally that I didn't even realize I was essentially going to film school from a very early age. I thought I was just hanging out with my family and Mom's pals at the studio and asking questions about things that piqued my interest.

Mom's projectionist friend who ran movies for us at the house, for example, was only too happy to teach me how to use the projector and other sophisticated equipment in our screening room when I simply asked, "How does this work?"

Uncle Bill had become a successful makeup artist, starting with feature films, including an Elvis movie, and eventually moving on to TV series like *The Waltons* and *Knots Landing*. I couldn't have cared less about movie star makeup, but Uncle Bill also knew how to create scars and bloody, gaping wounds and any other kinds of repulsive gore I could dream up. I had to know how to do that too.

Mom's stunt double on *How the West Was Won* was a fantastic guy named Loren Janes. He'd been a great friend to Carrie and me from the time we were barely old enough to walk, and who better to teach my buddies and me how to safely take a fall or get blown away by a shotgun blast or have a really convincing fake fistfight on-camera?

Mom had a Bell & Howell spring-wound movie camera that she used to film Carrie and our friends and me growing up on the MGM back lot at birthday parties and general play sessions. So one day she loaded Carrie and me and our friends and her camera into the Town & Country station wagon, drove us through the gates of MGM, and parked in front of the wardrobe building. Morton Haack, a world-renowned costume designer, led us into a vast warehouse filled with every imaginable costume and prop and turned us loose. "Like a kid in a candy store" doesn't quite describe what that was like for me— there isn't a candy store in the world that could compare with that warehouse as far as I was concerned. We boys pillaged the military uniforms and weapons, while Carrie and her friends headed straight for the nurses' outfits and first-aid supplies.

Then it was off to the Eastern European village on Lot 2, where Mom filmed us in a ferocious war sequence, very loosely based on *Where Eagles Dare*, with me leading the charge. We soldiers had to get wounded and killed over and over again to get attention from Carrie and the rest of the nursing staff, who kept losing interest in making a war movie and wandering off.

Mom and her Bell & Howell camera filmed our every childhood moment.

It was a great day.

We didn't have a clue as we drove out again through those giant iron gates and headed home that it would be the last film we'd ever shoot at MGM Studios.

What we soon learned was that MGM was about to be systematically dismantled by its new owner, Kirk Kerkorian. The plan was being orchestrated by MGM executive James Aubrey, entertainment attorney Greg Bautzer, and his partner, Sidney Korshak, whose reputation as the mob's man in Hollywood led the FBI to consider him "the most powerful lawyer in the world." The studio was being sold off, with proceeds from the real estate, costumes, props, sets, and so forth to be used as private equity for the construction of the MGM Grand Hotel and Casino, aka the largest hotel in Las Vegas.

Mom was heartbroken, along with countless other people who'd made some of the greatest movies in history on the MGM lot, who'd come to think of it as home, and who'd embraced those who worked there as their extended family. When it was announced that the costumes and props were going to be auctioned off, Mom did her damnedest to rally her show business friends to be there to buy as many of those treasures as possible, to keep them from being disbursed to God only knew where, to God only knew who—people who couldn't begin to appreciate and cherish them as much as she did. Very few of those friends showed up, but Mom was at that five-day auction every single day, from the minute the doors opened until they closed again, bidding her heart out, with me by her side on a couple of those days. And before long, countless racks of costumes and crates of props began arriving at 813 Greenway Drive, to be stored, catalogued, and adored in her rehearsal hall downstairs.

It was a massive, overwhelming collection that meant the world to my mother. She didn't know it would almost literally save her life someday. All she knew was that in her eyes, it was priceless Hollywood history, that it was safe and secure in her care, and that

Las Vegas, meet my children, Todd and Carrie.

eventually, somehow, somewhere, she'd find a way to share it with the movie fans she loved so much.

As for me, I was twelve years old when the MGM auction happened, so all *I* knew was that suddenly, right there in my own house, I had all the wardrobe and weapons I needed to make action movies. If I couldn't make them at the studio anymore, oh well. I had a gigantic backyard with a huge vacant lot right behind it, and Greenway Drive was a quiet out-of-the-way street with very little traffic. I'd make my movies at home and dare those studio suits to try to stop me.

Carrie and I came up with a police drama story line (okay, actually just the cops-and-robbers shootout part), and we recruited several enthusiastic friends to play the necessary cops, robbers, and nurses. We didn't let it stand in our way for one second that the only law enforcement costumes we had were British RAF uniforms, or that of the four guns in our collection, three of them were Western six-shooters. We were filmmakers, and filmmakers don't whine about what they don't have; they take what they do have and make it work.

The one necessity we were missing was ammunition for the new cache of weapons. The guns had arrived unloaded, with nothing to load them with. Probably an oversight. (Probably not.) I asked around, and at a friend's suggestion, I called a store called Ellis Mercantile. Why was I just now hearing about this place? They had everything—blanks, squibs, blood packets, *everything*. They were happy to help, and we were ready to start shooting (so to speak).

Armed with Mom's trusty Bell & Howell, I yelled, "Action!" and our first major production at 813 Greenway Drive was under way.

The scene was a shootout between two armed thugs and two policemen. When the thugs turned and fired at the cops, the cops shot back and dived for cover as Cop 1's arm began spurting blood. Cop 1 took aim and fired at Thug 1, who'd run into the street. Thug 1's chest erupted in a disgusting cloud of blood and tissue. And on it went with more blood and bullets flying.

When I finally yelled "Cut!" the casualties jumped up, the cast gathered, Nurse Carrie and her fellow RNs emerged from the bushes with me and the crew, and we began jumping around shaking hands and congratulating one another.

It doesn't look like much on paper, but what made it really remarkable is that we shot that entire sequence without letting ourselves even once be interrupted or distracted—because we were, after all, seasoned filmmakers—by the unexpected tour bus that had come to a dead stop in front of the house. The thirty or forty screaming, terrified tourists inside were crouched on the floor behind their seats, having obeyed the driver's order to "Get down!"—all of them believing that they'd accidentally driven into the middle of an actual gunfight. The windshield of the bus was dripping with blood and body tissue (raw hamburger), and I have to admit, the director in me couldn't have been happier with how repulsive it looked.

Not until the dead cops and thugs started getting up and Carrie and I stepped into view did the busload of tourists catch on that none of this was real. They started laughing, helping one another up, and reaching for their Polaroids. Then the bus driver, who'd settled back into his seat, recognized us and announced over the intercom, "Ladies and gentlemen, those are Debbie Reynolds's kids, Todd and Carrie Fisher."

The tourists immediately started cheering and applauding and taking pictures of us through the bus windows, prompting the cast and crew of the first official 813 Greenway Drive film production to line up and take a deep bow. We could still hear the cheers and applause as the bus drove away, and we happily kept waving until it disappeared.

They loved us, and we loved that they loved us. There's an old thespian creed that says, "Never turn your back on an audience." So, in keeping with tradition, we started checking the tour bus schedules and putting on shows for them once or twice a week for the next month or so. It was great. I'd found my niche.

Unfortunately, when I screened our footage from that first day, I wasn't happy. The actors had done their jobs perfectly—in fact, John Courtney had turned in an especially riveting performance as Thug 1. But compared to what I'd pictured, there was a quality, a richness, missing from the film itself. I knew exactly what the problem was: I needed a better camera. And I knew exactly how to get one.

Mom had always been willing and eager to encourage Carrie

and me in whatever healthy pursuits seemed to capture our interests, so I sat her down and explained my dilemma.

"What kind of camera is it you want, dear?" she asked.

That was a no-brainer. "A Beaulieu R16 with a twelve to one-twenty zoom," I told her, already excited about the "of course, dear" I knew was coming.

Instead, she threw me a curve.

"Dear, we all have to earn things in life, and I'm not sure you've earned a new camera yet. I'll tell you what—let me set up a meeting for you with Harry Stradling. If he says you're ready for a new camera, I'll be happy to take his word for it."

Fair enough. Harry Stradling was a friend of Mom's. He was also one of the best directors of photography in the business, with credits like *My Fair Lady* and *A Streetcar Named Desire* and *Funny Girl*, and he and Mom were working together on a half-hour television series called *The Debbie Reynolds Show*. I could learn a lot from him.

So there I stood on the set of Mom's show with Harry Stradling, confused about the roll of 35 mm film he was handing me—film for a still camera. Maybe he'd misunderstood.

"Mr. Stradling, I want to make *movies*."

He gave me a patient smile and a simple order. "There are twenty-four exposures on that roll. I want you to take twenty-four random still pictures and show me the contact sheet. We'll see where we go from there."

Meeting over. I didn't get it, but I wasn't about to argue with Harry Stradling. I took the film and left. I hope I remembered to say thank you.

I spent the next week or so taking twenty-four still photos. He wanted random, so I gave him random, everything from a shot of a sewer cover, to Grandma Reynolds talking on the phone, to Carrie by the pool. I was a nervous wreck while he studied every shot through a loupe magnifier. Finally he looked up and said, "Number seven."

He pointed to the seventh shot on the contact sheet, a picture of

our backyard on Greenway Drive. I studied it for a second. "Uh
. . . what about it?"

"Tell me why you framed it that way."

"I don't know, I just took it," I told him.

He handed back the contact sheet. "Todd, if you don't know,
then neither do I. If you don't have a reason for the way you
framed a shot, the shot's not worth taking. Motion picture film
runs at what amounts to twenty-four still shots per second. If you
can't show me twenty-four well-composed stills on a contact sheet,
how can you ever expect to manage the thousands of stills it takes
to make a movie worth looking at?"

I hated to admit it, but what he said was interesting and a good
point. It was also obvious that it wasn't leading to "So tell your
mom to buy you that Beaulieu R16."

"What do I do now?" I asked him.

He handed me another roll of film. "Try again," he said, and
then returned his attention to his set and his crew.

I was a little disappointed. I really wanted that camera. But at
the same time, this wasn't just about getting a camera, it was also
about learning to be a skilled cinematographer, and I was being
given a chance to learn from the best.

In the meantime, Mom arranged a meeting for me with veteran
director George Sidney, husband of her lifelong friend and mentor
Lillian Burns Sidney, Louis B. Mayer's right-hand woman.

"The movie camera and what you film is freezing time forever,"
Mr. Sidney told me. "The moments you film are captured forever.
A hundred years from now people will watch those moments and
understand what you're trying to say."

George Sidney and Harry Stradling had a passion for the art,
not just the fun, of filmmaking, and it was contagious. I apparently
took it to heart. Harry Stradling carefully studied every detail of
every shot of my second contact sheet, reached into his duffel bag,
pulled out a handsome, glossy brochure, and handed it over. He
didn't smile until he saw it register on my face that he'd just given
me a handbook on the Beaulieu R16 camera.

He couldn't have imagined how perfect his timing was. I'd been planning my next Greenway Drive production, a war sequence from the Clint Eastwood film *Kelly's Heroes*, and thanks to a round of golf, I'd just scored the war prop of a lifetime.

I started playing golf when I was seven years old. Mom was great friends with Lucille Ball, and Lucy had given me a set of golf clubs that Desi Arnaz Jr. had outgrown. I loved the game, and from the beginning I turned out to be good at it. As Eddie Fisher's son, I was half Jewish, and hard as it is to believe now, our neighborhood course, the Los Angeles Country Club, didn't allow Jewish players. So I'd play at the Hillcrest Country Club, compliments of Harry Karl's membership there, or I'd simply hop the L.A. Country Club fence with my tutor, a great guy named Ray Noack, and play a relatively inconspicuous three-hole section of the course over and over again until we'd had enough.

The better I got at golf, the more often Harry and I played together at Hillcrest with some of his very wealthy, very influential golf buddies. And the more we played with Harry's golf buddies, the more he enjoyed including me in making the round more inter-

Golfing with Harry in Spain.

esting with a few side bets here and there. He developed a simple series of signals, a stroke of either the right side of his mustache or the left, that would cue me whether to make a putt or miss it, or win a hole or blow it, depending on which way he bet. I never paid attention to how much money was on the line or how big a check Harry had to write when we lost. I just got a kick out of watching the looks on his buddies' faces when they found out I was pretty damned good for such a small young kid, and out of the fact that Harry and I almost always won.

So one day while I was putting together my second contact sheet for Harry Stradling, Harry Karl set up a golf match for him and me at Hillcrest—the two of us versus a Superior Court judge and his playing partner, neither of whom I'd ever met and both of whom seemed to think it was very cute that Harry had brought his little stepson along to play with the big boys. As usual, I had no idea what stakes Harry and the judge had agreed on for themselves, but the stakes between Harry and me were simple and irresistible, based on my having talked nonstop about the war movie I was planning to shoot. If we won, he'd buy me anything I wanted at the Santa Monica military surplus store. We quickly reviewed Harry's mustache signals as we drove our cart to the first tee, shook hands with our opponents, and teed up.

To give credit where it's due, the judge and his buddy were pretty good, and it was a close match. When I sank the winning putt on the eighteenth hole, I literally saw the blood drain out of the judge's face. (I found out later that my putt on the eighteenth had cost the judge $25,000. I was glad I didn't know that ahead of time.)

True to his word, Harry had Phil Kaplan drive us straight from Hillcrest to the Santa Monica military surplus store.

"We did pretty well today," Harry told me as we headed for the front door. (Ya think?!) "Whatever you want, it's yours."

I hadn't taken my eyes off the World War II M3 army tank parked by the entrance since we had gotten out of the limo. Kidding but not, I pointed at it.

"How about this?"

He shrugged a little, reached into his pocket for his money clip, and headed into the store. I couldn't believe it!

Neither could Mom when we got home.

Harry was in his chair in the den with his J&B, peanuts, and cigarette. I was pacing nearby, excited but nervous and ready to plead my case, while Mom detonated in Harry's face.

"A *tank*?! You bought him a tank? Who buys their child a tank?" She was so furious she couldn't even get her thoughts together. Finally she came out with, "How the hell much is a tank?"

I honestly thought this might help calm her down. "Mom, don't worry about that. It wasn't our money."

I saw Harry cringe a little. Mom glared at him like ice.

"What does that mean, Harry?"

He stalled a little by taking a long sip of his scotch.

"Answer me!" If looks could kill, he would have dropped dead.

"Honey," he explained, "it's just a scout tank, not a full-size tank. It's not as if it fires—"

She cut him off. "It's a *tank*, Harry! And don't change the subject. What did Todd mean by 'it wasn't our money'? Whose money was it? Where did it come from?"

I was naive enough to think this would make her feel much better. In fact, I was still proud of it. "We won it fair and square in a golf match, Mom. Some judge bought me that tank. Seriously, it didn't cost you a dime."

Harry sank a little in his chair. I'm sure I even heard a slight groan. Mom leaned into him even farther, and she lowered her voice, which was somehow even scarier.

"You know, Harry," she said into his eyes, "people all over town have been trying to tell me you're involved in a lot of high-stakes gambling, and you keep telling me you're not. So which is it?"

He looked right back into her eyes. His voice was so quiet I could barely hear him. "Dear, I swear, it's not like that."

She exploded again. "And you're not just gambling, you're involving my son? How dare you? How *dare* you?"

I'd never seen her so angry with him. I'd never even seen them argue, and I felt responsible for it. I managed a pleading "Mom . . ." to draw her fire, but she just turned on me and ordered me to go to my room, with an added promise that she'd deal with me later. I didn't doubt it for a minute.

I flopped down on my bed, very upset. I didn't know what the gambling part of Mom's rage was about. Harry was a gazillionaire, so if he liked to gamble every once in a while, what was the big deal? As far as I was concerned, the headline of that whole conversation was that she wasn't going to let me have my tank, and I couldn't handle that. I didn't just want it because it would be cool to have a tank, although, let's face it, what could be cooler? I wanted it, I *needed* it, because it would open up a whole new world of cinematic possibilities. All the way home from Santa Monica my head had been spinning with ideas for action sequences I could shoot with that tank, action sequences that could move me light-years ahead as a cinematographer. I had to have it.

But Mom had said no, that definitive, uncompromising *no* of hers that nothing short of divine intervention could change. And there was only one way to make that happen: I rolled off the bed, knelt beside it, and literally started praying out loud—the first time I'd ever actually prayed in my life—asking God to please, *please* help me get that tank. I promised to do anything He wanted, anything He asked. I promised to never help Harry cheat at golf again if it upset Mom that much, and to be the best, most protective, most loving son and brother Mom and Carrie could ever hope for. I promised that if He'd let me have that tank, I'd work so hard to become the great filmmaker He'd created me to be, but I couldn't do it without that tank. . . .

I have no idea how long I would have kept going if Mom hadn't interrupted from my bedroom doorway with a slightly incredulous "Are you serious? You're *praying* for a *tank*?"

I glanced up at her, told her that's exactly what I was doing, and moved to sit on the bed again. She crossed the room and sat next to me. "I'm sorry. I don't get it. I suppose it's a great toy, Todd, but what on earth is so important about this tank?"

I looked deep into her eyes, and I'll never forget that moment. It was the precise moment when I had the first epiphany of my life, my first soul-deep awareness of who I was talking to and what made her tick. She wasn't just my mom. She was Debbie Reynolds, a world-famous actress, singer, and dancer, the hardest-working person I'd ever known, with an appreciation for creative talent most people could only dream of. To her, creativity, and making art, were sacrosanct. She believed that, she lived it, and she taught it to Carrie and me. Suddenly I knew what to say—because I knew it would work.

I kept my eyes locked on hers and said, "I need it for my creativity, Mom. I need it for the art I'm trying to make."

She kind of tilted her head to one side, taking that in, and then pulled me toward her to hold me. She got it.

I was on a roll. I was pushing my luck, but I couldn't resist adding, probably a little overdone, "It's like that camera I've been asking for. It's not just for the hell of it, Mom. It's for my art, my creativity. I want to make movies like you, but from behind the camera."

She let go of me, her hands still on my shoulders, and studied my face. "What does Harry Stradling have to say about that?"

I reached over to my nightstand, picked up the brochure he'd given me, the brochure I'd already practically memorized, and handed it to her.

A few days later, John Courtney, a few other buddies, and I were gathered in front of 813 Greenway Drive, in nothing short of awe, to witness a crane lifting my new tank from a flatbed truck to the backyard; and I captured the whole thing on my new Beaulieu R16 movie camera.

I was the happiest boy in Beverly Hills. Mom seemed to enjoy watching my friends and me charging around the yard in that tank, Carrie couldn't have cared less, and Harry seemed a little distant but pleased with himself. The only person who had a problem with it was Elmer, our poor gardener, who, because tanks aren't exactly known for their ability to make sharp turns, would occasionally shriek out an agonized "The dichondra!"

Not long after the tank arrived, filming on Greenway Drive went on hiatus when Mom announced we were booked for another show at the Desert Inn in Las Vegas, for the first time in two years. Las Vegas had been one of our family's homes away from home since before I was born. Eddie Fisher first headlined there at the Tropicana in 1957, and I have footage of Eddie swimming with his baby daughter Carrie in the hotel pool. Debbie Reynolds made her debut at the Riviera in 1960. Harry and Mom and Carrie and I loved just hanging out in Las Vegas, whether Mom was working or not. We spent a Christmas there, if Christmas and Las Vegas in the same sentence isn't an oxymoron. It's where Mom became close friends with other headliners like Liberace and the Rat Pack and Louis Prima. It's where I got a glance of a very frail, haggard-looking Howard Hughes at the Desert Inn, when I was playing spy

The Desert Inn, our home away from home.

and climbed up a trellis and my head accidentally popped up at the edge of Mr. Hughes's balcony just a few feet away from him. (Yes, my mom did sit me down later and explain that it would be a *really* good idea not to do that again.) It's where we were always welcome and treated like royalty, and where a couple of decades later, one of Mom's greatest dreams would be shattered.

When I was about ten years old, Mom started including Carrie and me in her Vegas act. She'd taken guitar lessons for a movie called *The Singing Nun* when I was six or seven, so I took lessons right along with her. I'd sing and play the guitar in the Vegas act while Carrie, who had inherited her father's fantastic voice, sang and blew the room away, with Mom watching from the wings in tears of pride until it was time for her to join us. When my voice inevitably began changing in my early teens, I happily retired as a singer and simply stuck with my guitar.

Mom, Carrie, and I would gather in the music room on Greenway Drive, while Mom's friend and musical director Rudy Render (who'd known Uncle Bill since they served together in the Korean War, by the way) put a show together for us, along with storied choreographer Bob Sidney and composer Jerry Fielding, and rehearsed us for hours at a time. Mom and Carrie were really, really into it. I took more of a "sure, whatever" position on performing. But it meant so much to Mom for us to be together that I didn't try to get out of it. Debbie Reynolds headlining in Las Vegas was a family enterprise. Grandma Reynolds was the wardrobe mistress, and Uncle Bill was in charge of makeup. Mom's friend Pinky Babajian, who was so close she might as well have been family, was the hairdresser. Grandpaw was there because he belonged wherever we were, and so that he and I could play the Desert Inn golf course every day with Uncle Bill, who happened to be a scratch golfer.

From the first time we performed together when Carrie was barely a teenager all the way through the hugely successful national tour of *Wishful Drinking*, her one-woman show that started in 2007, she suffered from horrible stage fright before she set foot

The young Princess, 1971.

onstage. I'm not talking about normal pre-performance jitters, I'm talking about sheer panic. I remember standing with her in the wings, between the asbestos fire curtains and the brick wall, while Mom was setting up our entrance for the audience, and having to put my arms around Carrie to try to quiet her trembling. She was always so frightened that she wouldn't be as funny or as powerful a singer or as charismatic as she was sure audiences expected her to be—or, probably more accurately, as she expected herself to be. I lucked out. I wanted to do a good job for Mom and Carrie, but I didn't harbor any lofty expectations about myself as a performer. Carrie did, and they scared the hell out of her all her life.

Then she'd walk out onstage, the lights would hit her, and in an instant her terror would transform itself into sheer joy. She loved performing in front of a live audience as much as Mom did. I would watch them while we were taking our bows and marvel at how the cheers and applause actually seemed to nourish them, as if they were enjoying a gourmet meal or a rare bottle of vintage wine, while I'd just be thinking I was glad people liked the show and wondering how much longer I needed to stand there. I never really

related to what Mom and Carrie got from that applause—it simply
registered as a need they had that I didn't.

By the time we got to Las Vegas for Mom's show at the Desert
Inn in 1971, I was pretty much over the whole performance thing. I
had my new camera and my buddy John Courtney with me, and all
I wanted to do was take off with John to film some night shoots in
the tunnels under the hotel, where we'd planned to get some scenes
of us pretending to plant some explosives for a *Mission: Impossible*
sequence . . . or something . . . Doing the show was enough of
a holdup. Then I felt obligated to stand around backstage while
Carrie held court and Mom smiled her way through being fought
over by Howard Hughes's director of entertainment Walter Kane,
MGM's notorious fixer Sidney Korshak, and infamous mob boss
Anthony "the Ant" Spilotro—something about wanting their
"million-dollar baby" back at the Riviera where she started, and
their "friends in Chicago" not being happy about the Desert Inn
taking her away. Finally, when Mom and I were alone in our suite

On stage with Mom and Carrie at the Desert Inn.

one night, I sat her down and explained that I thought I could be more creatively stimulated and more valuable to the act by filming it rather than playing guitar in it. And besides, I was thirteen, and she wasn't likely to find a lot of thirteen-year-old boys who were really into having to wear makeup every night.

Again, she got it. In fact, she was great about it. I hung up my guitar and started filming her and Carrie onstage, and I loved it.

We followed up that 1971 Las Vegas stand with a trip to Europe.

Something was going on between Mom and Harry, kind of a cool distance that Carrie and I sensed but never really addressed with Mom. As I look back, it's clear that Mom designed that incredible first-class trip as a last-ditch effort to keep her marriage and her family together. It really was an unforgettable trip, a Debbie Reynolds masterpiece all the way; and I'm pretty sure we managed to take stills and home movies of every square inch of the European continent. Mom and Harry seemed to enjoy each other, and I thought that by the time we came home she was feeling better and more secure about where things stood between them.

Unfortunately, we arrived back on Greenway Drive to the news that the next step in dismantling MGM Studios was about to be taken—they were getting ready to bulldoze those magical back lots I'd grown up on, including the Western town where I'd had countless shootouts and killed God knows how many bad guys. It was obscene. It was out of the question. I had to save that Western town.

A family trip to Europe as Mom tried to keep her marriage together.

With Mom's permission, I rented some trucks from Sam's-U-Drive and rounded up all the drivers I could find. My friends and I dismantled the Western town, loaded the set pieces onto the trucks, and took them home to our backyard on Greenway Drive. I already had a huge room full of costumes and props, my own tank, and my own world-class movie camera. Now, incredibly, I had my own Western town. My buddies and I couldn't wait to start rebuilding it and adding as many storefronts as the space allowed—a general store, a Western Union office, a sheriff's office, even a hotel/house of ill repute, converted from Carrie's former playhouse. It took a whole lot of return trips to MGM, a whole lot of lumber, a whole lot of help from our security man Zinc (we didn't call him "the human crane" for nothing), and a whole lot of hard manual labor, and it was worth it.

Work was interrupted one day when Mom asked me to come into the music room. We needed to have a talk.

She and Carrie were sitting there waiting. Carrie always had this self-satisfied smile on her face when she knew something I didn't. She had that smile now. In fact, she was bursting.

I flopped into a chair, grabbed a piece of butterscotch hard candy from the crystal dish on the small coffee table beside me, and asked, "What's up?"

Whatever was going on, Mom seemed kind of serious about it, and for some reason she was having trouble saying it. Finally, in one breath, she came out with "You know, dear, we're having a few difficulties here, and I'm going to have to go away and do a show."

Okay. She'd gone away and done a show about a million times before. So? And as for the "few difficulties," that went right over my head—as far as I was concerned, things had never been better.

"I'm going to do a Broadway play," she said, "and I don't know how long it's going to last, but I'll be gone for a while."

Yeah? And?

She wasn't quite finished. "Carrie's coming with me. She's going to be in the chorus of the show. And if the play's a success, I'll send for you."

I could tell she wanted some kind of response. I think I came up with something like "Cool." Carrie, in the meantime, was enjoying every second of this.

Mom leaned closer to me and gave me her most positive, reassuring, Debbie Reynolds smile. "I just want you to know that everything's going to be fine. I'm going to fix it, okay? So please don't worry."

No problem, since I still didn't have a clue what the big deal was. I promised her I wouldn't worry, grabbed a handful of butterscotch candy to take to my crew, and headed back to work on the Western town.

In *Debbie: My Life* Mom wrote of me after that conversation: "He banged, he hammered, and instead of crying over the separation from his mother and sister, he took every bit of anger and frustration out by building."

I'm sorry, but she couldn't have been more wrong. I wasn't angry. I wasn't frustrated. I was having the time of my life. You might even say I was downright blissful.

4

TIME OF MY LIFE

Carrie and Mom together.

S o Mom and Carrie headed off to New York for Mom to star in a Broadway musical called *Irene*, and Harry and I stayed home on Greenway Drive. With only the two of us in the house, there was no need to keep the full roster of employees on hand; so Harry and I roughed it with just a bare-bones staff of seven, including our faithful housekeeper Mary Douglas. Other than that it was just me and Harry, two "bachelors" on our own, getting along great, each of us pretty much minding our own business (the operative words being *pretty much*). Harry seemed to be spending more time at home in the master bedroom, watching *Star Trek*, getting his daily haircuts and shaves and, oddly, a *lot* more manicures.

I was busy with my buddies, finishing work on the Western town and making movies in the backyard. When we weren't shooting anything that could conceivably involve a tank, we were making the best possible use of that Western town, including a dramatic reenactment of the final scene of *Butch Cassidy and the Sundance Kid*, starring me and John Courtney. (John's an executive at CNN now. He told me recently that he wouldn't be where he is today if it weren't for the upbringing he had at my house. No doubt about it, we both learned a lot during those years. A lot.) I did miss the endless fun of filming in all those magic worlds at MGM Studios, but there was a lot to be said for the convenience of waking up in

John Courtney and me, filming in the Western town.

the morning and walking out my back door into the magic world I was creating right there on Greenway Drive.

Eventually we moved on from Westerns, as we got our hearts set on filming the sequence in *Where Eagles Dare* in which Clint Eastwood blows up the guard tower. Time for another delivery from our trusty friends at Anawalt Lumber, who'd filled countless orders for the completion of the Western town; and in a couple of weeks, with a lot of long, sweaty days of manual labor, we built our very own guard tower. The military surplus store provided dummy hand grenades. Now all we needed was a way to make that tower explode.

As usual, it was Ellis Mercantile to the rescue. Not only did they have M160 explosives, they even had a trigger board so we could set the explosives off remotely, and they showed us how to use it.

We raced back to Greenway Drive, wired up that trigger board, loaded the guard tower with M160s, and were ready for "Action!"

One friend in a German military uniform from our endless supply of costumes took his place at the guard tower. Another friend manned the trigger board a safe distance away. John Courtney and I, in character, came running into frame on cue, lobbed the dummy grenade into the tower, our man at the trigger board flipped the switch, and BLAM!

The guard tower didn't just explode, it disintegrated. It blew a mile high and vaporized in midair. The deafening force of it knocked us down and shattered all the windows on one side of our house. We found out later that we'd accidentally overloaded the guard tower. One M160 translates to a fourth of a stick of dynamite. We'd used four of them. Okay. Good to know for future reference.

Finally, when our ears stopped ringing, I yelled out the obvious question—not "Is everyone okay?", but "Did we get the shot?" (We did. It was spectacular.)

We were in the house, assessing the damage from all those broken windows, when the doorbell rang. On her way to answer it, Mary called out to me, "Boy, you're in trouble now!"

John and I raced to that discreet vantage point through the window and the terrarium to the outside of the front door and saw two grim uniformed Beverly Hills Police Department cops standing there, one of them holding a charred, smoldering fragment of the guard tower.

We heard, "Is Mr. Karl here?" I had a pit in my stomach the size of Texas.

Mary asked them to wait there; and a few moments later Harry appeared, drink in hand and elegant as always, and greeted them, as calm and friendly as if he'd invited them over to watch a football game.

"Well, hello, gentlemen. What can I do for you?"

The cops were uncharmed. One of them held up the piece of blackened wood.

"Mr. Karl, we've had several reports of an explosion on your property, and this flaming piece of wood landed on the roof of the house next door."

The Sarnoff house. Sarnoff, as in Robert Sarnoff, head of RCA. My heart sank. I hadn't even had time yet to wonder where the disintegrated guard tower ended up. Horrible visions started flashing through my mind—handcuffs, the backseat of a squad car, a holding cell, the humiliating publicity . . . "Debbie Reynolds' Son Charged with Arson."

I was thinking of making a run for it when we saw Harry take the burnt, splintered evidence with a gracious "Thank you very much. I've got it under control," and close the door in their faces.

The cops stood there outside the closed door, obviously trying to figure out what had just happened and what they should do about it. Then, by some miracle, or because they simply wanted to save themselves a whole lot of paperwork, they turned and walked away.

Harry was our hero that day. He never said a word to Mom, or to me, about any of it. He even quietly had all those broken windows replaced. Moments like this made it impossible not to like the guy.

With Harry at home.

"Not worrying Mom" was kind of a running theme while she and Carrie were in New York. My life was a lot easier and a lot more fun that way, and with the logic of a teenager, I was sure that keeping my mouth shut would make her life a lot easier and a lot more fun too. I was actually doing her a favor, right?

Imagine her needless worry, for example, especially when she was three thousand miles away, if I'd told her that Eddie had bought me a gun.

And in Eddie's defense and mine, it wasn't as irresponsible as it probably sounds.

For one thing, my buddies and I had learned to shoot at Gold Arrow summer camp, where we earned our own NRA cards. I was a pretty good shot, and I was pretty responsible about gun safety (despite some highly publicized evidence to the contrary a year or so later).

For another thing, Eddie had a lot of experience with and respect for all sorts of firearms, thanks to his service in the Korean War as an army private first class. (He also entertained the troops in Korea, by the way, as did Debbie Reynolds. They didn't actually meet while Mom was there, but by all accounts, including his, the first time he saw her, he turned to his best friend, Bernie Rich, and said, "I'm going to marry that girl." Within a year or so, of course, he did.)

Eddie went to Vietnam several times to entertain the troops, with an officer's status—first as a major and later as a colonel—and a legitimate Defense Department military ID card. He was friends with a lot of generals, and he had a very strong, almost surprising sense of patriotism. I still have some of the souvenirs he brought me from Vietnam, from army pouches and patches to a captured Vietnamese flag with blood on it, signed to him by the soldier who captured it.

Eddie kept a gun in the nightstand beside his bed, and more guns all over the house, and he got a huge kick out of showing them off to me and my buddies. Finally one day he bought me a Remington .22, the kind of gun we'd learned to shoot at camp. We practiced target shooting in his backyard, we were never allowed to practice unsupervised, and I kept my gun at his place and kept my mouth shut that it even existed—Mom would have had Eddie's head on a platter if she'd known about that gun. I had guns on Greenway Drive from the MGM auction, obviously; but in Mom's mind those were just "props," and I wasn't about to break it to her that just because they shot blanks didn't mean they weren't real.

I appreciated the Remington and the war keepsakes Eddie gave me, don't get me wrong. But at around that same time, the man outdid himself when it came to memorable gifts. I never told him how memorable it turned out to be. As I look back on it now, I'm sure he would have loved it.

My dad, Eddie, and me, 1971.

Eddie invited John and me to his house one afternoon. He had a surprise for me, he said. And yes, he certainly did.

We walked into the living room to find a voluptuous, scantily dressed exotic dancer gyrating in front of a video camera on a tripod, with Eddie nearby, grinning from ear to ear. John and I froze in place the instant we saw her. We were two healthy, red-blooded virgins in our early teens, and we were mesmerized, in awe and ten or twelve other adjectives that apply to surging testosterone.

Eddie finally broke the silence, beyond pleased with himself. "Well? What do you think, boys?" He beamed. "Hottest model on the market. Think you can handle it?"

We exchanged a *what?!* look before we realized he was talking about the camera. I'm not sure if I was disappointed or relieved.

We headed home that day with the new Sony AVC-3200 video camera, complete with a half-inch black-and-white VTR recorder and matching black-and-white video monitor. Great present, great presentation!

It was my first video camera. John and I couldn't wait to see what kind of picture quality it had to offer. We set it up in our studio headquarters, aka the projection room, and we were in luck—we were getting ready to do a test shoot with it when John discovered a half-recorded videotape in the tape deck. We rewound a little, hit play, and our jaws hit the floor. There was that same exotic dancer, performing the same incredibly exotic dance, only this time, on that tape, she was completely naked. Thank you, Eddie, and thank you, God! We played it over and over again, gaping at it, probably drooling, wondering if Eddie had really tossed it in as a bonus gift he knew we'd come across sooner or later and *love* it.

Apparently not, as we discovered on viewing number eighty or so. Eddie's car suddenly came flying up the driveway and screeched to a halt at the front door. His valet/driver Willard raced in, frantic to exchange the tape Eddie had accidentally left in the machine for the blank tape he was waving at us.

Really? Eddie left a tape in the machine? We'd been so busy playing with my new camera that we hadn't even noticed! Of *course* we'll be happy to trade tapes!

The relieved driver handed us the blank tape, we handed him the tape we'd been thoroughly enjoying for the last half hour, and once he was gone John and I laughed our asses off reliving the whole crazy, abnormally normal day.

Again, don't get me wrong, I really appreciated that video camera, but there was no way around it: the picture quality didn't begin to measure up to the picture quality of a film camera. On the other hand, video was an emerging technology that needed to be investigated, and I could hardly insult Eddie by returning this very generous gift. (Read "no way was I handing back a $3,000 piece of equipment.")

So there I was with a top-of-the-line video camera and no idea what to do with it until another one of Harry's manicurists showed up. I had a brainstorm: maybe I could use it to solve the mystery of why Harry had started having so many more manicures since Mom and Carrie left town.

There was a tall corner table near the headboard of the oversize bed in the master bedroom. A ceramic doll with a lacy skirt sat on top of the table. I'd never paid a bit of attention to it before, but now it seemed as if it had been sitting there patiently waiting for me to grow a brain. I carefully placed the camera under the doll's skirt so that only the lens peeked out. Then I ran the video wire behind the table, along the baseboard, behind a dresser, and under the carpet into Mom's changing room, where John set up the recording machine and monitor. Whatever was going on between Harry and that parade of manicurists, I was going to find out once and for all.

It took some patience, which wasn't one of my strongest qualities. There was no way of knowing when a manicurist might show up, and I couldn't exactly sit staring out at the front door twenty-four hours a day without tipping everyone off that I was up to something. So I went on about my business as best I could, jumping every time the doorbell rang, waiting and waiting for what seemed like years. Finally, as if it was meant to be, all the pieces of the plan fell perfectly into place late one otherwise ordinary morning.

Harry was upstairs. John and I were downstairs. The doorbell rang. John and I hurried to peer out at the front door through the monkey ferns in the terrarium. An attractive brunette manicurist was standing there waiting. Mary answered the door, the manicurist asked for Mr. Karl, and Mary led her up the grand stairway to the master bedroom.

The instant they disappeared John and I zoomed through the maze of hallways, walk-ins, and bathrooms that led to the back entrance of Mom's upstairs dressing area. We planted ourselves in front of the monitor in the nick of time—the show was just getting started.

This might be a good opportunity to bring up a few glitches in Harry's relentless aristocratic facade. Besides his snoring and his chronic farting, he was also in the habit of sleeping, and gliding around in the privacy of the master suite, in silk pajama shirts and no pajama pants or underwear. I'm sure you can picture this without needing any further details. It wasn't pretty. Carrie and I had been making faces at each other about it since we were old enough to say "Ew." (If you want a more graphic description, Carrie handles it far better than I ever could in our documentary *Bright Lights*.)

So John and I watched breathlessly as Harry, in his usual nightshirt and no pants, sat down on the edge of the bed with his back to the camera. The manicurist removed all her clothes. She then knelt in front of him, obscured from our view by his large frame, and we saw that his nightshirt was being bunched up around his waist. We couldn't figure out what she was doing, except that it had nothing to do with Harry's nails. Whatever it was, it didn't take very long. When she was finished she stood up, got dressed, and left. Harry covered up, resumed his usual position in bed, and went right back to enjoying *Star Trek* and his J&B and soda.

John was as stumped as I was, but luckily we had a friend named Scott Zimmerman who knew everything there was to know about this kind of thing. (We never asked how he knew, he just did, and you don't question the reliable experts in your life.) We barely understood the general mechanics of sexual intercourse, and now we were being introduced to a whole new concept called oral sex. From his description, it sounded strange at first, maybe even unlikely, maybe even disgusting. Scott just smiled and said, "Don't knock it 'til you've tried it."

Needless to say, I thought about all this new information *a lot* over the next couple of weeks. I wasn't devising a plan, any more than I would have wasted time devising a plan on how to film a golf tournament on the moon. Why drive myself crazy thinking about something that was never going to happen?

And then the doorbell rang.

To this day I can't remember why, because it was so rare at 813 Greenway Drive, but somehow, for a series of reasons, I was home alone.

I wasn't about to answer the door until I made sure it wasn't the Beverly Hills Police Department or some disgruntled neighbor complaining about my filmmaking again, so I went to my post at the window and looked out at the front door.

She was young and blond. She was wearing a very flattering form-fitting top and a short skirt, and she was without a doubt the most beautiful woman I'd ever seen.

She rang the doorbell again, and I raced to the door but calmed myself when I got there so I could open it with that patented Harry Karl nonchalance.

"Hello," she purred. "Is Mr. Karl in?"

I was young, but I wasn't stupid. "I'm Mr. Karl," I said.

She laughed. "No, really, is he in?"

"No," I said, "no one's here but me."

She smiled, sweet and friendly. I think I smiled back. I'm not sure.

"May I come in?" she asked.

I opened the door wider and stepped aside. She stood in the foyer looking around while I closed the door. I noticed that her eyes settled on the bar, and she asked if she could have something to drink. If I'd been in my right mind, I would have known that she was hoping for something alcoholic. But I wasn't, so I helpfully led her to the kitchen.

"What would you like?"

She scanned me from head to toe and asked with meaning, "What have you got?"

I opened the refrigerator, trying to reconnect with reality. "Water? Orange juice? Milk?"

She hopped onto the butcher block island, unapologetically leaving her legs open just enough to make it impossible not to notice that (a) she wasn't wearing panties beneath her skirt, and (b) she was a natural blond. My legs were getting weak.

"Do you have a girlfriend?"

I didn't answer her—I'd lost my ability to understand English.

"Have you ever had a girlfriend?"

Somehow that penetrated, and I laughed nervously. "Of course. I've had a couple of girlfriends. Why?"

She put her hands on my shoulders, pulled me to her, and kissed me, with a lot of passion, a lot of expertise, and a lot of tongue. I thought my head was going to explode. When she finally pulled back a little, she looked into my eyes and breathed, "Have you ever been kissed like that before?"

I was pretty sure no one had ever been kissed like that before. By this point I'd lost my ability to even form words, so I just shook my head. She smiled and eased herself off the butcher block, letting her skirt hike up for a moment. Then, with her hands on my waist, she asked, "Where's your room?"

Heart pounding, barely able to breathe, I led her from the kitchen, through the pantry, through the dining room, through the music room, through the den, and down the hallway past Carrie's bedroom to my room. I will always remember it as the longest walk of my life. I had no idea what was about to happen, or *if* something was about to happen, or if something did happen, how the hell I would know that to do. Where was Scott Zimmerman when I needed him?

She sat down on the bed and politely listened while I nervously regressed to the age of five and started touring my bedroom, showing her my arrowhead collection and my war medals and my soldiers, pretty much everything but my sock drawer. At some point I looked over at her, and she patted the bed, inviting me to come sit beside her.

I did. She took it from there.

I believe there really is such a thing as too much information, so I'll leave it at that, except to say that at some point I learned what Harry's manicurist had been doing kneeling in front of him while he sat on the edge of the bed, and that "Don't knock it 'til you've tried it" were words to live by.

I'd had my first "manicure," and it exceeded anything and everything I ever imagined it would be. I told a few of my buddies all about it, of course. But I never told Harry, and I'm sure it goes without saying that I never, *ever* told Mom—no good could have come from that, for me or for Harry.

Harry had been his usual mellow self after Mom and Carrie left for New York, but when I stopped long enough to focus on him, he seemed kind of preoccupied, like something was bothering him. It probably says a lot about me and my relationship with him that I didn't call him on it and ask if he was okay.

One day, though, he apparently needed to get whatever it was off his chest, and he took me into his massive, crazy impeccable closet and opened one of the hidden drawers in a back cabinet where he kept some of his valuables. I vaguely noticed some slips of paper with amounts of money written on them, and some others with scribbled names and phone numbers, while he rooted around and pulled out a handful of tabloid articles he'd obviously cut out and stashed.

He handed them to me without a word. One headline read, "Debbie Leaves Harry Karl!" Another read, "Debbie Reynolds and Harry Karl Separated!" Still another read, " 'It's Over!' Says Debbie of Her Marriage to Harry!"

I finished glancing through them and gave them back to Harry with a shrug. "So?" I asked him. It surprised me that he looked so upset.

He hung his head, and I could barely hear him when he said, "I don't know what to do, Todd."

I was incredulous. "What to do about *what*? What are you talking about? Harry, since when do you believe anything you read in the tabloids? Mom's in New York doing a play, and some asshole reporters have decided to make up stories about it to sell more papers. What's the big deal?"

He actually had fear in his eyes. I'd never seen that before. "You really think your mother's coming back to me?"

"You're being ridiculous. Of course she's coming back to you," I said, done with this conversation.

He seemed cautiously relieved, smiled a little, and took a long sip of his J&B and soda. I noticed as I walked away that he put the tabloid articles back in the drawer rather than throwing them away, but beyond that, I didn't give the conversation another thought.

At least not then.

A few weeks later, Harry's friend Gregory Peters invited us

to play in a pro-am golf tournament at a course he owned in La Manga, Spain. I was on a major high when the tournament was over and we boarded a plane back to the United States, and with good reason—I shot my first hole in one while partnered with Hall of Fame golfer Gary Player. I was still floating on air about it when we flew into JFK, and not until then did I find out I wasn't heading on to California with Harry, I was staying right there in New York. Mom had promised that if her play *Irene* was a hit, she'd send for me.

Irene was a hit, and she sent for me, by way of Harry, either before or during our time in Spain. On one hand, it was a happy surprise. I'd missed Mom and Carrie, and New York City sounded like a great new place for me and my cameras to explore.

On the other hand, for some reason I didn't understand, saying good-bye to Harry there by the baggage claim carousel had the oddest weight to it, an intangible finality that made it feel as if it were happening in slow motion.

It felt like an ending, and I didn't know why.

5

154 EAST 74TH STREET

My first birthday away from Greenway Drive.

A car was waiting at JFK to take me and my luggage to 154 East 74th Street, the four-story brownstone between Third and Lexington where I'd be living with Mom and Carrie.

It was one of those reunions when you feel as if it's been a long time since you've seen one another, and as if no time has passed at all. Carrie and I picked right up where we'd left off, easy and playful, close enough to know what to expect from each other and what not to expect. Mom seemed edgy, almost too eager to make me comfortable and reassure me that she'd missed me and felt guilty about leaving me with Harry. And she was tiny. She looked as if she'd lost a good ten or fifteen pounds since I'd seen her, weight she didn't have to lose in the first place. But she was working her ass off starring in a Broadway musical. Yeah, that explained it.

They immediately presented me with a welcome-home gift, an adorable apricot teacup poodle. If I said, "Who's there? Who's

Mom taking a dip with my poodle, Killer.

there?" with a sense of urgency, that little poodle would attack anything within a ten-foot radius, so I named him Killer.

I arrived with nothing but my golf clubs and the clothes I'd packed for Spain. No problem. Mom had hired a guy named John Lebold to organize and catalogue her collection of MGM memorabilia. He'd helped me and my buddies haul things from the MGM back lot to Greenway Drive, and he and I had become friends. So Mom had arranged for John to help Mary pack up my whole bedroom full of stuff and ship it from Greenway Drive. These huge aluminum bins from the MGM wardrobe department, about six times the size of foot lockers, were waiting for me in my room next to Mom's on the second floor of the brownstone.

There were two bedrooms on the fourth floor. One was Carrie's. The other, when she was in town, was Joan Hackett's. Joan was a wonderful actress who'd become a good friend and mentor of Carrie's. Joan was very sweet, smart, and cerebral, one of the few people Carrie trusted. From the first day I got there it was impossible not to notice that Carrie was gravitating toward Joan and her *Irene* castmates, and away from Mom. Mom couldn't figure out why the distance between them was growing, let alone what to do about it. She kept trying to win Carrie back, and Carrie kept pulling further and further away; and it was Joan who convinced Mom that it might be a good idea for Carrie to start seeing a therapist. It was Joan who also encouraged Carrie to start keeping journals, which eventually led to Carrie's incredible writing career. Thanks to Joan, a poem of Carrie's even appeared in *Interview* magazine, Carrie's first published work. It's an understatement to say that when she was around, Joan was instrumental in helping Carrie in a whole lot of ways, at a time in Carrie's life when she would never have accepted help from Mom—as Carrie later said, "It's a teenager's job to find her parent annoying and ridiculous."

I couldn't make any sense of what the hell was going on between them, so I opted to stay out of it and went on about my

Carrie with her great friends Connie Freiberg and Joan Hackett.

business making myself at home in the brownstone. The third floor
housed a separate kitchen, a living room, and a guest bedroom.
Some of the aluminum bins John and Mary had sent from Greenway Drive contained my stereo system, my 16 mm projector and
screen, and everything else I needed to transform the living room
into a projection room. Mom had found a man named Angelo who
sold movies to her out of the trunk of his car at $200 apiece, and
almost immediately we revived our family tradition of watching
movies together, either in the projection room or in bed, and *never*
without popcorn, with *real* melted butter. (Popcorn was the only
thing Mom could cook, back in the days when popcorn had to be
made in a pan.) It was a family tradition we continued for the rest
of Mom's and Carrie's lives, and to this day I can't watch a movie
unless there's plenty of popcorn with real melted butter on hand.

I was promptly enrolled at the Professional Children's School,
which Carrie was already attending. I'm sure it's a great place, if
you can relate to cliquish ballerinas and male ballet dancers. Neither of us could, although to be fair, neither of us had ever been too

enthralled with the whole school thing to begin with. At best we thought of the Professional Children's School as a barely tolerable endurance test, but I did manage to find a couple of upsides to it.

For one thing, Mom gave us cab fare every morning to get to school. Carrie stayed with the cab option. I, on the other hand, quickly figured out that if I invested in the cheap bus or subway passes the school offered us students, I could pocket the cab fare and find something much more interesting to do with that money.

For another thing, I was leaving school one afternoon when I saw a guy around my age, with a lot of red hair, standing at the bottom of the stairs smoking a cigarette. I must have looked as miserable as I felt about having wasted yet another day in classrooms when I could have been exploring New York with my cameras, because as I passed him he kind of muttered, "Long day?"

I stopped and looked at him. It was probably more of a glare. He offered me a cigarette, which I declined.

"You into ballet?" he asked.

"No fucking way," I said. "I'm a filmmaker, not a dancer."

He seemed relieved. "Richard Landers," he said.

"Todd Fisher," I said, and we shook hands.

And that's how one of the most enduring friendships of my life began—two of the few straight male students at the Professional Children's School finding each other and becoming pretty inseparable for a long time to come. Richard's real last name was Friedlander, but he was fairly rebellious, didn't get along very well with his parents, and chose to go by Landers instead. He didn't talk much about them except to say that his dad was a press agent for the Yankees.

Richard and I were at the brownstone a few days later when Mom walked in. His back was to her, with his big head of red curly hair, and she greeted me with a cheerful, "Hi, dear. Aren't you going to introduce me to your girlfriend?"

Richard turned and looked at her. He was insulted, she was embarrassed, and from that awkward beginning they became such great pals that she came to think of him as her adopted son.

From the very beginning of our friendship, Richard made any number of invaluable contributions to my life. For example, I knew a lot about big band music—Cole Porter, Irving Berlin, Meredith Willson, you name it—but I knew virtually nothing about contemporary music. Richard did. We started making stops at a record store every day after school, where I happily spent my pocketed cab fare and, with Richard's guidance, amassed an impressive record collection of esoteric jazz, Frank Zappa, Tower of Power, all the best of the best in the early 1970s. One of Richard's and my favorites was Mike Oldfield's *Tubular Bells*. Carrie declared us "fucking geniuses" for appreciating it—high praise coming from her. (Of course, all three of us were loaded out of our minds when we listened to that song, so we may have overreacted.)

I knew virtually nothing about sound, beyond the usual top-of-the-line Radio Shack equipment. Richard did. In fact, he knew a lot. He showed me how much of a difference a great sound system could make in enjoying music and movies, and it blew me away. I brought home brochures of this amazing equipment Richard turned me on to and told Mom about this whole new movie and music experience I'd heard with my own ears at the stores he took me to. Next thing I knew, all the great equipment I'd been raving about, including—I loved this—Fisher speakers, was being delivered to the brownstone. It seems that Mom got caught up in my enthusiasm and surprised me with it, and she was as excited about the new sound system as Richard and Carrie and I were from the instant she first heard it. Richard, by the way, went on to become one of the top sound technicians in the recording industry, with a lot of stops along the way that he and I worked on together.

I knew absolutely nothing about marijuana. Richard did. I smoked my first joint with Richard, and I liked it. We invited Carrie to join us. It was news to me that she'd smoked pot before. Even when Richard wasn't around, Carrie and I would get stoned and listen to music together, and get stoned and lie in bed and watch movies together, and popcorn had never tasted so good. It's probably worth adding, because it's true, that if I'd known the path my sister was on, I would never in a million years have done any kinds of drugs with her.

Richard and Carrie and I were hanging out on the third floor of the brownstone one day when a very familiar aroma came wafting up the open stairway from the first-floor living room. This was way too bizarre for us to ignore. We flew down the stairs and into the living room, and there on the sofa, pleasantly chatting away, sat Mom, with a glass of wine, and this long-haired stranger, smoking a joint.

She greeted us with her usual cheerful, "Hi, dears." Then she gestured to the stranger and added, "Say hello to Richard Perry. We're just sitting here with my wine and Richard's marijuana cigarette talking about recording an album of the *Irene* soundtrack."

We said hello and headed back up the stairs in total shock—not over meeting Richard Perry, who was a huge record producer, but over Mom's casual acceptance of pot in her house. We'd been very careful to hide it from her that we were smoking it, but hey, maybe we were overreacting. Maybe next time we were hanging out together and she was having her wine, which she was drinking more and more often, we should just light up a joint and see what happened. On the other hand, maybe watching a guy in the music business smoke pot was a whole different thing from watching her own kids do it. Maybe it would upset her, and for what? So she could forbid it in the brownstone, which would leave us where, exactly? Was it really worth the risk? That settled it. It made much more sense to keep hiding it from her.

We were all at home one day when who should show up at the door but Tony Curtis. He and Mom had known each other since they did a couple of movies together in the 1960s (*The Rat Race* and *Goodbye, Charlie*). There had been some tension between them when Mom found out that Tony had been quoting his pal Eddie Fisher's claim that Mom was a "lesbian" and a "lousy lay." Mom had confronted him about it, they talked it out, Tony apologized, and while they were never good friends again, they were at least friendly.

Tony, it turned out, had just moved in across the street, and he'd come to say hello and invite all of us over for drinks.

At some point while Tony was showing us around his new place, Richard and I found ourselves alone with him. He stepped over to me, put his arm around my shoulders, and very discreetly dropped a couple of joints in my shirt pocket. I looked at him with a silent *Huh?*

He kept his voice just above a whisper. "Don't go to strangers," he said to both Richard and me. "Seriously, this is New York. Do *not* go to strangers. Come to me."

Thanks! Consider it done!

We definitely took him up on it, and we even reciprocated by hooking him up with a few trustworthy suppliers we connected with through school, who had better quality pot than Tony did. He appreciated it. Come to think of it, considering my track record on Greenway Drive, Tony Curtis may have been the first person in my life who enjoyed having me as a neighbor.

Thanks to Mom, I was earning enough money to afford my own marijuana and other incidentals—almost immediately after I arrived in New York, she got me a job selling programs at the Minskoff Theatre, where she and Carrie were doing *Irene*. I was perfectly happy to be working, and all these decades later I've come to appreciate something even more important about it.

Mom really was incredible, since Carrie and I were born, about doing everything in her power to make sure that we were included in her life as much as possible. She never sequestered us or treated us like accessories to be trotted out for photo shoots and then handed back to a team of nannies like so many other "show biz kids" we knew. Having a mom as hardworking and independent as Debbie Reynolds and knowing that wherever she was, she wanted us there too made me feel not just loved but *valued*, even when it came to something as seemingly ordinary as selling programs at the theater where she and Carrie were performing.

By definition, the three of us left for work together every night, and unless Carrie went out with friends after the show, we got

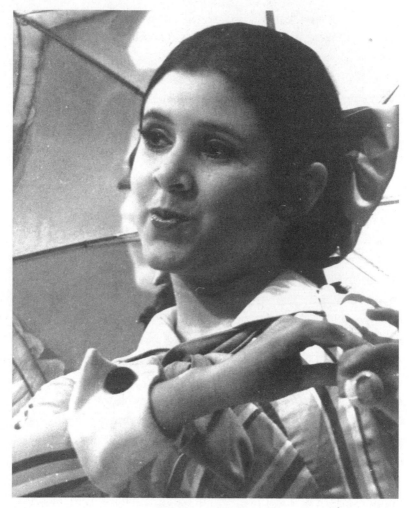

Carrie performing in *Irene* at the Minskoff Theatre.

home at the same time. Carrie would head to her room on the fourth floor, and Mom and I would grab our popcorn and her wine and lie in bed in my room with Killer, watching a movie.

So one night at about 1:30 A.M., there we were, home from the theater, going about our usual routine. Carrie was at a disco with Mom's friend and hairdresser Pinky Babajian. Mom and Killer and I were in my room eating popcorn and watching the Montgomery Clift/Elizabeth Taylor/Shelley Winters classic *A Place in the Sun*.

A commercial came on that had tap dancing in it, and I started wondering if maybe I should take tap dancing lessons. I'm a short guy like Donald O'Connor, and God knows he was great at it and loved it, so sure, even though performing was of zero interest to me, it might be kind of fun to give it a try. Mom was giddy to hear that I'd even consider it.

And all the while, I was absent-mindedly playing with my first-generation chrome Army Colt .45, a classic Western six-shooter, my favorite among the arsenal John and Mary had shipped from Greenway Drive along with everything else in my room. I was lying on my right side when I started twirling the gun, aiming it around the room at nothing in particular and generally being an irresponsible idiot. (In my defense, I knew there were no bullets in it, it was just loaded with blanks. Okay, full-load blanks, but still, no bullets.) Mom wasn't getting nearly as big a kick out of it as I was and asked me to put it away, so I reached over to lay it on the nightstand. Unfortunately, the hammer gently touched the edge of the table, and since there was no safety, the gun went off, with the barrel only a few inches from my right leg.

It shocked both of us. The sound was deafening. Our ears were ringing, and the room filled with a hazy, acrid smoke. The full-load blank blew a huge hole in my pants and my leg. My pants were slightly on fire for a second, and there were some powder burns and a lot of blood. I was in so much of a daze that I didn't feel a thing.

Rather than freak out as so many moms might have done, mine shifted into instant Girl Scout/take-charge mode, leapt up, yanked a pillowcase off one of the pillows, tore it in half (try that some-time—it's not easy!), and tied it around my leg for a tourniquet. Then she grabbed the phone and, because ambulances were noto-riously slow in New York, made an emergency call to the Checker Cab company we always used. She tried to carry me down the steep staircase to the first floor and our front door, but she weighed ninety-seven pounds, and adrenaline can do only so much, so I scooted down the stairs on my butt instead, while Mom wrote a note to Carrie and Pinky, something like, "Todd shot himself, we've gone to the hospital," and we were in the cab and on our way to New York Hospital in no time.

Mom knew enough about tourniquets to know she had to keep releasing it every few minutes so she wouldn't cut off circulation in my leg, and every time she released it in the cab, blood spurted all over the place. In the meantime, the cabdriver was completely enchanted to find Debbie Reynolds in his backseat—not only was he a fan of her movies, but he'd served in the Korean War and saw her when she was there entertaining the troops. He was so enchanted that he stayed with us at the hospital until I was settled into the emergency room.

I remember hearing the word *surgery*. I remember being given a shot of Demerol that made me stupid and loopy. I remember Mom looking down at me with tears in her eyes and saying, "We were just talking about you learning to tap dance." I remember watching the overhead fluorescent lights fly past as my gurney was wheeled to a room, and seeing what seemed like a million flash-bulbs going off through the glass hospital entrance doors as the press started gathering.

And I remember some cops showing up. A doctor had called the police, as required by law, to report that the hospital was treating a gunshot victim. I swear to you, the plainclothes detective who stepped up to question me was short and dark-haired, wearing a trench coat and holding a cigar. I was too out of it to talk to him coherently, so I have no idea what I said. In fact, I was so out of it that I started laughing because he looked and sounded exactly like he was doing a parody of *Columbo*.

Then he turned to Mom and said, "You're under arrest."

I found out later that while I was lying there, loaded on Demerol and whatever other drugs they gave me before, during and after surgery, I missed out on a whole lot of drama.

Mom was taken to the police precinct after refusing to leave the hospital until she'd visited me in my room. She was fingerprinted, along with a crowd of very surly hookers; she had her mug shot taken, without her makeup, eyelashes, and *Irene* wig, at 4:30 A.M., so that she looked like a reject from a very low-budget Debbie Reynolds look-alike contest; and she was booked for possession of an unregistered firearm.

Somehow, in the meantime, she'd managed to get in touch with Carrie and Pinky, filled them in on what was happening, and told them to go back the house. The police would be showing up to retrieve the Colt .45—but they weren't to let the police come in before hiding the other guns and ammunition Mary had shipped from California and flushing all the marijuana in the house down the toilet. (Carrie and Richard and I obviously weren't as discreet about that as we thought.)

Carrie and Killer went to sit with Mom at the police station while she waited to be interrogated. Pinky was sent to stay with me at the hospital, but they wouldn't let her in because she wasn't a family member, so she sneaked in through a service entrance and was there when I woke up from surgery.

Carrie, wrongly assuming that the press shared her droll sense of humor and knew when she was kidding, told reporters that "Todd wouldn't brush his teeth, so Mom shot him."

My Colt .45 was booked into evidence—and never seen again, by the way.

Mom, with the help of her attorneys, was arraigned and released. She went home, cleaned herself up, and was with me in my hospital room when a few photographers were allowed in. A photo of me in my hospital bed, smiling, with Mom by my side, made the front page of the New York papers, overshadowing the headline "Pablo Picasso Dies at Age 91." The tabloids had a field day speculating about what had happened, including an allegation that Mom had set this whole thing up (that is, shot her own son in the leg, I guess) as a publicity stunt to help boost *Irene* ticket sales.

The phone rang beside my bed. Mom answered it, turned to ice in an instant when she heard the voice on the other end, and handed me the phone with a clenched "It's your father."

It shocked me. Eddie never called. I'm sure my hello sounded like a question.

I heard, "Are you okay?"

I said I was fine.

"What happened?" he asked. "Why did she shoot you?"

I couldn't believe it. He actually thought there was a chance in hell that Mom had shot me. I didn't care what he'd heard or read in the papers, it pissed me off that he would even think such a thing. I explained exactly what happened and repeated that I was fine.

One of Eddie's most frequent exclamations to me since I was a child was some variation on "That's my boy!" I was his only male child, his "one boy." So that day's variation was "I don't want anything to happen to my only boy!" Loopy as I was, I remember feeling as if, whether he meant to or not, he'd managed to make this all about how it would affect him.

I was out of the hospital and back in the brownstone the next day. The surgeon told me that if I'd shot myself less than an inch farther left than I did, it would have dramatically changed the rest of my life; but as it was, I would fully recover. He was right. I was back to normal in no time.

As for Mom, her lawyers saw to it that she never went to trial, all charges were dropped, and she managed to get through the whole thing without missing a single performance of *Irene*.

Incidentally, a great postscript to this story happened seventeen years later. I was in New York with my second wife, Christi, on our way to introduce Christi to Eddie, who was living in a spectacular apartment with his fifth wife, Betty Lin. Christi and I hopped in a cab and gave the driver the address, and it was impossible to ignore the fact that he hadn't stopped staring at me since we settled into the backseat. I was getting ready to ask him if there was a problem when he said, "I know who you are. You're Todd Fisher."

I acknowledged that yes, I was. He gave me this almost rapturous wide-eyed smile as he reached for his glove compartment. "I got something to show you." He beamed.

And out of the glove compartment he pulled this old rag, filthy and stiff from some dried dark brown stains. He didn't just hand it to me, he presented it to me. I was understandably confused, wondering what I was supposed to say, and/or if maybe Christi and I should hop out and hail a different cab.

Then, with some combination of pride and sentiment in his voice, he explained. "That's the tourniquet that was wrapped around your leg the night you shot yourself. I'm the guy who drove you and your mom to the hospital."

I'm not a very emotional guy, but I was blown away—by all the "small world" clichés; by the fact that this man had held on to that torn, bloody pillowcase for almost two decades; and by the unbelievable opportunity I'd just been given to say a long-overdue thank-you to him for taking such good care of me and Mom during a rough, stupid, scary event in our lives.

I signed the rag, handed it back to him, and thanked him.

Believe it or not, I still have the pants I was wearing that night, but I'm more than okay with not having the tourniquet that went with them.

I was also back to my job selling programs at the Minskoff Theatre in no time, and I was in Mom's dressing room one night after the show when I noticed a check sitting in front of her on her makeup table. It was for a small, odd amount of money, and I asked what it was. She told me it was her cut of that week's program sales.

I picked it up and looked at it more closely. The total number of programs sold was written on the memo line.

"Mom," I said, "something's really wrong here. There are three of us selling programs for every performance, and this doesn't even reflect the number of programs *I* sold."

She asked me to repeat what I'd just said. I did better than that. I'd never mentioned it to her or my boss or anyone else, but I was having a running contest with myself, trying to outsell myself every week, and I religiously kept the tallies in a notebook I carried in my pocket. I pulled out the notebook and showed it to her. She'd been given her cut of a total of 1,425 programs for the previous week, at two dollars per program. I'd personally sold 1,503, not even taking the other two salesmen into account—the three of us together averaged sales of about 4,000 per week.

Mom said, "Come with me," and we marched down to my boss's office under a staircase in the theater. He was a short, stocky Italian guy whose name I've blocked out of my mind. There he was in his closet of an office, surrounded by countless boxes of programs, and he greeted Mom with an unctuous "Miss Reynolds. To what do I owe the pleasure of this visit?"

She gave him a terse recap of my conversation with her about the possibility of a "mistake" in the amount of her check and showed him the very thorough, accurate account in my notebook. He studied it for a long time, not one bit happy about it.

Then he looked her right in the eye and said, "Your son's a fuck-ing liar."

Mom went from zero to redlined in less than a second; she reeled back and punched him right in the face. It wasn't a girl punch. It wasn't a bitch slap. It was a full-on prizefighter punch that she ac-tually stepped into, and she knocked him to his ass on the concrete floor.

He was stunned. (So was I.) It took him a few breaths to recover before he got up as if he was going to come after her. She stayed right where she was, silently daring him to try it.

Enter Mom's bodyguard. His name was Bob O'Connell. If you put out a casting call for the biggest, toughest, most badass, ex-convict-looking bodyguard in town, Bob O'Connell would have had the part the minute he walked through the door. Bob stepped in and shielded Mom while he blocked the Italian from getting anywhere near her. She, in the meantime, was still trying to get in one more punch and yelling, "Out! I want him out! He's fired!"

The Italian wasn't finished either, and he was still flailing his arms and yelling as Bob roughly escorted him out of the office and out of the theater. The Italian headed straight to Mom's *Irene* co-producer Harry Rigby, who heard him out and called Mom to try to smooth things over and let the guy keep his job.

"I'll tell you what," she told him. "He can stay in charge of program concessions if that's what you want, in which case I won't be performing in *Irene* anymore. OR I'll keep on performing, he's out, and you can give the program concessions to my son. Your choice."

Needless to say, the Italian never came back. He tried to sue Mom for assault, but the judge laughed him out of court.

And that's the story of how I was put in charge of program concessions for *Irene* at the Minskoff Theatre, making $750 a week, in cash. It's also the story of how Mom was never stiffed on her cut of *Irene* program sales again.

So, feeling like the richest, happiest kid in New York City, continuing to make movies and getting better and better at still photography as well, I strolled one afternoon into a well-known rental and sales house for professional cinematographers called the Camera Mart.

I'd only been there for a couple of minutes when I froze in place, transfixed by a camera in a glass display of Arriflex cameras that seemed to be whispering my name over and over again while the angels sang "Hallelujah." This camera wasn't just another Arriflex, it was the Holy Grail of Arriflexes, my *dream* Arriflex. I tried to look casual when I finally tore myself away from it and asked the store owner how much it was.

He grabbed a pad and pencil, did some quick addition that included the whole package, and calmly announced, "Thirteen thousand."

I refused to give him the satisfaction of watching all the blood drain out of my face, so I simply nodded, gave him a confident "I'll be back" on my way out the door, and headed home to launch my campaign with Mom.

"*Thirteen thousand dollars?!*"

I hadn't heard that much incredulity in her voice since her unforgettable "You're praying for a *tank*?!"

She was far past needing to be convinced that I had talent as a filmmaker and that I was serious about it. She was only incredulous about the price. Finally she offered a compromise. "You save your money for a while and see how much you can come up with. Then maybe I'll help you."

Fair enough. Within a few months, thanks to the $750 cash per week I was making at the theater, I'd saved about $7,000. I counted it out for her one night. She smiled and reached for her checkbook. I handed her the $7,000, and I still have Mom's canceled $13,000 check made out to the Camera Mart.

Richard got interested in photography from hanging out with me. I took him to 42nd Street Photo, helped him pick out a still camera, and started working with him—it seemed like the least I could do to thank him for schooling me on music, sound, and marijuana. Of course, the more I taught him, the more I learned, and I ended up falling in love with doing photo shoots.

I took some publicity stills for *Irene*. I brought my camera along on a photo shoot with Mom and Carrie in Central Park for a magazine layout, took some shots of my own, showed them to the magazine editor, and ended up getting to do a photo shoot with Richard Avedon. That led to a photo shoot, with a crew, for *After Dark* magazine, which led to a lot more press work and some still work on a Jerry Lewis telethon that Mom did with her pal Sammy Davis Jr. Before long I got a call from a publishing company, asking me to go with a crew on a photo shoot for a book they were doing about Africa.

Africa! I was ecstatic! I couldn't wait to tell Mom!

Mom's reaction was an immediate, emphatic "No way." There wasn't a chance in hell she was letting me go off to Africa, and certainly not with a bunch of strangers.

I countered with an equally emphatic "Yes way." There wasn't a chance in hell I *wasn't* going off to Africa. This was a once-in-a-lifetime opportunity, and I wasn't about to miss it, whether she liked it or not. (I got pretty mouthy for a kid who wasn't even old enough to drive yet, but I did mention there was a trip to Africa on the line here, right?)

We finally arrived at a compromise—I could go if she could find a responsible adult, someone she trusted, to go with me. She ended up recruiting Bo Karl, Harry's son, who'd lived with us briefly on Greenway Drive. Bo was a photographer as well, and I liked him, so that was great with me.

It was an incredible trip, just extraordinary in every way. To make it even more extraordinary, toward the end of the book assignment I got an offer to stay in Africa for another two weeks to do a photo shoot for *National Geographic*. I was thrilled—so thrilled, in fact, that I forgot to tell Mom about it.

It seems that she and Carrie and Pinky had shown up at JFK to meet my scheduled flight, but of course, since I was in the middle of Zambia with *National Geographic* at the time, I wasn't on it. Mom put in a frantic call to the American consulate, and search parties were immediately dispatched all over Africa trying to find me when I didn't know I was lost. She'd given me an American Express card before I left, "just in case," but it never entered my mind to use it; so when they tried to track me by the credit card activity and found out

"Lost" in Africa on a photo shoot for *National Geographic*.

there wasn't any, they were convinced I'd been killed and eaten by some roving band of cannibals or something.

It wasn't until I was in the restaurant of a gentleman's club in Nairobi two weeks later, having some lunch before catching my plane back to New York, that I found out there was a problem. A whole herd of guys, including some officials from the consulate, came rushing up to me saying, "There you are! Thank God you're okay!"

I couldn't have been more confused. "Of course I'm okay," I said with a mouthful of food. "Why?"

They filled me in on the drama I'd caused while I was obliviously capturing stills and footage of the exquisite animals and landscapes of Africa. I had no defense, unless you count "Oops."

A limo driver with a sign reading *Fisher* was waiting at JFK to take me to home when I deplaned, but no one else was there to welcome me back. The reception at the brownstone when I walked in the door was, to put it politely, chilly. I'm not sure Mom even bothered to say hello or hug me or get up from the couch and put down her glass of wine before she leveled me with a rhetorical "Are you really so detached that you didn't think we'd be worried?"

I deserved that. I was wrong, and I felt terrible about it.

But oh my God, what a great trip.

We made a short film when I got back. It was called *The Guest*, about a guy who comes to stay with a friend for a week and is still there four months later.

It was a documentary.

In real life, actor and playwright George Furth, an old pal of Mom's who'd done an episode of *The Debbie Reynolds Show* with her, was going to be in town for a few days and wondered if he could crash at our place. Of course! He took over the spare bedroom on the third floor and made himself at home—and when I say "made himself at home," I mean that in every way possible. He had absolutely no compunction about helping himself to anything and everything in the house, coming and going at all hours on his own schedule, constantly raiding a refrigerator he never helped fill—you name it, George did it. At about the ridiculous two- or three-month mark, this became a running joke between Mom, Carrie, and me.

When George was still there after four months, Carrie and I got the idea to make a short movie about it and call it *The Guest*. And it's a testament to what a nice guy he was, and what a good sport, that he happily agreed to participate in it with us.

It was a fun, funny little project. George was hilarious at satirizing himself, ad-libbing reenactments of actual moments like meeting us on the stairs carrying food he'd taken from our refrigerator to put in his. I have a lot of respect for anyone who can satirize himself, and friendships were intact, with no hard feelings, when George left shortly after we finished it.

Other than filming *The Guest*, Carrie didn't seem to spend that much time either out of her room or out of the house at that point in our lives. She was isolating herself more and more, and her contempt toward Mom seemed to be escalating by the day. When she wasn't sniping at her—and with Carrie's brilliance and incredible sense of humor, her words could cut deep and leave scars that took a long time to heal—she was ignoring Mom as if she didn't exist. And if she didn't feel she'd done quite enough damage, she tried to spend her to death.

Carrie was always the first to admit that she was a compulsive shopper and never let a little thing like not being able to afford something keep her from buying it. When she was shopping with Mom's money, it gave her yet another opportunity to punish Mom for God only knew what. Carrie was gleefully out of control. The bills were outrageous, and Mom had no intention of refusing to pay them and run the risk of alienating Carrie even more. (I'll spare you and myself the obvious discussion about enabling, and rewarding, bad behavior.)

Buried in all that shopping, by the way, was an extraordinary side of Carrie I'm not sure she ever realized about herself. She certainly never wrote about it or gave herself credit for it. But throughout her life, a whole lot of the money she spent, whether it was hers or Mom's, she spent on other people. She had the most uncanny knack of noticing what someone liked, filing the information away in her vast mental catalogue, and buying it for them if she ran across it, no matter where in the world she was or how many years had passed since she last saw that person. She did it with close friends, but she also did it with casual acquaintances. For example, if she was in your house and happened to notice that, say, you had a collection of saltshakers or an affinity for movie-themed cocktail napkins, she'd think nothing of showing up at your door weeks or months later with a saltshaker or package of movie-themed cocktail napkins she had spotted in some little shop in Dubai or Singapore. It was remarkable and thoughtful and generous, and it always amazed me that she never seemed to notice it, as if it were something everyone did but just didn't mention it.

And of course, it was also a great built-in way for Carrie to justify some portion of those bushels of Mom's money she was overspending before she started overspending her own.

Mom threw Carrie a spectacular, no-expenses-spared, 1930s/1940s-themed seventeenth birthday party, first in a very posh restaurant and then home to the brownstone, in keeping with her tradition of outdoing herself on every special occasion. During the party Mom had too much to drink, got fairly boisterous, started unraveling a bit, and at one point twirled her skirt high enough that it was apparent she wasn't wearing panties.

I was there. I didn't think it was a big deal. Carrie, on the other hand, thought it was such a big deal that she referenced it in her book and subsequent movie *Postcards from the Edge* almost twenty years later. The "skirt-twirling incident," as we came to call it, seemed to escalate Carrie's animosity toward Mom and confirm a belief she held on to for a long, long time—that Mom was perpetually trying to compete with her. The truth is, she couldn't have been more wrong. *She* was perpetually trying to compete with *Mom*, which created a lot of her resentment and, for many years, put Carrie in the sad position of running hard to win a race that she didn't even realize she was running all by herself.

(I took Mom to the premiere of *Postcards from the Edge*, by the way. I remember a woman coming up to her when it was over and saying, "Oh, dear, I'm so sorry," to which Mom replied, "Oh, dear, it was only a movie." And in case you saw the movie and found yourself wondering, Mom never crashed a car and never got a DUI in real life—which, to be honest, isn't to imply that she never deserved one.)

Carrie and I were hanging out in her room one night when the subject of Harry came up. We started telling stories about him and laughing, and I decided she'd get a huge kick out of hearing about John Courtney's and my videotape surveillance of Harry and the manicurist. I was wrong. It made her livid. She went on a rant about how much she hated him and how glad she was that Mom was getting rid of him.

First of all, I told her, there was no reason for her to hate him. Okay, the manicurist thing was kind of sleazy, but it was also meaningless, just Harry being Harry, and underneath all his aristocratic weirdness, he was a good guy. And second of all, what did she mean, Mom was getting rid of him? Where the hell did she get that idea?

Slowly but surely Carrie started leaking bits of information about what had been going on for the past couple of years, while I'd been so obliviously busy having a great time. All those things I'd kept to myself because I didn't want to worry Mom paled in comparison to all the things she'd kept to herself because she didn't want to worry me. Carrie knew some of it and, being my big sister, had kept it from me as well.

By the time Mom's lawyers came to the brownstone to discuss her divorce from Harry, I knew enough to know that there was no way I was going to let her go through that meeting without me.

6

THE TROUBLE
WITH HARRY

In Central Park on one of our favorite photo shoots.

In October of 2016 I was in New York for a showing of our documentary *Bright Lights* at Lincoln Center, and on a nostalgic impulse, I went back to the brownstone at 154 East 74th Street the next day. I introduced myself to the owners and told them that Mom and Carrie and I lived there a long time ago, and they were kind enough to invite me inside to look around.

I walked into the first-floor living room, and I had an immediate visceral flashback to that meeting with Mom and her lawyers, right down to where everyone sat. It was so emotionally vivid that it might as well have happened earlier that day, probably because it was at that meeting, in that living room, where I made the transition, in just a few short hours, from a carefree, oblivious, self-absorbed boy to the man of the house.

The subject of the meeting was Debbie Reynolds divorcing Harry Karl. That day was the first time I'd heard that the word *divorce* was even being considered. I stayed on the sidelines of the meeting at first. Mom was poised and polite, listening very intently, and she looked so little surrounded by those stern, all-business lawyers. My shock over the whole divorce reality was immediately upstaged as the attorneys started detailing what it was going to cost Mom—she'd have to sell the house, she'd have to sell the cars, she'd have to sell her art collection, she'd have to sell her wedding ring, she'd have to liquidate her beloved MGM memorabilia . . .

I kept my mouth shut for as long as I could, but finally I raised my hand about shoulder high, like Tom Hanks in *Big*. One of the lawyers nodded at me to speak, and I did, seething.

"I've been sitting here for the last half hour listening to what Mom has to give up," I said. "What about Harry? What does he have to give up?"

There was a long silence. I couldn't make sense of what was going on, and I'll be the first to admit, I hadn't been all that interested in anything but being a kid until that day, that meeting, that silence. Now I was very interested. Now I cared, very much. If someone was bullying my mother—even if it was Harry, weirdness and all, the only father I'd known, and I did love him—I wanted to know everything about it, and there was no divided loyalty when it came down to a choice between Mom and him, or Mom and *anybody*.

I started asking questions until the meeting ended and kept right on asking Mom and Carrie for the next several days. The lightbulbs over my head lit up. Connections clicked into place. Unformed questions were answered, and my innocence vanished.

I grew up.

As Mom would explain to me in the days ahead, the first awareness that something was really, really wrong had come one day
in 1967 when a stranger rang the doorbell at the Greenway Drive
house. He was a credentialed FBI agent, and he was there to talk
about Harry.

It seems the FBI was investigating a cheating scam at the Friars Club involving a hole drilled in the ceiling of the card room
where high-stakes gin rummy was played. The accomplice hidden
in the attic would peek through the hole at the players' cards and
electronically transmit the information to his co-conspirators at
the table.

Harry wasn't one of the cheaters. He and such buddies as Phil
Silvers, Zeppo Marx, and Tony Martin were among the players
who'd been cheated out of what was rounded off to be around
$400,000; the five men behind the scam were ultimately arrested
and charged with forty-nine counts of conspiracy.

Mom hated gambling and knew nothing about it, but since
Harry was a very, very wealthy man, she took the position that he
could do what he pleased with his own money.

The FBI agent wondered if Mom was aware how much he gam-
bled. "Did you know he's been losing somewhere between thirty
and fifty thousand dollars a day for years?"

Mom hid her shock at that and repeated that what Harry did
with his money was none of her business.

Then he asked if she happened to know if Harry owned a
ten-thousand-dollar bill.

"Yes, I do know that. Why?"

"Because he lost it, in one card game," the agent told her, "along
with a lot of other cash, and a couple of mortgages with your signature on them."

He showed her the mortgages, which had been seized as evidence. She didn't understand. She signed papers all the time without giving them a thought, because she trusted the people who told

her to sign them—Harry; Irving Briskin, the business manager Harry had hired for her; and her agents and lawyers.

She confronted Harry, who told her it was all a misunderstanding. That explanation fell apart when the Friars Club cheating scandal hit the news; Harry was subpoenaed to testify against the scammers and admitted under oath that he'd lost hundreds of thousands of dollars at the card table.

When Mom asked him how he could let that happen and keep going back, he answered with a simple "It's mine to lose."

Harry had been completely supportive of Mom's determination to buy all those MGM costumes and props when they were auctioned off. The thing was, he told her they'd have to take out a short-term loan from the bank, because "everything is temporarily tied up in investments." This was the man who went into the marriage with about $21 million, talking to his movie star wife, who was earning about a million dollars a year. Mom was able to purchase those costumes and props thanks to a $180,000 bank loan.

It was shortly after her visit from the FBI that Mom was straightening Harry's closet drawers and came across a lot of little pieces of paper with amounts of money written on them—$200, $600, $800, $350, and so forth. I'd seen those same pieces of paper myself.

She asked him about them. He casually explained, "Oh, that's the cash Irving gives me every week."

Irving Briskin was giving Harry cash every week? As always, Harry had a ready explanation: "It's cash, something Irving can take off the top of some deals, that you don't have to report."

Mom understood "cash" and "that you don't have to report," but the rest of it was Greek to her. She didn't keep track of her investments. Harry and Irving did. When it came to tax returns, she just signed them after Irving filled them out. Harry had power of attorney over Mom's money. So did his secretary Ida. So did Irving Briskin. So did a man at her bank. All those people who knew a lot more about these things than she did could legally sign anything and everything on her behalf, and she was relieved to not have to deal with financial matters that made no sense to her to begin with.

Irving Briskin invested some of Mom's money in a hospital in Santa Monica, and he invested more in an invention called the Scopitone, which was kind of a jukebox that played very early versions of music videos in the 1960s.

It turned out the hospital was actually owned by Irving, not by Mom, and the Scopitone was, as Mom later put it, "so far ahead of its time no one bought it."

The last straw with Irving came when Mom's friend Rod Taylor was looking for a business manager. Mom recommended Irving, and Rod went to meet with him. Rod called her after the meeting, incredulous.

"I would never sign with that jerk," he told her. "He charges 25 percent! That's ridiculous!"

Mom truly had no clue what he was talking about. "Twenty-five percent of what?"

"Your income, Debbie! Twenty-five percent of every dime you make goes into his pocket for 'managing' it! You didn't know that?"

No. She most certainly didn't. She went to Harry and told him she had no intention of continuing a business relationship with Irving Briskin for 25 percent of her income.

Harry's reaction was "Well, you've been doing it for all these years, Mother, so why stop now?"

She left Irving Briskin. He settled with her for $300,000 in government bonds. She'd given every penny she'd made in the 1960s to Harry and Irving, a total of around $10 million. She had $300,000 left of that $10 million.

Oh, and those little pieces of paper in Harry's drawer weren't notations of cash Irving had made off the books and given to Harry. They were notations of cash Irving had given to Harry out of Mom's earnings, money she'd paid taxes on.

As I sat there letting Mom fill me in on all this, my mind immediately flashed back to a family lunch we had at the Hillcrest Country Club one day. Irving stopped by to say hello to everyone, and when he got around to Mom, she turned into a block of ice, froze him out, and refused to even look at him. I'd never seen her do that before to anyone, and it startled me. I asked her what that was about, and she said, "He stole from me." I was eleven years old. I didn't get it, but I remembered it. And unfortunately Irving's duplicity was just the beginning.

A few months after Mom left Irving Briskin, Harry had asked her for money. She wasn't working, and all she had was the $300,000 in government bonds from the Briskin settlement. Predictably, her first reaction was an emphatic "You must be kidding."

Harry had assured her the bonds wouldn't be spent. They were only to be used as collateral against a business loan he needed. Reluctantly, she gave them to him. She spent the rest of the day throwing up, sobbing, and lying in bed by herself.

She found out later that the bonds weren't collateral against a loan. They were a pledge against the loan, and they were called in. Gone.

Piece by piece, I came to have a whole new understanding of the last few years. We'd done the Las Vegas shows because Mom desperately needed the money—while I was busy complaining about having to wear makeup to go onstage. She'd made enough money from those shows to pay off the loan she'd taken out for the MGM memorabilia.

Though she'd taken care of the immediate financial distress with the Las Vegas shows, Mom was understandably still quite upset. She arranged to have a very private dinner with Harry's good friend Gregory Peters, the guy who invited Harry and me to the pro-am golf tournament in Spain a couple of years later. Gregory had always been a good friend of Mom's too, and she had his word that he would never mention a word about the dinner to Harry. She confided in Gregory that she was very unhappy and very confused by Harry's constant lies and half-truths. She hated putting Gregory in this position, but she needed the truth from him, whatever it was.

He was uncomfortable and hesitant to rat Harry out—he and Harry weren't just friends, they were also partners in a shoe factory in Spain. But Gregory had some issues of his own with Harry, and he could also see that Mom was in a lot of pain. So finally he opened up. He told Mom not only about the $1.7 million Harry had borrowed from him, which was more than Harry's half share in the shoe factory, but also about several trips he and Harry had taken to Las Vegas together, when he'd seen Harry lose hundreds of thousands of dollars at the tables, sometimes in a single night.

And to confirm another of Mom's suspicions, yes, there were other women in Harry's life. No one in particular, no one who meant anything to him, just brief random encounters when he traveled, or when his manicurists showed up on Greenway Drive.

Although it wasn't her nature to snoop, Mom went into Harry's closet when she got home from that dinner, and in a hidden compartment in the back of a drawer, she found several little slips of paper with women's names and phone numbers on them.

She didn't confront him yet—she was too stunned and disoriented to even begin to make decisions about what she was going to do. But she never slept with him again, using the excuse to Carrie and me that it was because of his snoring.

Then one day, a week or two after her dinner with Gregory Peters, Harry came to her with some papers for her to sign. She asked him what they were, which surprised him, since she'd been signing papers he handed her for more than a decade without asking a single question.

He told her it was "just a continuing mortgage for the beach house."

Mom had bought the land and built the beach house with the money she'd made on *The Unsinkable Molly Brown*. It wasn't a property she and Harry owned together, it was solely hers, and there was no mortgage on it, as far as she knew.

For the first time since she married him, she refused to sign the papers.

He seemed frightened and told her she *had* to sign them.

She didn't ask why, she just said, "No, I don't, and I won't," and she left the room.

Mom went to the wall safe in Harry's den one night to retrieve her emeralds to wear to a charity gala. The safe was empty. Every piece of jewelry in that safe, hundreds of thousands of dollars' worth, was gone.

She confronted Harry, who admitted he'd hocked it all.

He didn't apologize. He just took a sip of his J&B and soda and explained that "we" needed the money.

At that same time, he got another offer to sell the Karl Shoes business. He'd had a lot of other offers over the years and turned them down, but now his back was to the wall—he was dead broke.

A department store chain called Hartfield-Zodys was willing to pay $5 million in cash and stocks. It turned out Karl Shoes had millions of dollars' worth of outstanding debts to the State Street Bank of Boston, and as Harry's wife, Mom was a principal. Harry owned Karl Shoes outright, so he'd been able to personally borrow those millions by using the company as collateral. When Hartfield-Zodys took over Karl Shoes, that debt didn't go along with it. That debt was Harry's, and he—and Mom—owed every dime of it to the State Street Bank of Boston.

The day before she and Carrie left for New York to do *Irene*, Mom told Harry she was seriously considering getting a separation, and she wasn't sure when or if she'd be coming back to him. He was sitting up in bed watching *The African Queen* and barely looked away from the TV screen when he calmly told her, "Whatever you want to do is fine."

Which explained why he'd shown me those tabloid clippings in his closet one day, the headlines about Mom's leaving him and their being separated, and asked me so anxiously if I thought "Mother" would come back. I remembered how dismissive I was about it, telling him that of course she'd be back and asking when he'd started believing what he read in the tabloids. No wonder he hadn't answered me.

After getting a lot of referrals from a lot of trusted friends, Mom hired one of the most prestigious accounting firms in Los Angeles to help her get back on her feet financially and manage her weekly $15,000 paychecks from *Irene*. Unfortunately, the woman with the firm who was in charge of Mom's account ended up absconding with $160,000 of her *Irene* earnings. The firm stood behind its employee. Mom had to hire an investigative team to trace the embezzled money and sue the firm to recover it, and in the end the firm reimbursed Mom through their insurance company. The woman who stole her money in the first place was never prosecuted.

Mom's *Irene* paychecks were being systematically stolen by her accountant, and that weasel at the Minskoff Theater had to add insult to injury by stiffing her on her cut of the program sales? She hadn't punched him hard enough as far as I was concerned.

Her drinking and her weight loss had nothing to do with how hard she was working on *Irene*. As Carrie put it, Mom was "working her way through a nervous breakdown."

I couldn't believe how much she'd kept from me to protect me. Now it was my turn to do the same for her.

After days of discussion following the meeting with the lawyers in the brownstone living room, Mom finally decided it was time to go back to Los Angeles and take care of business. She'd accomplished all she needed to with *Irene*, including a Tony nomination, so she recruited her old MGM pal Jane Powell to take over the title role, and we headed back to Greenway Drive—Mom, Carrie, me, Killer, and Richard Landers.

Harry was out of the house by the time we moved back in and was living very comfortably in a beautiful condo in the Century City Towers, compliments of Mom. Some combination of the divorce and the financial stress had taken a toll on his health. On the rare occasions when he showed up at the Greenway house to meet with Mom and the attorneys, he was being chauffeured by Phil Kaplan and still immaculately dressed, but he was also looking frail and much older and walking with a cane.

Upset as I was—quite angry and beyond disappointed—I could never bring myself to hate him. In fact, there was a part of me that couldn't help but feel sorry for him. I'd loved this man, and I never doubted for a moment that he loved Mom and Carrie and me and the "family" we were together. His addictions to gambling and alcohol, and maybe sex for all I knew, cost him everything in this world he cared about. He was too proud and too weak to ask for help with his demons, and to man up and take responsibility for what he'd done. I didn't wish him ill. I wouldn't even have resented the fact that his lifestyle hadn't seemed to change a bit if I hadn't known that now Mom was paying for every dime of it.

By the time all the legal wrangling was over with and the final divorce documents were signed, my naive question about what Harry had to give up seemed like a bad joke.

In the end, in addition to footing the bill for his condo and his membership at the Hillcrest Country Club, Mom agreed to pay Harry alimony of $25,000 a year for five years, along with half of her earnings from *Irene* (because technically they weren't separated at the time she took the job) and a 10 percent "agent's fee" on her other earnings.

Her beloved emerald-green custom-made Rolls Royce turned out not to be hers at all. It was legally owned by Karl Shoes. When Hartfield-Zodys bought Karl Shoes, they also became the owners of the Rolls-Royce pink slip. Harry bought it back from them for $8,000 and promptly sold it for $18,000. Left without a car, which makes life virtually impossible in Los Angeles, Mom bought a 1968 Chevy Impala for $1,500.

Since California is a community property state, Mom became the lucky recipient of half of Harry's assets—that is to say, half of $0—and half of his debts—i.e., about $2 million, including what he owed the State Street Bank of Boston, his friend Gregory Peters, various other friends he'd borrowed money from over the years, and several suppliers and manufacturers left over from Karl Shoes.

She sold the Palm Springs house and insisted on putting the small amount left over into a trust for Carrie and me.

She refinanced the Malibu house and rented it out to cover the mortgage payments.

She sold all her artwork and silver.

She sold the only important piece of jewelry Harry hadn't found in the wall safe and pawned—her spectacular twenty-one-carat diamond wedding ring. It originally cost $200,000. She got $75,000 for it.

The one thing she refused to sell—in fact, fought like a tiger to keep—was her collection of MGM memorabilia. (Thank God, as it turned out.)

As for the Greenway house, my world for all my life, it was now owned by Gregory Peters and the bank. We were being allowed to stay, but only until the bank found a buyer.

A lot of Mom's friends and advisors urged her to file for bankruptcy, but Mom grew up believing that bankruptcy was a disgrace. She couldn't bring herself to do it.

She did an amazing job in public of being the unsinkable Debbie Reynolds, just as she'd done through her divorce from Eddie. In private, though, she was drinking too much, and she seemed to have two moods when she was drunk—either she was laughing and loud and almost obnoxiously happy, or she was maudlin and miserable, rambling endlessly about Harry and Eddie. I'd sit through the Harry and Eddie rants as best I could, and there's no doubt about it, they were tedious. But to Carrie, these slurred, self-indulgent monologues were like nails on a chalkboard. She made no secret of how much she hated them, to the point where she'd let out an agonized groan and rush out of the room when she saw one developing. I'm convinced to this day that it was Mom's drinking years that kept Carrie and me from ever becoming interested in alcohol. We might have an occasional beer or something now and then, but alcohol never had the potential to get a grip on either one of us.

A year or so after the divorce was final, I got a call out of no-where from Harry Karl, asking me to meet him at Trader Vic's, a landmark Beverly Hills restaurant that prided itself on its exotic Polynesian mai tais.

His grooming and wardrobe were as impeccable as ever, but his trademark aristocratic elegance was as thin and dissipated as his body. I was still angry with him. I was still disappointed in him. I still loved him, and I loved Mom even more for knowing that and not resenting me for it or trying to talk me out of it.

We talked about pretty much nothing for a while, until finally he took a deep breath and got around to the question that had prompted him to call me in the first place: "Do you think there's a chance that Mother and I can get back together?"

I nearly fell out of my chair. Mom used to call him an ostrich, always preferring to bury his head in the sand rather than face reality. I'd never seen a more blatant example of how right she was. I knew what he wanted to hear, but no way was I going to be unkind enough to give him false hope.

So I just leaned closer to him, met his eyes through his thick glasses, and said, "Dude, listen to me—that ship hasn't just sailed, it's caught on fire and gone down like the *Titanic*."

It was sad to see a flash of disappointment on his face, as if some part of him was actually holding out hope for a reconciliation with a woman who'd be spending decades trying to recover from their thirteen-year marriage.

We said good-bye in front of Trader Vic's that day and drove off in our respective cars. I spoke to him on occasion after that, but I never saw Harry Karl again. Several years later, on August 7, 1982, I got a call saying that Harry had unexpectedly passed away. I called Mom to break the news. I didn't start crying until I said the words out loud to her.

According to Carrie's account in her book *Shockaholic*, Harry had been walking through the lobby of the Beverly Hills Hotel when a guy came up to him, said, "Harry! Long time no see!"

and gave him a pal-punch in the arm. Harry was rushed to the hospital that night, due to a blood clot that had formed at the site of the punch. The blood clot traveled to his heart and killed him. I'm sure I remember that emergency heart surgery was involved. But whatever the specifics were, Harry was gone. I went to the funeral, staying in the back of the room and crying some more.

A few months later I drove Carrie to LAX, where she was catching a flight to London to shoot *Star Wars VI—Return of the Jedi*. Her plane was delayed a couple of hours, and one or both of us came up with the idea that, rather than spend that time hanging around the terminal, we could go visit Harry's grave at the Hillside Memorial Park near the airport.

Next thing we knew we were at his gravesite, with its simple marble headstone that read *Harry Karl—March 9, 1914–August 7, 1982*. We obviously hadn't brought flowers, so instead I teed up a golf ball and left it there.

There was something incredibly poignant about the two of us standing there together saying a final good-bye to him. He was the first death in our "family," the first death that hit so close to home. And for all the extraordinary amount of damage he'd done, he was also the man who'd never been unkind to us or even raised his voice to us or our mother, the man who was at least there when Eddie wasn't.

I had tears in my eyes. So did Carrie, which I think kind of pissed her off. She had never let herself be close to him, especially when it became so much easier to be angry with him instead. But in that moment, in that place, she felt the loss of the Fancy Man just like I did.

I don't remember saying a word at Harry's grave. I only re-member Carrie quietly repeating the description of him she'd come up with years earlier, as a comment on his snoring and fart-ing, that she was now offering as his eulogy: "He was a mass of noises."

We'd laughed at that in the past. Now we just smiled at it through our tears and then slowly walked back to the car, each of us lost in our own memories of Kent cigarettes and bowls of redskin peanuts and cut crystal tumblers of J&B and soda, and how safe we'd felt with that big, tall, quiet man when we were so little and happy at 813 Greenway Drive.

7

INNOCENTS ABROAD

Mom and Carrie in their London cabaret show.

So there we were, back from New York to 813 Greenway Drive, for however long it lasted. Most of the staff was still there—our housekeeper Mary, our laundress Leetha, our gardener Elmer, our security guy Zinc—and except for the fact that Harry was living a few miles away in his new condo in Century City, life seemed amazingly normal.

In spite of the Harry debacle, Mom, unsinkable as ever, was regaining her strength and her confidence. She was determined to keep our family afloat. *Irene* had broken every record on Broadway, and she was ready to put a new show together and hit the road to Las Vegas, Reno, and Lake Tahoe. And there was a new man in her life.

Bob Fallon was an old acquaintance from Los Angeles, a producer and businessman she'd known from the Hollywood Presbyterian Church and countless charity events. He was a man's man, a World War II bomber pilot, tall and good-looking, and he'd moved to New York after his wife, comedienne Marie Wilson, died of cancer in 1972. He came backstage to say hello to Mom after a matinee of *Irene* one day and asked her to dinner. It was all over but the paperwork between her and Harry, so she accepted. By the time we headed back to Los Angeles, she and Bob were in the early stages of a happy, sexually healthy relationship for the first time in her life. (Mom was never shy about discussing those things with Carrie and me, and with any reporter who happened to ask her.)

Carrie and I trudged back to school at Beverly Hills High, but as far as I was concerned, the headline when we got home in February of 1974 was that my sixteenth birthday was coming up and I could finally get my driver's license. John Lebold had taken me to get my permit, and a drunk driver crashed into us as we pulled out of the DMV parking lot, which gave me a fairly accurate preview of driving in L.A. Mom also signed Carrie and me up for driving lessons. I was into it. Carrie wasn't—she'd been legally eligible for her driver's license for over a year, and she wanted a driver's license but just wasn't excited about the process of getting it. She and I had the same driving instructor. He and I got along beautifully, but he ran out of patience with Carrie, who was—let's see, how can I put this delicately?—distracted when she was behind the wheel, to the point where she once drove our instructor up the driveway on Greenway, through the terrarium, and up to the front doors, stopping in the nick of time before blasting right on through them. When she finally did get her license, she crashed into a parked car less than a week later. I never let her drive when the two of us were going somewhere together, no matter how much eye-rolling she made me wait through in response to "Carrie, give me the keys."

I successfully got my license as a sixteenth birthday present to myself, and Mom arranged for Mr. Greenberg, who'd maintained our family cars for years, to bring a Porsche and a Mercedes to the house for me to choose from as my first car. They were both nice, but I wasn't as excited about either one of them as Mom expected. She asked what the problem was, and I dashed into the house and came back with a brochure of what I really wanted. I'd been to an RV show at Dodger Stadium the previous weekend, and I fell in love with a 1975 GMC Motorhome I'd seen there. Mom was mystified until I reminded her of a trip we'd taken in a motorhome when I was ten or eleven years old.

Condor Motorhomes had made a deal with Mom to send our family on an RV vacation to Ridgway and Ouray, Colorado, the Grand Canyon, the Painted Desert, and a bunch of other great places, on the condition that they could send a crew along for a series of photo shoots. Harry didn't come with us, but Mom, Carrie, Grandpaw, Grandma, and I spent a couple of weeks sightseeing all over the western United States, and I thought it was the coolest thing ever. (Carrie wasn't wild about it, but the rest of us had a fantastic time.)

By the way, one of the Condor executives even took me to Edwards Air Force Base in a custom motorhome, where I got to fly in a B-52 aircraft; see an HL-10 lifting body, aka a prototype of the Space Shuttle; and meet astronauts Bill Dana and Chuck Yeager. To no one's surprise, years later I started taking pilot lessons.

At any rate, Mom was still a little hesitant to give me an RV for my first "car," but as I pointed out to her, "With everything that's going on with Harry and losing Greenway Drive when and if it sells, if I have a motorhome, at least I'll always have a place to sleep and keep all my equipment."

It worked. A few days later Mom drove me to a GM dealership

near L.A., and I drove my brand-new GMC Motorhome back to Greenway a few hours later. I'd never driven one before, but I got the hang of it quickly. I loved that RV, and so did Richard Landers and my other buddies at Beverly Hills High when I started driving it to school. It became a great place to hang out during lunch breaks, and I insisted on showering in it after phys ed class rather than take showers in the locker room with a bunch of other guys. Mr. Militich, our gym teacher, who in retrospect was a lot like my pal Jeffrey Jones's character Ed Rooney in *Ferris Bueller's Day Off*, kept dragging me to the principal's office about that. I refused to back down from my position that as long as I didn't leave school property, was showered and dressed after phys ed, and showed up on time for my next class, what possible difference could it make to them?

In the meantime, Mom was hard at work putting together a spectacular Broadway show, with a cast of twenty, for her return to Las Vegas. The mafiosi at the Riviera had been fighting with Howard Hughes's entertainment company at the Desert Inn for Debbie Reynolds, their "million-dollar baby," and the Desert Inn won. Mom was happy to be back in Vegas and the Desert Inn. She loved her new show, she loved performing for a live audience, and she loved having an answer to the question that was constantly on her mind: "How am I going to support Carrie and Todd, and my parents, and keep my Las Vegas cast on retainer by myself?"

As soon as school was out for the summer, Richard and I hopped into the motorhome and drove to the Desert Inn to see Mom, where she was playing to sold-out crowds and cementing her status as the undisputed queen of Las Vegas. We stayed for a couple of days before taking the RV on its inaugural long-distance trip to the Spokane World's Fair, and it performed like a champion. (As I write this, I'm admiring that forty-two-year-old GMC Motorhome through my office window.)

There was big news waiting for us when we got back to Greenway Drive. Mom's new act had been booked into the London Palladium. It would be her first appearance on a European stage and

Departing for London with Mom and her fractured leg.

the first time a Vegas act had ever played the Palladium. It was huge, it was exciting, and it was another much-needed shot in the arm for her. Before we knew it, we were packing for England—Mom, Carrie, me, Richard, Grandpaw and Grandma, Bob Fallon, Rudy Render, Mom's conductor, nine dancers, and three singers—with rehearsals to begin immediately for her opening night on July 30, 1974. Mom had fractured her leg in Las Vegas, and her doctors told her she wouldn't be healed in time. She proved them wrong.

We all moved into the Savoy Hotel, and it was obvious from the minute we arrived that London was as excited to see Debbie Reynolds as Debbie Reynolds was to see London. Her two shows a night for the three-week engagement were already sold out, and the press was everywhere. Carrie and I started being chased by the paparazzi whether Mom was with us or not, which was a first for us.

The paparazzi even gathered at the Palladium for final tech rehearsals on July 29, the night before Mom opened, with Carrie on hand to make her solo starring debut. I did some filming with my trusty Arriflex, and then headed out to the entrance to wait for Mom's driver to pick me up in the Daimler limo and take me back to the Savoy for the night.

There was a tabloid feeding frenzy at the curb when I got there—a few feet away a throng of photographers was going crazy over Bianca Jagger, Mick Jagger's wife at the time, and she was playing them like a Stradivarius. I was paying only marginal attention to this circus and trying to stay out of the way when some of the paparazzi recognized me, splintered off from the herd, and walked over to get a few shots of me.

Bianca noticed that I was apparently of interest to the press and came rushing over to me. The rest of the herd followed her; and suddenly, with what seemed like a hundred flashbulbs going off in front of us, she pulled me into a long, passionate kiss for the tabloids to devour. And they did, while I reeled from the bizarre experience of waiting for my car one moment to making out with Bianca Jagger the next.

But wait. There's more.

When Bianca finally decided the paparazzi had enough to work with for the night and broke the kiss, she looked toward the curb and noticed that her limo had arrived.

"Mick's at home throwing himself a birthday party. Want to come?" she asked.

Let's see. Did I want to go with Bianca Jagger to a birthday party her husband, Mick Jagger, one of my rock 'n' roll heroes, was throwing? Why yes, as a matter of fact, I did. There was just one problem.

"I'd love to," I said, "but I'm with—"

She knew where I was going with that and cut me off. "Don't worry, I've invited your whole gang. They'll be there."

Problem solved. We raced through the clamoring stampede of photographers, hopped in the back of the limo, and sped away from the Palladium.

She immediately snuggled up next to me, lit a joint, took a long hit, and passed it to me. I took a long, welcome hit as well, and promptly launched into a major coughing fit. I'd smoked a lot of joints, and that had never happened to me.

"What the hell is that?" I asked as I handed it back to her.

She laughed. "It's called a blunt. Weed and menthol tobacco cut together."

I told her I didn't smoke tobacco.

"It'll get you crazy high," she said, and she offered it to me again.

What can I say? That night I smoked tobacco. Bianca and I shared the rest of that joint. She was right—I got crazy high and loved everything about it.

By the time we arrived at the Jaggers' massive mansion on the outskirts of London, the party was already in full swing. It was "holy shit!" everywhere I turned, lavish and completely over the top, the "sex, drugs, and rock 'n' roll" version of a Debbie Reynolds extravaganza. Long buffet tables were overloaded with huge bowls and plates of food, pills, powders, and joints. Glass trays were everywhere, covered with lines of cocaine, razor blades, and straws. Wall-to-wall people were laughing, drinking, smoking, snorting, and making out.

Bianca was a perfect hostess from the minute we stepped in the door, leading me to Mom, Carrie, Bob, and Richard, introducing me along the way to superstar guests like Keith Richards, Peter Frampton, and Jeff Beck. Mick Jagger quickly joined us, and I managed to restrain myself from telling him that the Rolling Stones had accompanied Richard and me through the RV sound system most of the way to Spokane and back. I found out later that, to his credit, Mick had told Mom that there were activities going on upstairs that her seventeen-year-old daughter and her sixteen-year-old son shouldn't be exposed to, but if Carrie and I stayed on the ground floor, we'd be safe. He was very nice to us and respectful to Mom, and I still look back on that and appreciate it.

Mom, Bob, Richard, and Carrie were having a great time on their own, and I decided to go explore the crowded back patio

Mick Jagger's birthday party with Mom and Mick's wife, Bianca.

and swimming pool, where a whole lot of people were busy doing things that were none of my business. I started down a hill that descended to a pond and a gazebo where more partying was going on and found a large woman in a floral tent dress coming up the hill toward me. She was out of breath, and I stopped and asked her if she was okay.

She glanced at me, not smiling, and said, "What's it to you, honey?"

"I'm sorry," I told her, "you just look like you might need some help, that's all."

She softened a little and admitted, "It's a bit of a climb."

I'd already recognized her, and I was trying to contain my excitement, but I heard myself blurt out, "I have to tell you, I love your music!"

"You know who I am?" She didn't sound surprised, or annoyed.

"Of course I know who you are! You're Cass Elliot! Mama Cass! I'm a major fan of yours!"

She just smiled a little and nodded, so I went right on gushing.

" 'Oh, Lord, Won't You Buy Me a Mercedes Benz?' is one of my all-time favorite songs!"

"And you are . . . ?" she asked.

"Todd Fisher."

"Never heard of you, Todd Fisher," she said coolly.

I deserved that. "Mercedes Benz" wasn't a Mama Cass song. It was a Janis Joplin song. I meant to say "Dream a Little Dream of Me," which Mama Cass made famous and was one of my favorites too. But it was too late to backpedal now. In fact, all things considered, it was gracious of her to end the conversation with an added "Enjoy your evening" and a wink before continuing her trek up the hill.

Other than that, believe it or not, it was a star-studded but fairly uneventful birthday celebration, and we stayed for only an hour or so before going home to the Savoy to get some sleep so we'd be as rested as possible for opening night.

We were completely shocked when we woke up the next morning to the news that a few hours after the party, Cass Elliot had passed away—not from choking on a ham sandwich, as a lot of tabloids cruelly claimed, but from heart failure. By all accounts, she'd left the party alone, and no one including us had seen her drink any alcohol or do drugs of any kind. It was so sad, and I was glad I'd had a brief chance to meet her, even though I'd managed to make an idiot of myself in the process.

(Unfortunately, that kind of thing has happened to me throughout my life. I once told Lauren Bacall how much I loved her in *Casablanca*. She graciously informed me that she wasn't in *Casablanca*—that was Ingrid Bergman. I ran into her several times over the years, and despite her reputation as, let's say, not the warmest actress in Hollywood, she was always very sweet to me.)

The tabloid headlines were predictably screaming with the Cass Elliot news and misinformation the next morning. But coming in a close second in the world of late-breaking bulletins were those photos of me and Bianca Jagger "passionately" kissing in front of the Palladium. I had to hand it to Bianca, she really knew how to work the press. The phone in my hotel room was ringing off the hook as friends saw the morning papers and called, laughing, to give me a hard time about it, and I told them, laughing, to eat their hearts out.

On about call number twenty, I answered the phone to hear a vaguely familiar voice asking if I was free for lunch.

It was Eddie. He happened to be in London on his way home from Jamaica and was hoping we could get together. I was so surprised I almost dropped the phone. I hadn't heard a word from him since his call to New York Hospital a year or so earlier to ask why Mom had shot me. I admit it, a small part of me wanted to just say "no thanks" and hang up to let him know I was tired of having him drop in and out of my life at his convenience. But a bigger part of me kept hoping that one of these days, one of these times, maybe we'd really connect in some way that would mean something, and last longer than the door at his house closing behind me. I mean, here he was in London, and he didn't have to call, but he did. He didn't have to invite me to lunch, but he did. Baby steps, right?

We met at a café near the Savoy Hotel. Eddie was already there when I arrived, tan and sporting a shiny new bad facelift. I sat down across from him at a small table. I can't say I was hopeful about his agenda, but I was open to whatever it was, and I was curious.

I had to stay curious for only a few seconds. Before a waitress had even arrived at the table to take our drink order, Eddie beamed at me, handed over a folded newspaper he'd been holding in his lap, and said, "Bianca Jagger, huh? That's my boy! A real chip off the old block!" He punctuated it with a hybrid of an arm around my shoulder and a congratulatory slap on my back.

Oh, my papa. (Or, as Carrie occasionally paraphrased it, *Oy, my papa.*)

I unfolded the paper. Sure enough, it was one of the tabloids, with a photo of that meaningless publicity stunt in front of the Palladium the night before. He wanted to hear every detail of what the article described as my "romp" with Bianca Jagger. And that's all he wanted to hear—not how I was doing, not how Carrie was doing, not how Mom was doing after her highly publicized divorce from Harry, not how school was going—nothing. Just how the seduction of a beautiful, famously married woman by his "only boy" had gone down.

I told him exactly what had happened and exactly what hadn't. He didn't believe me and kept pressing, but I wasn't about to embellish the story for his entertainment—if anything more than that kiss had happened, he was the last person I would have told. He would have loved it. He also would have found a way to take some kind of genetic credit for it, and there was no way I was going to give him that.

It was a short lunch, after which we said good-bye and headed off in separate directions.

He never did get around to "How are you?"

At least he was predictable.

Mom and Carrie's opening night at the Palladium was a phenomenal success. I got lots of footage of their arrival and of both of them onstage, and you couldn't begin to tell that before the show, as usual, Carrie was a complete wreck.

As Mom described it in *My Life*, "Born with a great voice, [Carrie] absolutely killed the audience; brilliant and wonderful in her Edith Piaf way—the opposite of me. I was there with the beads on, singing and dancing and chattering away. Carrie walked out, quiet as could be, belted out a song and killed 'em. When she finished, they gave her a standing ovation. I cried in the wings."

A typical review read: "Debbie Reynolds is the gold of vaudeville. She has presented us with her daughter Carrie Fisher—the platinum of vaudeville."

It was thrilling, and we were all ecstatic after the second show when we headed to La Valbonne Club in the West End. La Valbonne Club was one of the hottest nightclubs in London in 1974, and they'd invited our whole Palladium gang for an opening night celebration.

The club was crowded and noisy and very posh, and the pa-

The billboard for Mom's London show at the Palladium.

trons went crazy over the arrival of Debbie Reynolds the instant we stepped inside and walked down the long entryway to the hostess podium. I was enjoying watching Mom bask in the cheers and applause until I looked up and focused on the hostess. From that moment on, in my mind, there was no one else in that room but her and me.

She was absolutely gorgeous, with long blond hair, full lips, and a perfect body. She was professionally friendly and cordial as she greeted us and led us to our table while Richard and I exchanged *wow!* expressions behind her back. She came to the table several times to check on us, and then, at some point, my dream came true and she sat down beside me.

Her name was Sarah. I'm sure she told me how long she'd
worked at La Valbonne, and a bit about herself and her background; it was just hard to hear her over the noise of my head exploding. What she did say that managed to penetrate was that her
father had fought in World War II as a pilot in the Royal Air Force.

I had my in. Before I knew it, I was regaling her with my vast
knowledge of the RAF, England's role in the second World War,
World War II in general, my collection of military medals—you
name it. And to my profound relief, she was impressed that she'd
met someone with a genuine appreciation of her father's distinguished history. I think she thought I was well read. I wasn't
about to tell her that actually I'd just watched about a thousand
war movies about a thousand times, including *Battle of Britain*.
Why get bogged down in details when we were off to such a good
start?

And thus began the first great affair of my life.

I was sixteen. She was twenty-seven.

I know. But in England at that time age was a nonissue, and it
was most definitely consensual. My sexual experience was limited
to the manicurist on Greenway Drive and a girlfriend at the Professional Children's School in New York I briefly dated. Sarah was
light-years ahead of me in that area, but I'm a quick study.

Mom had no objections. She got Richard his own room at the
Savoy rather than sharing a room with me so that Sarah and I
could have our privacy, and she recruited Bob Fallon to give me a
lecture on condoms and sexual responsibility. Sarah's parents were
fine with it too. I met them. Her dad and I had some great talks
about his World War II experiences. Her mom couldn't have been
lovelier and more welcoming. I'm not sure it would have mattered
if our parents had disapproved, but this was so much easier than
having to sneak around.

Sarah and I disappeared into my hotel room, and for several
days it was just us, a lot of sex, and a lot of room service at the
Savoy. I was one infatuated teenager. I was also a teenager with a
previous commitment I might have canceled if I hadn't been look-

ing forward to it so much and if Mom hadn't gone to the trouble of arranging it.

Richard and I weren't doing the sound for Mom's show at the Palladium. Beyond taking a lot of footage and stills during rehearsals and on opening night, we had no responsibilities there. So while we were planning the London trip back on Greenway Drive, we'd decided it was a perfect opportunity for a jaunt through Europe. Mom bought us first-class Eurail Passes, which meant we could hop on any train, anytime, anywhere until the passes expired; and she made a hotel reservation for us in Monte Carlo on a specific date and booked our flight back to London so we wouldn't be wandering aimlessly around Europe for weeks or months with no deadline—especially with my "lost in Africa" stunt still pretty fresh in her mind.

It wasn't easy to tear myself away from Sarah. But a guy's got to do what a guy's got to do, and we needed to come up for air at some point, after all. So off Richard and I went on a trip that could have been called Europe Without Your Parents. We fell asleep on our ship across the English Channel and woke up in Amsterdam, where some of the ballerinas we knew from the Professional Children's School were touring with the New York City Ballet. They snuck us into their dorm rooms, which was great until we were busted by their chaperone and thrown out on our butts. We toured the Heineken brewery in Holland, not because either one of us cared all that much about beer but because it was there and because we could. We got drunk enjoying the beer tastings and slept in the bushes. We traveled through Switzerland and Germany, where I decided I could happily spend the rest of my life in the hot springs in Baden-Baden.

Finally the day arrived when we were due to check into the hotel Mom had booked for us in Monte Carlo. We were very low on cash by then—it felt like much more of an adventure to backpack our way around Europe and rely on our resourcefulness than it would have been to just pull out the $10,000-limit American Express card Mom had sent with me "for emergencies."

All of which is to say that, to put it politely, Richard and I looked like a couple of scraggly, long-haired, homeless bums when we strolled into the Hôtel de Paris, one of the most elegant hotel/casinos in Monte Carlo, to check in. We were only a few feet into the lobby when we were approached by an incredibly unfriendly hotel employee who tried to escort us right back out again. It took a good ten minutes to get anyone to even speak to us, let alone listen to our explanation that we had a reservation and that it was arranged for us by my mother, Debbie Reynolds.

Private discussions were held among the employees out of our earshot. Phone calls were made. And suddenly—what do you know?—we were welcomed with the most transparent effusiveness I've ever seen, to such a ridiculous extreme that a bellman literally knocked me to the floor trying to remove my backpack so that he could carry it for me.

I've never been back.

Eventually we caught our plane back to London after one hell of a great trip. I loved it, but I also couldn't wait to see Sarah again and pick up where we left off. In fact, I had bigger plans than that. We were all booked on a flight to L.A. in less than a week, and I'd decided that I was going to ask Mom if I could bring Sarah back to Greenway Drive with us. For one thing, Sarah had already told me that she'd never been out of England (or "off this green rock," as she put it) in her life, and she'd always wanted to see America. For another, more selfish thing, I was infatuated and loving every minute of being with her and having sex with her, and I didn't want it to end with a wave good-bye at Heathrow in just a few short days.

Now all I had to do was convince Mom that it was a great idea, once she'd worked her way through the drama that had started between her and Carrie while Richard and I were gone.

8

CULTURAL EXCHANGE

Mom on the set of *The Pleasure of His Company*
with longtime friend and mentor Fred Astaire.
(The Pleasure of His Company, 1960 © 1978 Sid Avery)

had prepared a very persuasive speech to talk Mom into letting
me bring Sarah home to Greenway Drive. As it turned out, I
didn't need it.

To my surprise, it was fine with her, on one condition: Sarah
and I had to promise that this was nothing more than a sexual

relationship and that neither of us had any intention of falling in love. Seriously? I was sixteen, with the depth of a wading pool. I was having sex whenever I wanted with a beautiful twenty-seven-year-old woman. She was fun and attentive and smart, and she seemed to be as excited about sex as I was. Love wasn't even a passing thought in my mind.

Mom apparently thought this was a great opportunity for me to get an education, so to speak, from an experienced older woman who was socially presentable and, in Mom's opinion, looked like Brigitte Bardot. (She wasn't wrong.) She implied more than once that she suspected Sarah might be a "professional," but she abandoned that theory when she never received a bill for Sarah's "services."

Grandma Reynolds, on the other hand, couldn't be bothered with simply implying anything, ever. She had no filter, and she was damned proud of it. She made it crystal clear that she found Sarah and my relationship with her disgusting, and she was horrified at Mom for approving of it. There's nothing quite like sitting beside your new girlfriend at a large family dinner and having your grandmother pointedly announce, as her contribution to a lighthearted, facetious conversation, that "Todd likes hookers."

Grandpaw got a kick out of the whole thing. He thought Sarah was cute, and he liked her. Grandma was sixteen when he married her, so he really didn't understand what all the noise was about.

Richard Landers hadn't appreciated being dislodged from the hotel room he and I were sharing when Sarah first came along, but he just started hanging out with Carrie instead. And Carrie's only reaction was to relentlessly grill me for information about exactly what Sarah and I were doing while we were holed up in that Savoy Hotel room for hours and hours at a time. She wanted every detail, no matter how minute. I wouldn't give her anything more than "Wouldn't you like to know?" and she would respond with a loud, no-kidding-around "Yes! I would!" She never did get it out of me.

She probably would have tried harder if she hadn't been preoccupied with a whole new development between her and Mom.

It seemed that while Richard and I were Eurailing and filming our way from Amsterdam to Monaco, Carrie was announcing to Mom that as soon as their Palladium engagement was over, she was officially ending her blossoming singing career. She'd taken it upon herself to audition for London's Royal Central School of Speech and Drama, and even though the school wasn't known for its enthusiasm about American students, she'd been accepted.

On one hand, Mom was disappointed. She'd believed with all her heart in Carrie's potential as a singer and recording artist. Carrie did have a spectacular voice, and Mom had invested an enormous amount of time and money in seeing to it that Carrie had the best of the best vocal coaches and trainers in the business. The thought of never getting to perform with Carrie onstage again and watch her continue to blow away one audience after another made her incredibly sad.

On the other hand, Mom had witnessed Carrie's pre-show stage panic (*stage fright* doesn't begin to do it justice) night after night. She also knew that singers often had a shorter shelf life than actresses. Mom never considered herself to be a very good actress and had always wished she'd had a chance to really study that craft and be formally trained. Carrie had just been given that chance, at a very prestigious school—an opportunity too good to pass up. It meant that Carrie would be on her own for the first time in her life, thousands of miles away from home and from us, but Mom would never have stood in the way of Carrie's creative pursuits, any more than she'd ever stood in the way of mine.

Carrie had already made her screen debut in *Shampoo* with Warren Beatty, although it hadn't been released yet. Mom had reluctantly given her permission for that to happen, despite her reservations. Warren's hobby at the time was hitting on every attractive woman in Hollywood, including Mom, and she wasn't sure she wanted him anywhere near her attractive seventeen-year-old daughter. And then there was Carrie's first line in the script:

"Wanna fuck?" Was that really an appropriate way for Carrie to make her screen debut?

But in the end, Mom read the *Shampoo* script and loved it, and Warren promised her he would never lay a hand on Carrie—a promise he kept. When I ran into Warren at the 2017 Academy Awards, he clarified a couple of details about that promise. First, when he and Mom discussed her concerns about Carrie appearing in *Shampoo*, she took his hand and said, in her sweetest Debbie Reynolds voice, "If you touch her, I will take out a hit on you," and they laughed. Second, and more important, he believed her. And with that, Mom agreed to let Carrie make that movie, and she never regretted it, nor did she ever doubt that Carrie had all the talent and potential she needed to enjoy a very long, successful acting career.

So it was decided. All of us, including Sarah, would head back to Greenway Drive. Sarah would stay until I started school in late September. Mom would be home for a week before flying to New York to begin rehearsals for a three-month national tour of *Irene*, and Carrie would start packing for her return to London and the Central School of Speech and Drama.

A few days after we got home Mom hung up from about her eightieth phone call and went to Carrie's room to proudly announce that everything was all set for London, including her apartment rental and her plane reservations.

To which Carrie, who was lying on her bed reading, looked up and casually replied, "Oh, I'm not going." She'd decided to stay home instead and figure out what she wanted to do.

Mom was incredulous; and for the first time, by her own admission, Mom said no to Carrie. There was no way she was going to let her turn her back on a prestigious school that was her idea to begin with, a school that she'd had to audition her way into, where she'd get first-class training that most aspiring actors would kill for, just so that she could hang out in Beverly Hills with her friends "figuring out what she wanted to do" and probably charging lunch every day at La Scala. Mom believed in Carrie's talent and future too much to back down this time. End of discussion, case closed.

Carrie and Warren Beatty on the set of *Shampoo*.

Mom left for New York. Two nights later Carrie called her and repeated, "I'm not going."

Not only did Mom still not back down, she gave Carrie an ultimatum: "You're going to do this or you're going to have to support yourself."

Both of them told me later that their phone argument lasted for six hours. How you keep an "I'm not going!"/"Yes, you are!" debate going for six hours I don't know, but I do know that instead of going to bed, Carrie went straight to LAX, caught the red-eye to New York, and showed up at Mom's hotel room door first thing the next morning to continue the battle.

In the end, it was Carrie who relented. She flew back to Los Angeles, finished packing, and caught her scheduled flight to London to attend the Royal Central School. She made it clear to Mom that she hated her for forcing her to go, and Mom was devastated that she'd lost the little girl she literally loved more than life itself. She convinced herself that she'd expected too much from Carrie by confiding in her about her problems with Harry, and that collapsing into a corner with a bottle of wine had destroyed Carrie's belief that there was nothing her mother couldn't handle.

Through all the drama between my mother and my sister, my loyalty never wavered—I chose me. I was back home on Greenway Drive, my favorite place on earth, with my gorgeous, very sexy older girlfriend, and I wasn't about to let anyone, not even Mom and Carrie, keep me from enjoying every minute of it.

In fact, it worked out brilliantly for me. By the end of August, when Mom was in New York, Carrie was off to London, and Richard Landers was back east visiting his parents, it was just Sarah and me, alone with the staff in that glorious house, the king and queen of Beverly Hills. Now I was the one hitting the intercom button and saying, "Mary, fix me a drink." Of course, instead of bringing me a J&B and soda, she was bringing me a cut crystal tumbler of Orange Crush, but still, what a life.

Then, as if it's possible to improve on perfection, it was all over the news that on September 8, 1974, Evel Knievel was going to try to jump the Snake River in Idaho on a rocket-powered motorcycle. Sarah and I could take a road trip in the RV to witness history in the making, and I could bring along my camera equipment to capture the whole thing on film. Brilliant! What could possibly go wrong?

We spent the first night of the journey in Las Vegas, compli-

Happy together before Mom "forced" Carrie to go to London.

ments of the Desert Inn, who were only too happy to accommodate the son, and his guest, of their "million-dollar baby," Debbie Reynolds. Our royal treatment from Greenway Drive carried right on over to the Desert Inn that night, and we were, pardon the expression, very happy campers.

Then it was on through the high desert and wide, open spaces from Nevada to Idaho—breathtaking, no one else in sight for mile after mile, night skies full of stars that went all the way to the horizon. Sarah had never seen anything like it on the "green rock" she came from. But instead of the gasps of awe and excited curiosity I was expecting, the trip inspired her to go into a complete and total meltdown. This wasn't a simple "I'm not really into this motor-home thing" or "I prefer urban scenery, thank you." This was fearful, sobbing, inconsolable hysteria. I kept pointing out high-lights of the landscape as we rolled along, but she wasn't having it and refused to even glance at them. I thought maybe it would calm her down if we spent a night at a hotel (which I admit I resented—I didn't mind spending the money, but who needs a hotel room when you already have your own fully stocked bedroom on wheels?). I was wrong. It didn't help one bit, and we were both in pretty foul moods by the time we pulled into Twin Falls, Idaho, for the big event.

The couple of days before the event were busy and fun. I had special access to a lot of areas that were off-limits to the general public, and I had a good time filming the festivities and the crowds that surged to around 20,000 people. I admit I didn't pay much attention to whether Sarah was having a good time. There was a good time to be had, and I figured it was up to her to take advan-tage of it, or not.

The day of the jump was amazing. The tension and anticipation in the air were palpable, and the spectators were almost as deafen-ing as the rocket-powered engines of Knievel's motorcycle when he revved them up and took off. Unfortunately, his parachute de-ployed too soon, and Evel Knievel was famously unsuccessful in his attempt to jump the Snake River.

It set the tone for my long trip home with a woman who wanted nothing to do with any part of being there. At that point, I felt ex-actly the same way. I was pissed off, and I couldn't wait to get this whole fiasco over with; so I drove nonstop, for more than twelve hours, from Twin Falls to Greenway Drive. Sarah was sound asleep in the RV when I pulled to a stop in the driveway. Zinc came out to meet us and asked if he should wake her up. I said, "No, leave her there," walked in the house and went to bed.

She was full of remorse and apologies when she woke me up

later that day and tried to seduce me into forgiving her. I let her give it her best shot, but it was way too little, way too late. I was marginally polite but cold to her for the next couple of days until it was time to drive her to LAX for her scheduled flight back to England, and I was relieved to see her go.

I never saw or spoke to Sarah again.

Now, let me just say that when I look back at the situation more than forty years later, I acted like an intolerant sixteen-year-old asshole about the whole thing. I couldn't imagine not loving a road trip in my motorhome, let alone being so fearfully, hysterically opposed to it. It occurs to me that it was the beginning of my tendency to compare the significant women in my life to my mother. Mom enjoyed every minute of traveling and sightseeing and camping out on every trip we ever took in an RV. How could Sarah, or anyone else, not enjoy it as much as Mom and I did? I ultimately came to believe that all relationships can be forecast in a motorhome in a matter of days—either they'll go down in flames or they have potential. (My wife Cat and I spent our first three getting-to-know-you months together in my current RV, and she was as content and at home in it as I was. I rest my case.)

So Sarah was gone, Richard Landers was back, and it was time for us to start our senior year at Beverly Hills High. I wasn't into it, and I seriously doubt that I would have graduated if it hadn't been for a great professor named Dr. Emanuel. He recruited Richard and me into a program that let us off the hook for normal class schedules and allowed students like us, who were already developing skills and getting on-the-job experience in the entertainment industry, to keep working and get credits for the experience. I was a card-carrying member of IATSE (the International Alliance of Theatrical Stage Employees) by then. I promise you, if and when Mom needed Richard and me to do her sound on the road, for example, there's no way we would have turned her down in favor of a bunch of classes that had nothing to do with where we knew our lives were headed. I would have dropped out before I would have let that happen, so I really do owe Dr. Emanuel big-time for my high school diploma.

In the meantime, though Carrie was loving going to school in London, she wasn't about to stop punishing Mom for forcing her into it. Mom never heard from her, and when she worked up the courage to call, either Carrie would be curt and dismissive or she'd refuse to come to the phone at all. Carrie's infrequent letters to Mom always started with a polite update or two, followed by "Oh, and don't forget to pay my credit card bills and my $1,000 phone bill." (In today's money, that would be a $5,000 phone bill, for calls to almost everyone in the States except our mother.)

Mom thought maybe it would help them reconnect if they were face-to-face again, so she went to London to visit her. Carrie wasn't thrilled. She made it clear from the moment Mom arrived that she didn't want her there. She and her flatmate threw a party at their apartment one night, and just before the guests were due to arrive, she told Mom it would be better if she stayed in her room. Mom spent the evening alone with a bottle of wine while Carrie and her friends partied on the other side of the closed guest-room door.

"I don't want to be here," Carrie kept telling her, despite the fact that it simply wasn't true. "I'm only here because you're making me be here, so congratulations. You got what you wanted."

After two weeks of Carrie's relentless hostility, Mom gave up and flew home to California in a lot of pain. She never called or wrote to Carrie in London again, while she struggled to make peace with the obvious reality that Carrie didn't want to be Debbie Reynolds's daughter anymore. She wanted to be Carrie Fisher, with her own separate identity, and she wasn't ever going to let Mom's shadow darken her path again.

Carrie stayed in school in London for almost a year. When she flew back to the States, she opted to stay in New York for a while with her great friend and mentor Joan Hackett. Part of Mom was grateful for that—she'd had two older women in her life, Lillian Burns Sidney and Agnes Moorehead, who'd been great friends and mentors to her since she had first set foot on a sound stage, so she loved knowing that Carrie was blessed with a special relationship like that too. The rest of Mom, though, was deeply hurt to know that Carrie was choosing to grow so close to Joan and so far away from her.

And so this was how things were in November of 1974.

Mom and Bob Fallon were back from the *Irene* tour.

School was rolling along at Beverly Hills High, thanks in large part to Dr. Emanuel and no thanks to the principal's ongoing resentment of me and my motorhome.

Carrie was in London getting fantastic training as an actress at the Royal Central School of Speech and Drama.

Harry was presumably enjoying his J&B and soda in the Century Towers condo Mom was paying for, right across the street from the Hillcrest Country Club, where, thanks to Mom, he never lost his membership.

We were all settling in to our new definitions of normal when the world turned upside down again.

Part of Mom's deal in her divorce from Harry was that we could stay on Greenway until the bank sold the house and Gregory Peters got some of the money Mom (in other words, Harry) owed him.

We were finally given notice: 813 Greenway Drive was officially sold, and we had three days to vacate. Three days, to clear out of a house we'd lived in and loved for fifteen years.

We didn't have time to think or feel. We had work to do.

Mom had seen this coming, obviously, and she'd been frantically looking for a rental house she could afford. It wasn't easy in Beverly Hills, but she was determined to have me finish school at Beverly Hills High. She finally found an affordable house at 619 Oakhurst Drive—perfectly nice, obviously much smaller than the Greenway house, and most of all, available immediately. Mom hated it. She found it dark and oppressive. She also decided that's why God gave us paint and wallpaper. She was determined to make the most of it and not waste her time and energy complaining, especially when, during this three-day move, she was also rehearsing a new stage act so she could hit the road again in order to keep the Oakhurst rent paid.

I still remember the surreal experience of walking around the Greenway house putting price tags on things that had been part of my world forever and putting other things I treasured into impersonal cardboard boxes. Predictably, I guess, the new owners weren't interested in having a Western town in their backyard, so that magical place we'd rescued from the MGM bulldozers, worked so hard to transport and rebuild, and captured on miles and miles of film was dismantled and destroyed. With a lot less square footage to work with on Oakhurst, we moved most of the Greenway furniture to North American Storage. A whole crew was there to help—Zinc, John Lebold, Richard, Mom's old set decorator friend Jerry Wunderlich, and plenty of others—which made it easier to focus on the task at hand and separate myself from the reality of what was happening.

The most serious consideration was where to house Mom's memorabilia collection. There was a lot of talk in the industry at the time about a Hollywood museum finally getting under way, possibly at the Harold Lloyd estate. So Zinc, John Lebold, and I carefully moved those treasures to the safe proximity of the Carr Building on Hollywood Boulevard next to Grauman's Chinese Theatre.

On our second day of moving I was packing up the massive amount of equipment in the projection room. I'd long since turned it into my production studio as well, and even moved my mattress in there and started sleeping in it. It had become "my room."

I looked up at one point to see Mom standing in the doorway watching me. She looked sad and exhausted, and after a moment she walked over, took my hand, and sat me down next to her in the front row of theater seats.

"I know it's hard for you to give up this projection room, dear," she said with tears in her eyes. "But don't worry, we'll build another one someday."

Of course. Instead of feeling sorry for herself, as she had every reason to do, she was concerned with comforting me.

"I'm not worried about it. I know we will," I told her, and I meant it. In the meantime, as long as we had a bed, popcorn, and real butter, she and Carrie and I would be watching movies together for the rest of our lives.

I was surprisingly okay about leaving the Greenway Drive house. God knows I'd loved it there and made memories that would last a lifetime. But I knew that sooner or later it was going to be gone, and when we were hit with the three-day notice to vacate, it was almost a relief that the "other shoe" had finally dropped.

All that mattered to me by then was my faith in my mom and in the connection between us. Since that meeting with the lawyers in the New York brownstone more than a year and a half earlier, Mom and I weren't just mother and son anymore, we were a team; and as a team, no matter what happened and certainly no matter where we lived, we could get through anything together.

It was late afternoon on the third and final day of the move. Zinc and I dropped off the thousandth truck full of boxes at Oakhurst and went back to Greenway to load up truck-full number thousand-and-one.

When we pulled up to Oakhurst again an hour or so later, we were stunned to find what looked like a fleet of cop cars filling the street and the driveway. We raced inside, where Mom, Mary, and Bob were huddled together among the mountains of boxes in the living room.

Mom tells the story in *Debbie: My Life*. I wasn't there and she was, so I'll defer to her description of what happened while Zinc and I were gone:

> It was just about dusk when I got over to the new house. I felt that coldly blank feeling that comes with turning your back on a whole way of life, knowing it's gone and still not believing it.
>
> Walking from the car up to the front door, halfway up the walk, I remembered I'd forgotten to bring my new costumes in. I went back and opened the trunk of the car. As I was taking my things out

of it, a very well-dressed man walked up to me from behind, put a gun to my forehead and said, "Get in the house."

I thought he was kidding. It was the kind of thing you only see on television; not on some quiet, sedate, tree-lined street in Beverly Hills.

"What is this, a joke?" I said, half laughing. "Who sent you?"

Just at that moment Bob Fallon drove up, got out of his car, and walked up to us. Oh, I thought to myself, Bob's in on the joke.

"Is there any problem?" he asked the man with the gun.

The guy turned around, with the gun on both of us. I was still kind of chuckling about it. It was so real and unreal—like maybe a scene out of *Candid Camera*.

Bob looked at the gun, looked at the guy, and said, "This isn't funny, Debbie. It's not a joke."

Then the guy said, "Go in the house."

So we walked into the house, with him right behind us. In the front hallway, the man ordered us to get on our knees. In the meantime, another man appeared from outside. He had a longer gun.

"Where's the money?" he said.

"You can see we're just moving in," I said. There were boxes everywhere. "There's no money here."

"This is a rich house!" he said. "In a rich neighborhood," he growled.

Then, with his friend still covering us, he went into the kitchen, saw Mary, grabbed her, and pulled her into the hallway with us. Mary, who had a towel in her hand, threw it over her face, fell to the floor, and started screaming:

"I don't see nuthin'! I don't see nuthin'! Don't kill me, please don't kill me!"

The sight of Mary, crouched on the floor, screaming out from under a towel, was hilarious. But by then I knew laughing was too risky. And the man, who happened to be the same skin color as Mary, said, "We ain't killing you, sister." Then he looked right at me like: "But I'm killing you. You're going."

I didn't have my towel, so I couldn't throw it over my face. This man was very handsome—and I couldn't help noticing he looked like Johnny Mathis.

Fallon, seeing me look at him, kept grumbling under his breath: "Don't look at 'em, don't look at 'em!"

"Where's your jewelry?" the man with the longer gun asked.

"I don't have any jewelry," I said. "There's nothing here! We're just moving in."

Then they wanted all the cash.

Bob had about two hundred dollars on him. And Mary had about a hundred and sixty I'd given her for groceries, so they turned that over.

The other guy ran upstairs and found a bunch of junk jewelry that I used in my Zsa Zsa and Mae West imitations. He brought that downstairs, triumphant.

"That's just *fake*!" I said. "You don't want that."

"It *looks* good," he said, giving me a suspicious eye.

"I'm telling you, it's fake," I advised.

Then they wanted me to dump out my purse, where I happened to have my good pearls with a diamond clasp and some jade jewelry. So I poured it all on the floor. Lipstick, cigarettes, lighter, keys, Kleenex, wallet, and the jewelry.

The first guy took one look at that and said, "And that's probably junk jewelry too!"

"Yes!!" I said.

He believed me! thank God, and thus I was allowed to keep the little that Harry Karl and the banks couldn't get their hands on.

When the men decided they'd got all there was to get, we were told to go into the bathroom. With the guns pointed at us at all times, we were very compliant. All of us thought for sure they would then shoot us through the door. It was only reasonable—I'd seen their faces.

It was a tiny guest bathroom under the hallway stairs, almost like a narrow closet. Bob had Mary climb up on the toilet and stand up close to the wall. I pressed myself against the other wall and, sweating beads, we waited for the bullets, praying.

Ten minutes went by; nothing. Had they left? We couldn't tell. Twenty minutes; nothing. Thirty, forty, an hour passed. All that time we stood there stiff with fright, afraid if we opened the door they would be standing there and shoot us, which was not very likely, of course. Finally we opened it a crack, all of us shaking like leaves.

They were gone. They'd taken the cash and left.

Everyone was a wreck. Mary got out the brandy and we all had a drink. We couldn't believe it; we'd moved into our new home only hours before, and we were still alive.

"It just goes to show you," Mary said, "even when you're on a real good roll, you can still get rolled." The three of us had a good laugh.

Zinc and I got there just a couple of minutes after the cops arrived. Zinc, Mom's fiercely loyal security guard, never quite forgave himself that he wasn't there when she so desperately needed him. Mom assured him that it might have been better that he wasn't—since he was always armed, it could have escalated into a real tragedy.

As grateful as I was that everyone was shaken but okay, it took me a long time to get the image out of my head of my mom with a gun to her head. And I couldn't help but smile a little and shake my head that even at gunpoint and terrified, Mom had still managed to convince these thugs that the only good jewelry she had left was fake and not worth stealing.

To the best of my knowledge, the two gunmen were never caught.

Welcome to our new home on Oakhurst.

Let the new games begin.

9

619 OAKHURST DRIVE

Carrie upstaging me as usual on my birthday.

ife at 619 Oakhurst Drive was filled with a lot of friends, RV adventures, filmmaking, as much sound engineering as school would allow, Mom's going back on the road, Carrie's return from London, even meeting the girl who would become my first wife. In other words, I was so busy living and moving ahead that I had no trouble putting 813 Greenway Drive in my rearview mirror.

Maybe it was an aftereffect of my several months with a girl-friend eleven years older than I was, or maybe it was from missing Carrie—in case you haven't noticed, I don't spend a lot of time psychoanalyzing things. But whatever the reason, I found myself connecting and reconnecting with friends who were more Carrie's age than mine: Pat Boone's daughter Debby; Debby's good friend Donna Freberg, the daughter of brilliant comedian/satirist Stan Freberg; Bing Crosby's son Harry; Dean Martin's daughter Gina; Buddy Ebsen's son and daughter, Dusty and Kiki; our new neigh-bor Shirley Jones's son and stepson, Shaun Cassidy and David Cassidy; and José Ferrer and Rosemary Clooney's sons Gabriel and Miguel Ferrer.

It was a great group, stimulating and adventurous and an end-less amount of fun; and Miguel and I had so much in common that we became especially close. We both knew the upside and the downside of having famous divorced parents. Our mothers were both movie stars and singers who were very popular in the nightclub circuit. (In fact, when Debbie Reynolds and Rosemary Clooney were booked literally across the street from each other for club dates in Reno, Nevada, Miguel and I drove up in the RV to see them. We won $12,000 in the casino and blew right through it before we headed back to L.A., so we were also both young and dumb.) Our mothers were both warm, loving women who thrived with housefuls of kids around. (In addition to her other memora-ble talents, Rosemary Clooney was a world-class hugger, and she loved to cook as much as Mom didn't.) Miguel and I both loved playing golf, and we were both, let's say, open-minded when it came to having a good time.

Oh, why sugarcoat it? We were wild as deer.

Perhaps because of this, it was also at Oakhurst that hard drugs came along, and Miguel and I pretty much tried them all. We even had what we came to refer to as "The Lost Weekend," when we hooked up with a set of pretty blond actress twins, loaded the RV with plenty of weed and cocaine, and spent sev-eral days skiing in Aspen. "Lost" was an accurate description.

On the set of *Nightlight* with Miguel Ferrer in 1982.

By the time we got home, neither one of us remembered much of it at all.

There were a lot of trips to the beach in the RV, which essentially became a party bus; and when Mom's Malibu house wasn't rented out and she wasn't there, we partied there too. And while I can't sit here with a straight face and claim that I never overindulged, I'd learned from a previous experience to pay just enough attention to know when to stop.

I'd flown home from New York for the Christmas holiday while Mom and Carrie were there doing *Irene.* John Lebold; my old school pal Major Brunk; my former tutor Ray Noack, who was now just a good friend; and I had come up with a great idea for a film called *Kohoutek*, the comet that entered Earth's solar system in 1973 and became an international (and overrated) sensation as the world anticipated its arrival. In our film, a man (to be played by Ray Noack in his acting debut) would go off in search of Kohoutek and, on discovering it, find himself going back in time.

Mom and Harry still had Harry's big, luxurious house in Palm Springs when we made that trip, so John, Major, Ray, and I headed there—armed with lots of equipment, tequila, and weed—to shoot our film. The night before cameras were set to roll, we partied, and I woke up the next morning lying the wrong way on my bed, with no idea how I got there, or even, for the first several minutes, where the hell I was. I was sure someone must have carried me in there, but no, I asked the guys, and they assured me that I'd just walked into my room at some point the night before and passed out.

I know that's not uncommon in the drug and alcohol world. There are people who are so accustomed to it that they don't think a thing about it. But I hated it. I swore I would never lose control and pass out like that again, and I never did. No matter how hard I partied and how loaded I got, I lucked out when it came to knowing when to put on the brakes, which I'm sure is why I never found myself in danger of addiction—that, and the fact that in several areas of my life, I'd become a control freak, and built some walls to protect myself emotionally when I was in danger of being blindsided and overwhelmed. Handing over control to drugs and alcohol or letting them chip away at those walls and leave me vulnerable was out of the question. So there's no moral superiority or highly advanced intellect in my refusal to give in to a genetically predisposed addiction. I'm just too damned self-protective, and needless to say, all things considered, I'm grateful.

Maybe if I'd been more sensitive, I would have been more vigilant when it came to Carrie. Starting with all that weed in New York, I'm not sure I ever tried a drug that I didn't first try with her. I do remember that a friend of hers was her angel dust supplier. I did angel dust with her once. It had a nasty, edgy effect on my head and hers. We got mind-bendingly high way too fast on way too little of it, and I told her I never wanted to see that guy anywhere near her again.

At the same time, we had a dentist who gave us Percodan when we had any major dental work done. Carrie really, really liked Percodan. I hated how it made me feel, so I didn't think a thing about filling my prescription and giving it to her. I was her brother, after all, and I loved her—why not give her something she enjoyed so much? How harmful could it be when it was prescribed by a medical professional, or several eager-to-please medical professionals who were happy to have Debbie Reynolds's daughter as a patient, or "friends" who could get their hands on Percodan when doctors weren't cooperative? Her psychiatrists and therapists had been giving her all sorts of mood-stabilizing medication since we were in New York, trying to help her control her feelings and mute the voices that were always going on in her head. Those professionals knew what they were doing a lot better than I did, right? Who was I to question their judgment, even when they didn't seem to be helping my sister a damned bit?

In other words, I did the same thing Mom had done when Carrie was a little girl who couldn't sleep—when over-the-counter medication didn't work, she turned to our pediatrician, who gave her a prescription for something "safe" that would help. It came from a doctor, so it must be okay.

No excuses, nor do I kid myself into thinking that if it weren't for me, Carrie would never have had a drug problem, or that she wouldn't have started combining Percodan with prescribed psychopharmaceuticals as part of her daily routine. It's just one of those things I look back on and wish I'd had more of a clue while I was busy having all that "fun." She and I were both doing our own thing and having a great time when we were together. It wasn't clear to me at that point that she actually had a problem, but I was aware that she was moving faster and further into the 1970s drug realm than I was.

In the meantime, Richard and I were hard at work developing our sound engineering skills, with the significant help of the equipment Mom invested in at the Audio Engineering Society (AES) convention and the advice of some of the experts in the field we met there. And in December of 1974, a month after the move to Oakhurst, we took the RV to do sound for Debbie Reynolds's show at Harrah's Lake Tahoe Resort and Casino.

Bill Harrah, the resort and casino's owner, was an incredible friend to Mom. He loved her. It wouldn't surprise me to find out that he wanted to marry her. When she played his clubs, he always invited us to help ourselves to his ranch on the middle fork of the Salmon River, accessible via its private airstrip and Bill's Twin Otter airplane. It was an amazing place where Mom could really relax and "recharge her batteries," and she, Richard, Killer, and I spent some great times there between her club dates.

I'm sure Bill Harrah made a far more lasting impression on Mom than he ever knew, along with Mom's cherished pal Agnes Moorehead.

Bill had a world-renowned collection of best-of and one-of-a-kind cars. He cherished every one of those cars, and it was a very high priority of his to protect his collection for an intended museum that would keep it intact for future generations. He had a dream team of attorneys to handle the paperwork and ensure that

Mom, Carrie, Eddie, and me, 1958.

Mom and Eddie on their honeymoon, 1955.

Carrie at two years old and me at one year old.

Mike Todd, Liz Taylor, Mom, and Eddie at the Golden Globes in 1957.

Gene Kelly and Debbie at rehearsals
for *Singin' in the Rain*, 1951.
(Courtesy of Warner Bros. Inc.)

With Mom and Carrie in
Palm Springs.

Mom with me at age three and
Carrie at age four.

Carrie at eight years old and me at six and a half years old at the Greenway house

Eddie and me at Carrie's birthday party, 1964.

With Harry, Carrie, and Mom during Christmas at the Greenway house, 1964.

Harry, Mom, Carrie, and me at the Greenway house
during Christmas, 1966.

Carrie and me during Easter at the Greenway house, 1968.

ABOVE LEFT:
With Mom and Carrie in
Ouray, Colorado, in 1969.

ABOVE RIGHT:
Carrie in Europe, 1971.

Carrie modeling for *After Dark*
magazine, 1973.

Carrie and Mom in Europe, 1971.

Carrie taking a picture of me on our European vacation, 1971.

Carrie on our European vacation, 1971.

Carrie in the Greenway house, 1970.

With Harry, Mom, and Carrie at the Greenway house, 1970.

Mom and Carrie in New York City, 1972.

With Mom at the beach house, 1979.

With Mom at Christmas in Malibu, 1979.

Riding with Eddie.

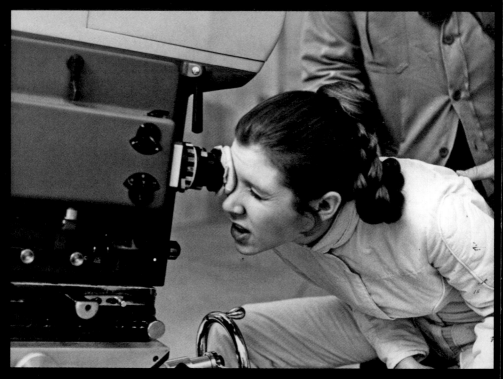

Carrie as Princess Leia on the set.

Carrie
messing
around with
Harrison
and Mark.

Carrie clowning
around between
takes on the set of
Return of the Jedi.

On the Redwood forest *Return of the Jedi* set with Anthony Daniels
and Harrison Ford (top) and George Lucas (bottom).

his wishes would be respected and carried out in the event of his death.

He died suddenly during heart surgery in 1978. Based on Mom's and my conversations with him, I believe it would have horrified him to know that when the Holiday Inn subsequently acquired the Harrah's resort chain, they also acquired the car collection and sold off the bulk of it at a series of auctions, scattering $100 million worth of his treasures to the winds. It took a lot of very vocal outrage by a lot of Bill's influential friends to persuade the Holiday Inn to donate what came to be called the Harrah Collection, almost two hundred of his cars, to establish the National Automobile Museum in Reno.

Mom had seen something similar happen a few years earlier when Agnes Moorehead passed away from uterine cancer. Mom and Agnes were so close from their days together at MGM that when she knew the end was coming, Agnes asked Mom to be the executrix of her will. Agnes had specifically told Mom that she was leaving her house in Los Angeles to her ninety-four-year-old mother, who lived in Ohio and had never been interested in moving to the West Coast. "She'll never want to live in my house," Agnes told her, "but you'll sell it. Between that and my residuals from *Bewitched*, she'll have so much money she'll never have to worry about a thing."

Agnes's mother came to Los Angeles for the reading of the will. The first page and the last page, the one with Agnes's signature, reflected what Mom knew Agnes's wishes to be. The pages in between were completely different. Her mother was left the furniture in the house. Elizabeth Montgomery inherited a piece of jewelry. The sapphire ring Agnes had wanted Mom to have wasn't mentioned. It presumably went to Agnes's lawyer, who got everything else, including the house and every dime of the *Bewitched* residuals.

At Agnes's mother's request, Mom auctioned off the furniture, for a total profit of about $30,000. Shortly after the estate was settled, the lawyer sold the house for more than $1 million.

Those two stories, both of them very close to home, hit Mom

hard, particularly when it came to her memorabilia collection. She'd fought like a tigress to keep from losing it to Harry's creditors in the divorce, and she was fiercely determined to keep it perfectly preserved and intact for a Hollywood museum she could share with the millions of fans around the world who cherished the movie business, its history, and its icons as much as she did. Bill and Agnes were smart, sophisticated people who were sure they'd taken every possible precaution to protect their estates and their heirs. Neither of them had any idea that they actually needed to be protected from the people they counted on to protect them.

It was in memory of those two friends who meant so much to her that from as far back as the 1970s, one of the driving forces in Mom's life was maintaining control over her extraordinary collection to make sure it ended up exactly where she intended.

By the time we got back from Mom's successful Harrah's appearance, Richard and I were more fired up than ever about designing sound systems. With her enthusiastic approval, we came up with the idea to take the impressive amount of equipment we'd collected and use it to convert the three-car garage on Oakhurst into a recording studio. Oakhurst was a rental house, but if Mom didn't care, neither did we. We recruited Tom Hidley from Westlake Audio, whom we'd met at the AES convention, to help us design it, and we worked hard, creating something elaborate and sophisticated enough that even our Beverly Hills High professor Dr. Emanuel was impressed when he came to have a look.

It was also slow going, thanks to a lot of distractions—we had a few classes to attend, some of Mom's tour dates to work, and partying to do.

And last but certainly not least, Carrie came home from London.

Things were still pretty icy between Mom and Carrie, but not for lack of trying on Mom's part. She was well aware of the fact that when Carrie left, we were living in the Greenway house where Carrie grew up. But Carrie was coming back to Oakhurst, a house she'd never seen before, a house that meant nothing to her. Mom tried to create a special bedroom for her, starting with a treasured item from her MGM memorabilia collection—the bed Marlon Brando slept in when he played Napoleon in the movie *Désirée*. We came to call it the Désirée bed, and Carrie kept it for the rest of her life.

Carrie and I sat on the Désirée bed and talked about the weirdness of the transition from Greenway to Oakhurst while she was unpacking in her new, much smaller room. We realized that, considering all the time we'd spent in New York and London, we'd both separated from Greenway Drive years earlier. For all the cherished memories we shared there, Greenway Drive was where we were children, living with Mom and Harry, in an innocent, spectacular, privileged world that no longer existed, where toy soldiers and Girl Scout badges and bicycles were relevant and the household staff far outnumbered the actual residents. As vast as the Greenway house was, especially in comparison to Oakhurst, we'd oddly, in a way, outgrown it, and we were okay with that. And even if we weren't, there was nothing to be done about it, so we might as well accept it.

In honor of Carrie's finally getting her driver's license, Mom brought home another classic piece from her collection, this one

619 Oakhurst Drive.

the red 1952 MG-TD from the Cary Grant/Marilyn Monroe movie *Monkey Business*. It would have been a spectacular first car for Carrie if it hadn't been a standard transmission. As it was, driving an automatic transmission took more concentration than she typically had to offer. Add manually shifting gears to the process and it's impossible to guess how many innocent lives would have been lost with Carrie on the road, assuming she could have made it out of the driveway in the first place.

In the end, everyone but Carrie drove that 1952 MG-TD, and Carrie settled for a perfectly nice dark blue Mercedes 450SL convertible, the front of which was personalized with her trademark dings within a few short weeks.

Shortly after she got home Carrie wrote a story for what became our most complicated, ambitious film project to date. It was called "You're You," and it was about a girl who was living in the shadow of her mother. (Where she came up with that premise, I have no idea.) The director was Josh Donen, whose father Stanley Donen directed Mom in *Singin' in the Rain*. I was the producer and director of photography, armed with my Arriflex. Richard did sound. And our esteemed cast consisted of Mom, Carrie, Cher, Natalie Wood, and Natalie's husband Robert ("RJ") Wagner. Mom had actually dated RJ early in her career, before she met Eddie Fisher. She was crazy about him, but they went their separate ways when she couldn't allow herself to sleep with him unless they were married. She never did stop thinking of him as the ideal man. Even in her last days she still had her young girl's crush on him.

Carrie also wrote the theme song for the film. The last line of the chorus went "There's no room for demons when you're self-possessed." (Years later I reminded her of those lyrics, which she'd long since forgotten. She loved that line so much that she had it printed on a rug that became a staple of her dining room for the rest of her life.)

We shot a scene in Carrie's bedroom in which Carrie, sound asleep in her Désirée bed, is having a nightmare, sure that she can hear tap dancing in the closet next to her bed. She gets out of bed, scuffs her way to the closet, and throws open the door to find Mom, in her red sequined tuxedo, singing the Brown/Freed song "Gotta Dance!" just as she did in *Singin' in the Rain*, tap dancing away with her trademark Debbie Reynolds smile.

Eventually, there's a scene in which Carrie dies, from either an accidental overdose or a deliberate suicide. The funeral was shot in the Wagners' backyard, with RJ, Natalie, and Cher, the only mourners, standing beside her coffin, crying. We included an impressive crane shot of the funeral, and the coffin itself was full-size and completely covered with white feathers.

When we finished shooting the funeral scene, we loaded the coffin back into the RV, which served as our production vehicle, and I headed up Sunset Boulevard to return it to the rental place. We'd discovered when we picked the coffin up that it was a little too long for the RV, to the point where it stuck out the back by a foot or two, so I swear to you, I drove very carefully in both directions. I'm still not sure how I managed to clip a truck on the return trip, but neither I nor anyone who saw it happen will ever forget the sight of that full-size, feather-covered coffin exploding all over Sunset Boulevard in the heart of Hollywood. I've wondered ever since what the hell the hundred or so drivers around me thought that was.

Somehow, *You're You* didn't lead to Carrie's stardom. What did was a movie she auditioned for and booked shortly after we wrapped *You're You*.

Before long she was off to London to start shooting *Star Wars*.

Mom went on tour with a successful revival of *Annie Get Your Gun*, at the personal request of Irving Berlin.

And through the grace of God and Dr. Emanuel, not necessarily in that order, I graduated from Beverly Hills High and was promptly dispatched by Mom on a brief trip to London to check on my sister.

It's an understatement to say that Carrie's reaction to filming the first *Star Wars* movie was consistent with the reaction of the cast in general: it was fun to work on, having a job was better than not having a job, and if it turned out to be another B movie, sci-fi box office bomb, as a lot of Hollywood was predicting it would—oh, well, on to the next, with the usual prayers that there would be a next. Their fate was in the hands of director George Lucas, a man who thought Princess Leia's "cinnamon bun" hairstyle was a great idea and didn't want Carrie to wear a bra under her costume because "there's no underwear in space."

I went to the set at Pinewood Studios a couple of times during the week I was there, and sure enough, it was impossible to tell that cinematic history was being made. Until it made its way into the brilliant magic of postproduction, *Star Wars* was a lot of scenes shot on partial sets in front of a blank blue screen, actors waving silent weapons around and Carrie delivering lines like "Into the garbage chute, fly-boy." The current running joke among the cast is to say to the press, usually not with a straight face, "Of course we knew we were part of something huge!" But in 1976? Of course they didn't. They couldn't have.

It was also impossible not to notice that Carrie was completely entranced with her castmate Harrison Ford. I'd never seen her so smitten, and to be honest, it was pretty adorable to see her like that. I knew he was married. I knew he was fourteen years older than she was. But I was seventeen, it was the 1970s, and from my perspective, it was an innocent infatuation. When she confessed to me that they were having a fling, it never entered my mind to judge her or lecture her. I just remember asking, "What could possibly come of this?" And the truth was, that wasn't on either of their minds. Neither of them had any illusions that they had a future together. They were simply acting on a strong mutual attraction while making a movie together, as if that's not one of the oldest stories in Hollywood. Beyond that, my only other thought about it was that there was no way I was going to tell Mom.

Of course, forty years later, after I unearthed some journals of Carrie's that Mom had preserved and stored away for her, Carrie decided to turn the journal about the making of the first *Star Wars* movie into a book called *The Princess Diarist*, including an exposé of her affair with Harrison. She used to joke that we were a family who wore our underwear on the outside of our clothes—from the time we were born, our most private family dramas had played out in the tabloids—so Carrie didn't have a reliable yardstick when it came to the concept of "too personal." This was the first Mom had heard about Carrie and Harrison, and she was very opposed to Carrie's writing about it, even though Carrie had given Harrison a heads-up that she was doing it. Predictably, *The Princess Diarist* made countless tabloid headlines and became a *New York Times* bestseller. What Harrison and everyone else may not know is that Carrie went to Mom after the book became such a big deal and said, "You were right, I shouldn't have told that story." For what it's worth, Harrison, she really did regret telling the story of that affair.

Once I was finished "checking on my sister in London" for a week, I flew back to L.A. and headed to Utah for a summer course in audio and visual electronics at Brigham Young University—just me, Richard, and my pal Major Brunk, off for yet another adventure in the RV.

Unfortunately, only two of the three of us made it all the way to BYU. We stopped in Las Vegas for a night on our way, and Major lost his tuition money in the casino. So Richard and I pressed on without him, and it was more than worth the trip. The course was great, we learned a lot, and we became good friends with a classmate named Art Kelm, who went on to become the vice president, general manager, and chief engineer of Capitol Studios in Hollywood's iconic Capitol Records Tower. But back then he was just a smart, talented guy who shared Richard's and my passion for the technological end of the audio and video industry; and when our BYU course ended, did we have a job for him.

When Mom's *Annie Get Your Gun* tour ended, she started putting together a huge new act for a countrywide tour, to be followed by Las Vegas and finally Broadway, produced by Bob Fallon. It was spectacular, and very complicated for us sound guys, by far the biggest challenge Richard and I had ever tackled. Art was a perfect addition to the team, and the three of us came up with a brilliant solution to that challenge—through a company called Edcor, we invested in the new technology of wireless mikes. We loaded ten of them into the sound truck, piled into the RV, and joined the *Debbie Reynolds Show* caravan to Dallas.

Opening night. The venue was filled to capacity. The curtains opened to reveal a dazzling battery of singers and dancers posed on and around a massive grand staircase that Busby Berkeley would have killed for.

Cue the orchestra. A few chorus boys up front sang, "Broadway rhythm's got me, everybody dance!" The music built. More members of the chorus joined in, leading to the singers and dancers on the staircase, working their way up the stairs, singing, "Gotta dance!"

Finally the spotlight hit the top of the stairs, thirty feet high, where Debbie Reynolds suddenly appeared, sparkling in her red sequined tux, and belted out, "Gotta dance!"

Probably. Except that no one heard her, because not a single sound came through her wireless mike.

She and the chorus pressed right on through the whole show, their mikes cutting in and out, while Richard, Art, and I, the Three Amigos, scrambled around like idiots trying to fix whatever the hell the problem was.

It was a disaster. We apologized to Mom and everyone else over and over again after the show, and the next day we flew the head of Edcor and their chief engineer to Dallas to help us iron out the glitches. The rest of Mom's tour went beautifully, so that by the time we got to the Desert Inn in Las Vegas we were on a roll and, thanks to Mom's clout, achieved a longtime goal of mine. It never made sense to me that the soundboards in Vegas showrooms were separated from the performers by a wall of glass, monitored through speakers that sounded nothing like the ones in the showroom. Why not position the sound engineer and mixing console in the showroom itself, hearing exactly what the audience was hearing and making adjustments accordingly? It made sense to Mom, but it made no sense to the Desert Inn. They weren't about to give up a perfectly good VIP booth to make room for us and our sound equipment. Mom had to pull rank and go straight to Hughes Hotel Entertainment chief Walter Kane, and in the end, just like magic, we were working from a prime booth in the showroom.

The show did make it to our old stomping grounds, the Minskoff Theatre on Broadway, to mixed reviews. I'm not even a little objective about this, but I'm pretty sure I noticed an elitist attitude on the part of some of the critics, kind of a scoffing "What's a Vegas show doing on Broadway?" tone that bothered me a lot more than it bothered Mom. She always wanted to delight her fans, of course, and she would never have brought a show to Broadway or anywhere else if she didn't believe it was worth their time and trouble. But she was still in full-blown damage-control mode, still working hard to earn her way out of the debt Harry had left her in, and there was no quit in her.

Richard and I got home to Oakhurst more determined than ever to finish our garage recording studio. It was coming along brilliantly, if we did say so ourselves. We had great equipment. Between our studies at BYU and touring with Mom, we knew what we were doing. We'd be there for Mom when and if she needed us, but we had a lot of realistic, doable ideas about how we could branch out and attract new clients. We were unstoppable, right?

Yeah, we thought so too. It seemed as if everyone was pulling for us, with the sole exception of the Beverly Hills Building Department. Not only were they not pulling for us, they shut us down. Permanently. Something about property-line setbacks, like setbacks were more important than art. We were outraged. They didn't care. I would never give them the satisfaction of knowing that they inadvertently did us a favor.

As luck, fate, or whatever would have it, we were still angrily dismantling our garage studio when we happened to hear about a Marin County keyboard player/songwriter named Lee Michaels who was going through a rough time and needed to sell his full-size mobile recording truck. A recording studio in a truck? So we could record anywhere we wanted? Who needed a garage?

We flew up to Marin, went to the guy's house, looked at the truck and its contents, made a deal, and drove back to Oakhurst in a five-ton studio on wheels, with an incredible microphone collection and some great outboard equipment. Between what we bought from Lee and the state-of-the-art technology we'd snared at the AES convention, by the time we were finished, we'd put together a mobile recording truck that was genuinely one of a kind and the best of the best.

Mom was excited for us and supportive as always, and she invited her weed-smoking record producer friend from New York, Richard Perry, to come have a look. Richard had just finished producing Ringo Starr's solo album and brought that and some other tapes to listen to through our playback system. He was impressed enough that he suggested we bring the truck to the Roxy that night to record Leo Sayer. We did. Leo Sayer was great, so were we, and we were off and running.

Westwood Music's Fred Walecki, who's still one of my best friends, brought Gerry Beckley, cofounder of the band America, to see the truck. (That visit was cut short when Gerry broke out in hives after smoking the joint Fred brought and Fred had to drive him to the hospital.) Fred sold guitars and equipment to everyone in the music business, and it was thanks to him that we got a gig with the Beach Boys. I remember calling Fred one day when we needed a guitar solo for a song we were recording. Fred sent over this kid in his late teens. We'd never heard of him, but we decided to humor him out of respect for Fred. He was amazing and nailed it on the first take. His name was Steve Lukather, and we heard a lot about him when he went on to become lead guitarist for a band called Toto.

We recorded Stevie Wonder, we were hired to archive and mix all his master takes, and we found ourselves becoming friendly with him and hanging out at his studio on a one-week job that went on for months. Neil Bogart, founder of Casablanca Records, started

Richard Landers, Art Kelm, and me in our mobile recording studio.

booking us for sessions with his new rock band Angel and other clients, and a Showtime miniseries with the Hudson Brothers. In what seemed like no time at all we were making a thousand bucks a day, with the added luxuries of meeting some of the greats in the music business and loving every minute of what we were doing.

I was on such a roll that I decided it was time to move out of Oakhurst and find a place of my own. I was almost eighteen. I had my own money coming in. I'd even figured out that having an RV as my only form of transportation wasn't really all that practical, especially in L.A., and bought myself a Lotus Elite. (The salesman neglected to mention when he sold it to me that Lotus Elites require being driven as fast as possible, regardless of the speed limit. I'll spare you the details; but after six speeding tickets in six months, a judge told me he'd dismiss the charges against me if I sold that car, and I took him up on it.)

I moved into a rental house off of Woodrow Wilson and Mulholland. I'd just finished loading the Lotus with the last of my stuff and was standing at the door on Oakhurst saying good-bye to Mom, who was at the top of the stairs, crying. I remember wondering what the big deal was, and pointing out that I wasn't leaving her, I was just getting my own place, maybe twenty minutes away. But she was devastated, and I didn't get it.

Carrie was technically still living at home, rarely there and barely speaking to her when she was there, but I didn't get it.

She'd ended her four-year relationship with Bob Fallon when she found out that their "exclusive" relationship wasn't exclusive on his part after all, but I didn't get it.

I was just excited about being out on my own for the first time and having my own thriving business, so "getting it" wasn't anywhere near the top of my priority list.

Oddly, it wasn't moving out, but my new mobile recording studio venture that caused the one and only real fight Mom and I ever had.

Mom's company name was RayMax (in honor of her parents, Ray and Maxene). I used the name RayMax Recorders when these $1,000-a-day checks started coming in. Next thing I knew, her New York financial advisors stepped in and insisted on managing RayMax Recorders money, trying to tell me how to spend it and how to invest it, even though they knew nothing about my business or me, for that matter. A letter from a RayMax lawyer arrived, addressed to me, essentially telling me that, since I was running my company through Mom's corporation, they had every right to essentially commandeer and control my income.

I redlined and hired my own lawyer to respond with the legal version of "This is my business, that I started, so fuck off!"

I took it personally, deeply offended at the suggestion that I wasn't bright enough or responsible enough to handle the money I was making from my own company. Mom took it personally, deeply offended that I was stubbornly refusing advice from a team of experts she'd brought in to help me.

For the first and only time in our lives, Mom and I stopped speaking. I knew I was right. She knew she was right. It was hard on both of us, and finally she suggested that we go to a therapist together to see if they could guide us through this painful impasse. I agreed, probably thinking it was a great idea—Mom wouldn't believe me when I told her how out of line she was, so maybe she'd believe a therapist.

We sat down together in this guy's Westwood office. He asked one question. I don't even remember what it was. But next thing Mom and I knew, we were pouring our hearts out to each other and talking about our feelings instead of legalities, with lots of apologies and "That's not what I meant." It was like a beautiful dance, two people who were essential to each other finding their way back together where they belonged. After about ten minutes the therapist said, "I've never seen a better relationship between two people in my life. All you two need to do is talk." He left us alone in his office, and we walked out an hour later, closer than ever and promising never to let anyone or anything, including our genetic stubbornness, separate us like that again.

There's a Mark Twain quote that goes "When I was a boy of fourteen, my father was so ignorant I could hardly stand to have the old man around. But when I got to be twenty-one, I was astonished at how much the old man had learned in seven years." Make a couple of age and gender adjustments in that observation and it's a perfect description of Mom and me at that point in time. She was exactly right—she'd handed me a group of very smart, very experienced investment experts whose advice was undoubtedly worth taking, but I insisted on spending my $1,000 per day on labor and new equipment, basically just pissing it away.

I was just as stubborn and just as wrong when it came to listening to Mom about my personal life. I was resolutely, steadfastly marching straight for a cliff. Mom saw it coming, and she tried to warn me, but I knew what I was doing. And what did she know, anyway? It's not as if she had any experience with choosing the wrong person.

10

THE WRONG GIRL

Clowning around with Carrie, while Mom ignores both of us.

om didn't like Donna Freberg from the minute I started dating her. Neither did Carrie. For one thing, Carrie had been acquainted with her for years through school and mutual friends and wasn't impressed. For another thing, I think sometimes females can instinctively pick up on qualities in other females that we guys tend to gloss over, and Mom and Carrie could spot a spoiled, high-maintenance Beverly Hills drama queen from a mile away. I should have paid attention, but I was in what I was young, crass, and indelicate enough to call a "pussy trance," where all logic flies out the window, your IQ drops to double digits, and you don't have the sense God gave a gnat.

Early in our relationship I took Donna to the beach house to spend an evening with Mom and Jerry Wunderlich. Donna took offense to some imaginary slight, stormed out the door, and took off on foot down Pacific Coast Highway in the middle of the night. I leapt up to chase her, and Mom said, "If you go after her now, you'll be doing this for the rest of your life. Think about it."

Got the picture?

I didn't.

I'd been vaguely aware of Donna through mutual friends over the years, but I didn't really know her until we became reacquainted through Debby Boone. Donna and Debby were very close, and there are few people I think more highly of than Debby Boone. Debby knew that Donna had issues and was devoted to trying to help her. Debby was also engaged to Gabriel Ferrer, my sidekick Miguel's brother, so we all spent a whole lot of time together; the more time we spent together, the more entrenched I became in the "pussy trance."

Donna was a factor in my moving out of Oakhurst and into my rental house. I definitely wanted my own place by then, and I also wasn't comfortable bringing my girlfriend home to a mother and sister who didn't want her around. Donna didn't move in with me. In fact, because Debby had started taking her to Bible classes, she wouldn't sleep with me until and unless we were married. I couldn't figure out what one thing had to do with the other, but it actually worked for me for quite a while. I was enjoying my freedom and my independence, seeing other girls and in no hurry to make a commitment to Donna or anyone else. One thing I knew about myself beyond a doubt was that when I make a commitment, I stick to it. I have my faults, but disloyalty isn't one of them. I was raised by Debbie Reynolds, not by Eddie Fisher, and never in her life did Debbie Reynolds turn her back on a commitment.

I was also pretty proud of myself for how self-sufficient I was living alone, for a guy who'd grown up with a full, attentive household staff and never had to wash a dish or do his own laundry in his life. The biggest adjustment was that without Zinc, the security staff, the trained guard dogs, the motion lights, and the alarm system that protected us twenty-four hours a day on Greenway Drive and Oakhurst, I was fearful. I spent a lot of sleepless nights listening for the slightest sound, getting out of bed to triple-check the locks on the doors and windows and staring at doorknobs almost expecting them to turn. One night I was so convinced someone was coming to get me that I left the house and drove around all night. Finally I got two Samoyeds, Noah and Sheba, who barked like crazy if a leaf fell in Seattle, and they made me feel safe enough that I actually started getting some sleep again.

I loved those dogs, but my landlord wasn't nearly as endeared to them as I was, and I was given a notice to move. Mom had sold her and Harry's big house in Palm Springs, and she used part of the proceeds to put a down payment on a house for me on Cedarbrook Drive, off Coldwater Canyon. It was a small, simple house, and the mortgage payments were a stretch; but the mobile recording business was doing well, and Noah, Sheba, their newborn puppies, and I were happy there.

In the meantime, Carrie moved out on her own as well, to a condo in Century City Towers. It happened to be in the building adjacent to where Harry was living, but it was a big, well-populated complex, so they never ran into each other. She'd finished shooting *Star Wars* and moved on to several other projects—*Star Wars* was in postproduction for a year, and no one knew yet that it would become a phenomenon. She was starting to feel secure about her own identity, separate and apart from Mom's, and her movie career gave the two of them more in common, so the ice between them had slowly begun to thaw. It wasn't consistent—it wasn't as though Mom could exhale and say, "Thank God that's over." But it was a start. There was even a small party to celebrate Mom's

Eddie, fresh from rehab, at my Cedarbrook house.

birthday when Carrie arrived after dinner and asked Mom to step outside, where a shiny new green Cadillac Seville was parked in the driveway.

"I just bought it," Carrie told her. "What do you think?"

Mom said, "It's gorgeous, but green? You don't even like green."

Carrie smiled at her. "No, but you do. Happy birthday. I love you, Mother." She opened the driver's door and handed Mom the keys.

Mom never forgot that moment, and she clung to it at those times when Carrie would suddenly stop speaking to her—again—and Mom would wonder—again—what she'd done to make her angry.

There wasn't ever a time when Carrie and I weren't close, which gave me a front-row seat to the best and the worst of what was going on with her. She could be the most brilliantly fun sister in the world, sensitive and compassionate and my best friend, and then turn on me in the blink of an eye and be angry and cruel and insensitive for no apparent reason. I had the advantage of never not having her as my sister and never not having her as an essential part of my reality, so no matter what was going on with her, I didn't judge it or analyze it, I just accepted it as Carrie being Carrie.

So it was a shock, but also not a shock at all, when I got an urgent call from her landlord at Century Towers telling me to get to her condo ASAP. It seems that no one had seen or heard from her in a couple of days, and someone had finally asked the landlord to check on her.

I can still feel the cold chill that surged through me when I raced into Carrie's condo that morning. She was fully dressed, lying facedown on the floor, not moving, vomit all over the place around her. I rolled her over and held her, and after a few minutes that seemed like hours she opened her eyes, looked at me without focusing, and slurred out, "It's a wacky, mod-a-go-go world."

She was out of it, and she'd obviously overdosed, but at least she said something. I rushed her to the emergency room, where they did some routine tests, gave her some medication, and released her. She told me as I drove her home that she'd taken more than her usual amount of Percodan from wherever and whomever, along with her usual prescribed mood stabilizers and—oh, yes—some acid.

I didn't make a big fuss over it. Drugs and Carrie were old news to me, after all. Whatever brought it on, it was over and she was okay, so what else mattered? Maybe she got carried away unwinding from a TV movie she'd just finished shooting. Maybe she'd partied too hard. Or maybe she'd gone overboard calming her nerves about an upcoming event she'd been both looking forward to and dreading—in just a few short weeks, I was taking her to the 20th Century Fox lot for a cast and crew screening of *Star Wars*, several days before its premiere at Grauman's Chinese Theatre on May 25, 1977.

Carrie was a wreck the night of that screening at Fox, that's for sure. I stood with her outside the back entrance of the theater while she paced and chain-smoked and panicked. What if this outer space B movie was a total disaster? What if she and her cinnamon-bun hair became a typecast laughingstock, and no one in the business ever took her seriously again? This could be the end of her career for all she knew, and then what would she do?

It took so long to get her to go inside that by the time we finally slipped in the exit door and settled into our seats in the front row, *Star Wars* had already been rolling for a minute or two. Along about the time that the battle cruiser flew overhead, I leaned over and whispered to Carrie, "This is no B movie." We didn't speak another word to each other or even glance away from the screen until it was over, except for her brief cringe when she broke into an English accent while talking to Darth Vader. And when it was over, we were both speechless, wide-eyed, and to understate it, blown away. George Lucas was clearly a genius, *Star Wars* was clearly a game changer, a triumph, a whole new level of science fiction filmmaking; and Carrie clearly wasn't just in that movie, she stood shoulder to shoulder with it, which was a triumph in itself. After the long silence between us, I turned to her and said, "First thing in the morning I'm buying stock in 20th Century Fox." I did, by the way, and I never regretted it.

The *Star Wars* premiere at Grauman's Chinese Theatre was no less of a jaw-dropper. We'd been to more than our share of red-carpet premieres in our lives. We'd seen lines of people stretching down Hollywood Boulevard. We'd heard fans cheering and applauding as the stars emerged from their limos and made their way through the gauntlet of reporters. But nothing had even come close to the frenzy and the full-blown fanaticism we experienced that night.

We had no idea where this sensation was headed or how long it would last, but there was no doubt about it, Carrie and her career were going to survive *Star Wars* after all. Ecstatic and relieved, she was looking forward to whatever came next.

In the meantime, with both Carrie and me out on our own, Mom found the Oakhurst house too big and empty, and she let it go when the lease was up. Grandpaw and Grandma had moved to Palm Springs, into the small house she'd owned since she and Eddie were married and had managed to hold on to through the Harry divorce debacle. So when she wasn't touring and the beach house was rented out, Mom had no home base. Her belongings were in storage and/or with Carrie, various friends, and me; but she wasn't about to stay with either Carrie or me—as far as she was concerned, we had our own lives now, away from her, and she didn't want to intrude. Sometimes she'd stay in hotels. Sometimes, in the middle of the night, she'd knock on the doors of a small handful of special people like Bob and Margie Petersen, who'd known her since her MGM days, understood her pain, and simply welcomed her without asking questions.

And sometimes, when she was very upset and probably had too much to drink, she'd just drive for hours and hours, through Beverly Hills or the Valley or Bel Air or Hollywood, feeling hopeless and exhausted, and finally park on a quiet street, crawl into the backseat, and go to sleep.

Early one morning I looked out my window at Cedarbrook to see Mom's car parked in the driveway, with her sound asleep inside it. I woke her up and asked her what the hell she was doing and why the hell she hadn't come in the house when she got there. She mumbled something about seeing Donna's car out front, and she and Donna didn't get along, and blah, blah. I told her she was being ridiculous, brought her inside, and put her to bed. It broke my heart to see her lost like that. The drinking part didn't really frighten me. Obviously I knew it wasn't good for her, but it had been going on for years, and it was just a fact that she sometimes drank more than she should have. She never let it interfere with her life or her career, though; and in a way, at that stage in her life, I even kind of understood it.

Mom was going through a lot. She took it very hard that both of her children were off on their own. Loving and taking care of Carrie and me had been her number one priority since the day we were born, her greatest purpose. We'd been the center of her universe, and now we'd moved on. The three most significant men in her life—Eddie, Harry, and Bob Fallon—had sought out other women, despite her best efforts, and made her feel like a foolish, inadequate failure. She was also struggling with her growing awareness that she might not always be able to rely on show business to provide her with a living. She had finally paid off enough of Harry's staggering debts that she could start setting some money aside for her future, but she'd still need a reliable income.

What evolved in the mind of this former aspiring gymnastics teacher was the idea that she could start a school for people who wanted to learn what she'd come to know best—the entertainment industry. If she could find a clean, solid building with enough space for classrooms and rehearsal halls, she could pass along the vast amount of knowledge her amazing career had provided her and create a source of income to fall back on if and when show business decided someday that it was done with her.

After a lot of searching, she found an old post office building in North Hollywood. It was one story, solid as a rock, 19,000 square feet full of large spaces and a forty-car parking lot. She bought it, and a year later the fully renovated Debbie Reynolds Studios opened for business, with Mom's old friend, MGM stand-in, fellow dancer, and personal assistant Margie Duncan at the helm.

Now all she needed was an affordable place to live, as close as possible to DR Studios. She found it just a few miles away, in the form of a modest brick English-style bungalow on La Maida Street in North Hollywood. It needed a lot of work, but Jerry Wunderlich, the indispensable Bob O'Connell, and a whole crew of us pitched in and transformed it into a home she could settle into and call her own when she wasn't on the road.

As she wrote in *My Life*, "I could sit there by myself on the floor of my own little house, and talk or laugh or sob for hours, or until I'd fall asleep—waking up in the morning not remembering how I'd ended up there. Many a night, a lonely night, I hoisted that bottle and tipped the wine into the crystal goblet and sipped it until there was no night left."

While all that was happening with Carrie and Mom, I was going through plenty of changes of my own—most notably I got in touch with my Christian faith.

Mom had exposed Carrie and me to both Christianity and Judaism when we were growing up. She never tried to dictate our beliefs, and what we believed as children was that the services we went to in both faiths were endless and boring. Other than that, I didn't really give much thought to religion at all.

By the time Donna and I got involved, she was under the kind, loving wing of Debby Boone, a devout Christian who started taking her to Bible studies and Sunday worship to help her with phobias. Debby was a member of the Church on the Way, where her father, Pat, was an elder and where Donna had responded to an altar call and committed her life to Christ.

One Thanksgiving, to be supportive, Miguel and I went to a service at the Church on the Way with Donna, Debby, and Gabriel. Rev. Jack Hayford was delivering the sermon. In the ten years or so since he'd been pastoring there, the membership had grown from eighteen people to around ten thousand. That wasn't hard to imagine after hearing him speak. He was great. His message was simple, straightforward, and thought-provoking. There was no dogma, no sanctimonious preaching at his congregation, none of the time-share-salesman approach I'd seen from a few televangelists I'd stumbled across while flipping channels. Instead, Rev. Hayford simply seemed like a compassionate, nonjudgmental guy who'd found peace and joy through

God and was inviting us to let him guide us toward doing the same.

"If you believe in God and want Him to be part of your life, just let your eyes meet my eyes and invite Him in."

I did. So did Miguel, and several other members of the congregation. Rev. Hayford moved around the sanctuary, met each of our eyes, and said, "I see you. I acknowledge that."

It took a while for Miguel and me to make a formal conversion to Christianity, but that Thanksgiving was the beginning of it, the moment when we each said what boiled down to "Okay, God, if you're willing to move in my life, I'm willing to let it happen."

A few weeks later, I was hired as a recording engineer by a record producer named Frank Wilson, who'd produced hits for everyone from Marvin Gaye to the Temptations to the Supremes, and he invited me to a Christian retreat the following weekend in the mountains at Lake Arrowhead. I wasn't really that into it, but I wanted to keep working with Frank, so sure, if a Christian retreat a couple of hours away would score some brownie points with him, why not?

The pastor that weekend was Dr. E. V. Hill of the Mt. Zion Missionary Baptist Church in Los Angeles. He was a hellfire-and-brimstone preacher, very articulate, passionate, and committed to his faith. He had insights into the Bible and the life of Christ that actually made sense to me, and that had never resonated with me on a deeply personal level before. He was an extraordinary speaker, and I was glad I'd accepted Frank's invitation to hear this man and really listen. Dr. Hill kept trying to get me to publicly embrace Christianity, but as moved as I was by him and his messages, I couldn't make that commitment yet, not until I was sure it was utterly, completely sincere.

The weekend was over, and I was driving back down the mountain, processing everything I'd heard in the last couple of days, when out of nowhere, I had the sensation of something heavy falling on me. It's hard to describe, but it was like I suddenly "got it" and my whole body felt it. For the first time, the meaning of the messages and Bible verses I'd been hearing all my life weren't just words anymore; they were living, breathing truth. I had this startling, crystal-clear understanding of why Christ had come for us. The concept of a father's love, a love I'd never known before, was waiting for me through Jesus if I'd simply accept it, be grateful for it, and celebrate it by living it.

I'm sure it had been at least a decade since I'd shed a single tear, but now I started to cry. I literally had to pull the car over as the full force of it hit me like a huge, cleansing wave—this Father, the Father of my soul, was mine, unconditional, always accessible, always believing in me whether I believed in Him or not. It was an epiphany, and a deep one. When I was able to drive again, I headed straight to Mom's house to tell her about it, and we cried together.

Mom couldn't have been happier that I'd found my way to Christianity. Her faith had given her strength and support all her life, and she loved knowing that I was now armed with that same powerful arsenal. It also gave us yet another thing in common and deepened a relationship we didn't know could be any deeper than it already was. As for Carrie, she just got a kick out of it. She started referring to me as her "born-again brother" and observing that "Todd turned out normal except for being a born-again Christian." Many years later, when she was asked by the press if I was still a born-again Christian, she replied, "I once fixed my brother up with Beverly D'Angelo, and you can't be born again and date Beverly." (Beverly and I both found that hilarious, by the way.)

I started exploring and investigating. I hung out with Frank, who became a minister, and I went back to the Church of the Way, wishing the hymns and the formality of the services moved me more than they did. But they didn't diminish my curiosity and my eagerness to learn. There wasn't a question in my mind about my faith anymore. I was just looking for a place to feel it and share it that didn't involve looking at my watch every few minutes wondering how much longer I had to sit there. A visit to the Vineyard Church, pastored by Kenn Gulliksen, felt much more like it—the worship music was alive, rock and roll, and there wasn't a hymnal in the place. I don't think I looked at my watch even once.

Part of my exploration led me to Ken Copeland, a massively popular televangelist. His ministry was based on a positive foundation of love, healing, and abundance, unlike so many TV preachers whose message seemed to be "Send us money, or God will send you straight to hell." In addition to his enormous television following, Rev. Copeland attracted thousands to conventions all over the country, so I went to one of them to check it out.

I met Ken Copeland and was very impressed with him and his ministry. I was standing backstage on the last day of the convention, listening to his sermon and the enthusiastic roar of five thousand of his devoted followers, when a woman approached me and introduced herself. She was Jan Crouch, and like Rev. Copeland, she and her husband, Paul, were mega televangelists. They didn't just have their own show, *Praise the Lord*, they also owned the Trinity Broadcasting Network, the largest Christian television network in the world.

"I love your mother," she said.

I assured her that I did too. And then, just making conversation, I told her that Mom had been a Christian all her life, and walked the walk every day of her life, but she'd stopped attending church when the Nazarene Baptists kicked her out for being a movie star. By the time we finished talking, Jan Crouch had invited me to be a guest on *Praise the Lord*. I warned her that I didn't think they were ready for me on their show, from what I'd seen of it, but she insisted, so I accepted.

With no prep and no pre-interview, I walked down the stairs of their set, where Paul and Jan Crouch were waiting for me. We were live, on the air, when I was greeted with the question "Why, according to our ratings demographics, are young people your age not interested in watching our show?"

It caught me off guard. I finally asked, "Are you sure you want an honest answer to that on live TV?"

They said they were sure. I doubted it, but I went ahead anyway.

"You're preaching to the choir," I told them, "and there's nothing about *Praise the Lord* that young people can relate to. Paul, you're sitting there in your Sears powder-blue polyester suit; Jan, you've got your 1950s hair and makeup; and the set looks like the lobby of a Ramada Inn." I could hear the crew quietly snickering offstage. "The music is unrelatable, you make Christianity seem like a boring, humorless stream of clichés, and it feels like the most important message you're trying to get across is 'Send us your money.' So when it's all said and done, why would my generation tune in?"

Incredibly, instead of taking out a restraining order on me, Paul and Jan Crouch asked me to create a special for the Trinity Broadcasting Network that would attract a younger audience. I said yes in the blink of an eye, provided they'd give me complete creative control, including the demands that (a) the traditional donation phone number not appear on the screen, and (b) the TV listings had to categorize the show as comedy, not religion. I believed then, and I believe now, that with very rare exceptions, when you're trying to get a point across, people are more receptive to humor than they are to somber, droning speeches, no matter what the subject matter.

I called my show *Nightlight*, and its model was the *Saturday Night Live* format, a series of irreverent skits satirizing traditional televangelist shows. I directed. Actor Jerry Houser wrote and played a character named Reverend Hype, staring intensely into the camera, begging for donations, while a home viewer's "sin-o-meter" pinned in the "Danger Zone." My guest stars, aka the Nightlight Players, were Miguel Ferrer and Wendell Burton.

We were a hit, we had a great time, and the Trinity Broadcasting Network wanted more. We ended up doing a total of five shows, with Mom, Carrie, Dan Aykroyd, Rene Russo, Donna, her dad Stan Freberg, the Eagles's Bernie Leadon, Johnny Rivers and his wife Christi, Dion, and several other friends joining in as guest

Left: Directing a skit on *Nightlight* with Dusty Ebsen.
Right: Behind the scenes with Henry Cutrona and Mom filming a *Nightlight* skit.

stars. During a network telethon I did ask our viewers for money, but I was very specific about it—I said, "God doesn't need your money, but if you like what we're doing on *Nightlight*, your donations can help us produce more episodes." When I had reason to believe that we were being given only a fraction of the extraordinary amount of money we'd raised, and I wasn't about to mislead our viewers about where and how their money was being used, the Crouches and I parted ways.

For the most part, though, *Nightlight* was a really satisfying experience, and it definitely had a huge impact on another new venture that made its debut at the very same time.

The seeds of that new venture were planted when I started doing some sound work with Debby Boone's musical director/bassist, a guy named Henry Cutrona. Henry and I had met during a trip to see Debby on tour in Lake Tahoe in the wake of her monster-hit song "You Light Up My Life." Henry was a hippie, a really talented musician, and someone I liked and related to immediately. He also happened to be the assistant pastor of a church in Glendale and the lead vocalist/acoustic guitarist of Gentle Faith, a Christian country rock band. Henry and I started doing a lot of projects together and spending a lot of time together. It was the most natural thing in the world for us to find ourselves pontificating about anything and everything to do with Christianity—Christ's condemnation of the Pharisees and the Sadducees for worshiping traditions instead of worshiping God, the fact that Jesus was too busy caring about people to care about the buildings they gathered in—you name it, we could carry on for hours about it, and whatever "it" was, we were always on the same page.

The next most natural thing in the world for us, out of all those conversations, was to come up with the idea of starting our own church. It would be nondenominational, liberal, nontraditional, charismatic, unregimented—basically a 180-degree turn from everything we found off-putting about the "organized religion" services we'd been to. If we had a founding philosophy, it was probably, "Judge not, lest ye be judged."

We called our church The Hiding Place, based on the Bible verse "You are my hiding place; You preserve me from trouble; You surround me with songs of deliverance" (Psalms 32:7). Our first service, in Studio F at Mom's new DR Studios, coincided with the airing of the first *Nightlight* special. The next week we were swamped, and The Hiding Place took off from there. We outgrew DR Studios, outgrew the Beverly Theatre in Beverly Hills, and ended up at the Emerson Middle School in Westwood, with an average congregation of a thousand people.

Our services were informal and all about celebrating our faith. The music was primarily live rock, provided by some of our musician members—Johnny Rivers, for example, who was a regular, along with his wife, Christi, played guitar for us, along with Eagles cofounder Bernie Leadon, who was also one of my guests on *Nightlight*. Baptisms were performed anywhere from hot tubs to the Pacific Ocean. Our doors were open to everyone, and we prayed for anyone who needed us. Henry's many friends came. My friends Donna, Miguel, and Dusty Ebsen were there every week and literally hundreds of newcomers started joining us, from "industry" people like supermodel Rene Russo to "civilians" from every walk of life.

There was no preaching at The Hiding Place, just messages about hope, empowerment, and significant life lessons we'd learned and wanted to pass along. The first time I spoke at The Hiding Place I told the story of one of the most fundamental principles in my family's life. Ironically, it came from Grandpaw, the quietest, most plainspoken of us all; it was a lesson that was first ingrained in me when I was six or seven years old.

I was visiting my grandparents' house in Burbank. Grandpaw was painting a picket fence beside the driveway, and even though I'd never read or even heard of *Tom Sawyer* at that point, I thought it looked like fun and asked if I could help.

He was more than happy to have me join him, but he made it clear before I picked up a brush that, "If you're going to paint this fence with me, you're going to stay with me until it's finished."

I agreed to that without a second thought and jumped right in. But after about an hour, the novelty had worn off. Like most kids, my attention span was nonexistent. I was bored and ready to move on to something else, so I held out my paintbrush to Grandpaw and said, "I'm done. I can't do this anymore."

He looked at the paintbrush without touching it, then looked me in the eyes and simply said, "There's no such word as *can't* in this family."

He went back to painting. After a moment or two to process that, I went back to painting too, and I was proud when I finished that fence with him.

Since the day that happened I had thought a million times about how much that one statement of fact from Grandpaw explained about my mom. She'd been raised on "There's no such word as *can't* in this family" from the day she was born, and as far as I'm concerned, she never proved it more than when she was nineteen years old and under contract to MGM Studios.

It was early spring in 1951 when Louis B. Mayer called his young star Debbie Reynolds into his office and informed her that she was going to be starring with Gene Kelly and Donald O'Connor in a movie called *Singin' in the Rain*. It sounded great to her—she was a big fan of both men. But when Gene Kelly was introduced to his new leading lady and she told him honestly that she danced only a little and that she wasn't really a singer, he wanted no part of her.

It didn't matter. Louis B. Mayer was the boss, and nobody, not even Gene Kelly, could override his decision. Debbie Reynolds was going to be the female lead in *Singin' in the Rain*—period, exclamation point, end of discussion.

Mom had exactly three months to make the transition from a girl who danced a little to a girl who could hold her own in a major motion picture with two seasoned pros who'd been dancing all their lives. They assigned three dance teachers to work with her in shifts, and she started tap dancing eight hours a day. Gene Kelly would stop by to watch, offering a lot of criticism and not a single compliment. Her feet were blistered and bloody, she felt utterly defeated and overwhelmed, and she spent a lot of those lessons dancing with tears flowing down her cheeks.

One day after a long, hard session on the sound stage, she was alone, literally lying under the piano, sobbing her heart out with her face buried in her hands, when she heard a male voice ask, "Why are you crying?"

The words came gushing out of her. "Because I'll never learn how to do this. I can't do it anymore. It's so hard. I feel like I'm going to die."

"No, you're not going to die," the voice gently assured her. "That's what it is to learn how to dance."

Mom lifted her head and saw the pant legs of the man standing beside the piano. She moved enough to look up and see who it was.

It was Fred Astaire. He reached out a hand to help her up. "You come watch me," he said. "You watch how hard I work. I don't cry, but I do get frustrated and upset and I'm going to let you watch."

Fred Astaire, one of the greatest dancers of all time, who never let anyone, not even Louis B. Mayer, watch him rehearse, led her to his rehearsal hall, where he was getting ready to start shooting *Royal Wedding*. His choreographer, Hermes Pan, was there, along with his drummer; and Astaire went to work on some of his dance routines. He was a perfectionist and a taskmaster, and when he got thoroughly frustrated with what he was doing, Mom was sensitive enough to know that it was time for her to leave.

She walked back to her sound stage that day with a whole new

Mom never hid her admiration for the iconic Fred Astaire.

attitude. She'd learned that she wasn't alone after all, and that if what she was learning was hard for Fred Astaire, it was okay for it to be hard for her too.

And through all that intense, relentless work and all that physical and emotional pain, the one thing that never entered her mind was giving up. "There's no such word as *can't* in this family."

"So next time you're confronted with a huge challenge you're sure you can't handle," I concluded to the group, "watch *Singin' in the Rain* and let my mom prove to you that the word *can't* doesn't belong in your vocabulary or anyone else's."

The Hiding Place gave me some of the most gratifying, humbling years of my life. I still hear from people to this day who tell me it was at The Hiding Place that they found Jesus, and that The Hiding Place changed their lives forever.

It changed mine too, in more ways than I could ever have imagined.

11

FOR BETTER OR FOR WORSE

Eddie showed up for his "only son's" wedding to Donna Freberg.

Donna Freberg and I were married on February 15, 1981.
Ken Copeland officiated.

Donna moved in to the Cedarbrook house, and we set
about learning that, for better or worse, no magic transformation
happens from one end of the church aisle to the other—the person
you dated almost always turns out to be the person you marry. But

I took my vows seriously, with every intention that Donna and I would be spending the rest of our lives together, and I assumed she did too.

She was very smart and articulate, and she had a good sense of humor. We had a close circle of funny, talented, stimulating friends, so there was a lot of laughter and a lot of fun to be had on Cedarbrook Drive. The marriage didn't change a thing as far as my relationships with Mom and Carrie were concerned. There were very few invitations from them to us, but I spent as much time as always with my mother and my sister. As for any drama between them and my wife, I simply took my usual "do not engage" position.

There was also the added bonus of having Donna's dad Stan Freberg as a father-in-law. He was a brilliant satirist, a genius he applied to his writing, his recording career, his radio show, his TV commercials, even his success as a puppeteer, and we became very close. He hired me to do sound and video production work for him and let me direct. He happily volunteered to be one of my guest stars on *Nightlight*. One of my favorites of Stan's quotes: "My records aren't released—they escape." He even taught me how to shave. I loved that man and remained friends with him until his death in 2015.

Another part of the Donna package was her tendency to be as high maintenance as Mom and Carrie had predicted. She had a long list of phobias that seemed to me to require a lot of attention. Maybe I would have had more patience with them if I hadn't had my own share of crises to deal with that were scaring the hell out of me.

Star Wars had obviously become a hit, far beyond everyone's wildest imaginations. Carrie had moved out of her Century City condo and bought a house on Lookout Mountain off of Laurel Canyon. She was traveling all over the world, she was overwhelmed by her sudden status as a full-fledged movie star, and she had all the friends, admirers, and drugs a girl could ever want. She and Paul Simon, who met while Carrie was filming *Star Wars*, were in the midst of an almost Shakespearean on-and-off love affair that included a short-lived marriage. At any given moment she might be experiencing the highest of highs or the lowest of lows, having nothing to do with what was going on around her.

It may sound odd to say about my sister's husband, but neither Mom nor I ever knew Paul Simon very well. The vast majority of their relationship happened back east, surrounded by Paul's circle of New York intellectual friends; and it seemed as if the brilliance, intensity, and volatility they had in common, the traits that attracted them to each other from the beginning, made it impossible for them to stay together for any length of time. As Carrie confided in me more than once, their relationship became more about the problems than the people.

"We were in a way defined by our objections," she said to me. "They gave us color."

When their on-and-off relationship was on, Mom and I could both see that Carrie was more immersed in Paul than happy with him, more involved in the high emotional pitch of it than in love, which made it hard to cheer them on. But let's face it, I was married

Roger Birnbaum, George Lucas, and Charlie Wessler
by Carrie's side at her wedding to Paul Simon.

to Donna, and Mom had Eddie and Harry on her roster of husbands, so who were we to throw stones about questionable choices in a partner?

In fact, Mom was always fascinated by the parallels between her and Carrie. They'd both been catapulted to stardom by one definitive film—*Star Wars* had done for Carrie exactly what *Singin' in the Rain* had done for Mom. Mom was nineteen when she shot *Singin' in the Rain*. Carrie was nineteen when she shot *Star Wars*. And they'd both been married for the first time to short Jewish recording superstars, despite Frank Sinatra's warning to Mom when she fell in love with Eddie: "Whatever you do, don't marry a singer." Mom wasn't wrong—it was a little uncanny.

I was at home on Cedarbrook late one evening when a call came from the Century City Hospital emergency room. "I have your sister here," a doctor I happened to know told me. "She's stable, but she's obviously taken something, we just don't know what."

I was out the door and on my way before he even finished that last sentence.

One of Carrie's doctors approached me the minute I rushed into the emergency room. They'd already given her charcoal to help clean out her system, and they were seriously considering the further precaution of pumping her stomach.

I didn't hesitate. "She tends to get away with this stuff and not take it seriously, so I say give her a night to remember." In other words, absolutely, pump her stomach.

I found my sister in one of those private ICU cubicles surrounded by curtains. She was lying on her side. The lights were dim, her bed rails were up, and she looked like a little girl, small, helpless, and pale.

I knelt down, got close to her face, and whispered, "There are two phone calls I never want to get, and I just got one of them."

She burst into tears. She knew she'd come close to dying, and she was scared.

After getting her stomach pumped and spending a couple of days in the hospital, Carrie went straight into the rehab facility in Century City. She was going through yet another phase of not speaking to Mom and didn't want her there. (I had no idea why. I tried to talk to Carrie about it, but she got so agitated that I dropped the subject.) So I was the only "family" at group therapy and meetings where the family was allowed to interact.

I remember an early indoctrination session where one of the doctors talked about tough love. "Addicts are going to do what they do, and there's nothing you can do to stop it," he said. "Leave them alone."

It was a concept I couldn't grasp, and I told him so. "I'm sorry, but if I find my sister unconscious on the floor in her own vomit, there's no way I'm going to leave her alone. I'm going to throw her over my shoulder and get her help." I knew too many people, particularly too many "children of," who'd died in the wake of their parents' well-intentioned tough love. I couldn't imagine living with myself, or Mom living with herself, if we took the "leave her alone" approach and lost Carrie in the process.

The doctor pronounced me a classic enabler and told me to run, not walk, to the nearest Al-Anon meeting. I didn't say it out loud, but I thought to myself, "At least I call Carrie on her bullshit. If I'm a classic enabler, Mom must be the cover girl for *Enabler Monthly Magazine*." But I really wanted to understand what I should and shouldn't do to be the brother my sister needed, so I went to several Al-Anon meetings.

As a Christian, I respected the Al-Anon position that dealing with addiction is between the addict and his or her higher power. On the other hand, I think that the higher power very often operates through those of us on earth. I'm a fan of the old saying "Believe in God, but row for the shore." I came away from those Al-Anon meetings appreciating the spirit of the organization but still struggling with the day-to-day behavioral definition of enabling.

That overdose and trip to rehab were the ones Carrie wrote about in *Postcards from the Edge*, by the way. Some of it was absolutely accurate, and some of it was exaggerated or fictionalized for dramatic purposes, like Mom wrecking her car while driving drunk. If I recall the real story correctly, the Dennis Quaid character who dropped Carrie off at the emergency room was actually Don Henley of the Eagles; and the actress he slept with on the same day he slept with Carrie, played by Annette Bening, was Beverly D'Angelo. (And yes, he really did use the "you smell like Catalina" line on both of them.) Carrie and Beverly went on to become great friends. Oh, and the doctor played by Richard Dreyfuss, who pumped Carrie's stomach, did send her flowers and try to date her. Granted, this was a decade or two before eHarmony.com, but trolling for girlfriends in the emergency room? Seriously?

There was another undeniable factor adding to Carrie's fear when she came to in that emergency room. I still remember how hard it hit Carrie, as it did a lot of people, when John Belushi died of a drug overdose. Carrie and John had been friends since they did *The Blues Brothers* together, if not longer, and they got even closer during the time when she was engaged to Dan Aykroyd, who loved them both. She said she was looking around at the crowd at John's memorial service and the thought crossed her mind: "All these people who I'd seen do drugs with him, and you know what they were thinking? Hoping? That what he died of was not what they liked to do best."

I actually spent some time with John the night before he died. Johnny Rivers and I walked into On the Rox, a club on the Sunset Strip, and there sat John at the bar. I'd met him several times before, but I hadn't seen him in quite a while, so I went up to him and shook his hand. "John, hi, it's Todd. Carrie's brother."

He asked how she was doing and then launched into a very loaded riff about how upset he was that Carrie had broken her engagement to Dan to go back to Paul Simon.

"I really wanted Carrie and Dan together," he told me.

"Yeah, me too," I said. I meant that. Carrie and Dan were cute together. They had fun together, and there was a lightness about her when she was with him that never existed with Paul. Dan was a terrific, laid-back guy, the polar opposite of Paul's intensity, and I'd been pulling for him and Carrie from the minute they'd started seeing each other.

John and I talked about that for a few more minutes before he announced, "I'm speeding my ass off. Got anything to bring me down? A Valium? Anything?" He'd been drinking a lot, trying to level off, but it wasn't working.

I explained that I didn't do drugs anymore, so no, I had nothing on me at all. He was really agitated about Carrie and Dan's breakup, and we kept talking for a while before he headed off to

Carrie and Dan Aykroyd during their brief, happy engagement.

the bathroom, where he obviously managed to score something. By the time he came out again, he'd quieted down, and he was sweating.

My last image of John was our waving good-bye to each other as I pulled out of the On the Rox parking lot at two A.M. and watched him get smaller and smaller in my rearview mirror as I drove away.

It shook me to my core when, less than twelve hours later, a friend walked in the door of The Hiding Place and said, "Hey, did you hear John Belushi died?"

It wasn't only that I'd just seen him that made me have to sit down to process the news. It was also knowing how much alike John and Carrie were, both of them hoping the right combination of drugs might give them a break from a relentless mental chaos most of us can't begin to imagine.

A couple of years earlier, when Carrie was twenty-four, she'd been formally diagnosed as bipolar, which both explained and complicated things. Various therapists in New York and L.A. had mentioned it as a possibility, so it didn't really hit us like a bolt out of the blue. Mom and I had seen this evolve for a decade by then. It was like living with someone on a roller coaster: sometimes she was riding it by herself and all you could do was watch, and sometimes you were on the ride with her. Now at least we had a specific name, an actual medical condition, to call it, as opposed to "Carrie's moods," or "Carrie being Carrie," or "that damned Percodan, Carrie's drug of choice." As we understood it, the symptoms of drug addiction can mimic the symptoms of bipolar disorder and vice versa, so it wasn't just a matter of what we were dealing with, it was a matter of which we were dealing with, before we could even get around to how to deal with whichever it was.

It was scary for all of us to learn that Carrie was suffering from something that may or may not be curable, at a time when the medical community had very little understanding of bipolar disorder. It broke Mom's heart to think of Carrie having to go through this uncharted bipolar journey alone, knowing that all we could do was embrace her and hang on. But if that's where we were, that's where we were; and wherever we were, there was never a doubt that we were going to be there together.

Since Carrie was a child, the constant noise in her head had made her prone to being overwhelmed by her own mind; and she used to say that drug use was her way of "putting the monster in the box," kind of "abbreviating" herself. Once she was diagnosed, she tried to make peace with her bipolar disorder, thanks to a psychiatrist named Beatriz Foster, by naming her two moods. Roy was what she called her "wild ride of a mood," and Pam was the one who "stands on the shore and sobs."

I know there were times when Carrie felt as if her ability to function came down to a choice between doing drugs or being at the mercy of Roy and Pam, and what the hell kind of choice is that? I'll always be proud of her for speaking about it so openly, and for using her brilliant sense of humor to get the point across without turning people off.

In the meantime, Mom was still hard at work touring, with Richard Landers and the rest of her usual crew by her side, when she suddenly announced she was getting married again.

She'd gone to Reno to tape a television special called *Classic Cars and Classic Stars*, a tribute to her late great friend Bill Harrah that featured the world's largest antique car collection. Everyone from Bill Cosby, Sammy Davis Jr., Jim Nabors, and Rip Taylor to the governor of Nevada went to the cocktail party after the show, and Mom was sitting at a table with a group of friends when a man approached her and asked her to dance.

His name was Richard Hamlett. He was a tall, good-looking man with remarkable Arnold Palmer–blue eyes, silver-gray hair, and a soft southern drawl. They danced, he joined her at her table, and at the end of the evening, they exchanged phone numbers. She went home to Los Angeles, and he went home to Roanoke, Virginia, where he was a real estate developer.

Three months later he called her. She was fifty-one years old; and thanks to Eddie, Harry, and Bob Fallon, she'd resigned herself to the idea that her years of romance and falling in love were behind her. But here, out of nowhere, was this very attractive man, asking her to dinner in Las Vegas, where she was scheduled to be at a convention publicizing her new exercise video *Do It Debbie's Way.*

She said yes.

They had a lovely dinner.

Over dessert, he asked her to marry him.

She was incredulous and pointed out the obvious—they barely knew each other. He corrected her. She barely knew him, true enough, but between her movies and the press, he'd known and loved her for as far back as he could remember. He'd just never dreamed he'd be lucky enough to meet her, and now that he had, there wasn't a doubt in his mind that he wanted to marry her.

She said no, of course, but she agreed to a date for the next night. They dated for a few months after that second night, "Tammy" was in love again with the man he presented himself to be, he kept asking her to marry him, and one day she called him and said yes.

Mom's great friend Ruta Lee gave Mom a copy of a prenuptial agreement she'd used, to protect herself "just in case." The agreement was the size of the Los Angeles phone book, and Richard signed it. That seemed promising, right?

Mom was booked to perform on a Caribbean cruise for a week that May, so she and Richard decided to have a small, simple wedding at the home of her friends Nancy and Joe Kanter in Miami and spend their honeymoon on the ship. Grandpaw was eighty-one and too frail to make the trip from Palm Springs, so in his absence I inherited the honor of giving Mom away—to a man I'd never met until I got to Florida.

Carrie was supposed to fly in from London the day before the wedding. Life hadn't been going smoothly for her since she got out of rehab. She and Paul Simon had ended a marriage that lasted only a few months. She'd confided in me that she was using again; and as if that weren't complicating things enough, she was recovering from surgery after a rough, emotional tubular pregnancy, which had been a drama of its own.

Carrie had called me one day from New York, alone in the hospital from this tubular pregnancy. I jumped on a plane and flew there without even knowing which hospital she was in, but I knew who would know. I headed to Paul's apartment, and sure enough, he was home—not with my sister where I thought he belonged. I strongly suggested he accompany me to Carrie's bedside, which he did. But needless to say, that incident hadn't exactly endeared me to him.

Carrie was also having a hard time with the fact that Mom was getting married again, especially since she didn't know Richard Hamlett any more than I did. So instead of catching her flight from London to Miami, she called Mom and said she couldn't make it. Mom wasn't as disappointed as she was worried about her fragile daughter.

Richard and I were properly introduced as soon as I arrived in Miami. Mom was right: he was a handsome man, and a smart one, and he seemed charming enough with that Virginia drawl of his. But I'd had a front-row seat to what Mom had been through with her previous husbands, so I sat Richard down for a beer in the hotel lobby bar.

"My mom has been through a lot in her prior marriages. I was much younger then. I'm older now. I'm not anticipating any problems here, but I want you to know, if anything like that should ever happen again—and I'm not saying it's going to, but if it does—you'll have me to deal with."

He laughed.

(I reminded him of that conversation several years later. He wasn't laughing then.)

It was a simple, pretty wedding, and Mom looked radiant in her pale green dress, with flowers in her hair. At the reception I noticed that she seemed a little preoccupied; sure enough, behind all those smiles for her new husband and her friends and the cameras, she was concerned about Carrie and asked me to call her in London.

Carrie and I talked a little before I passed the phone to Mom, who started with her usual greeting that Carrie and I never stopped smiling about: "Hi, dear. It's your mother. Debbie."

They chatted for a couple of minutes, with Mom telling Carrie how much she missed her and Carrie telling Mom she'd caught a bad cold on one of the many planes she'd been on in the past few weeks. Then Mom passed the phone to Richard so Carrie could say hello to "your new stepfather."

By the time Mom finished the call with a cheerful "I love you. Wish you were here," I could see she was frightened. If Carrie thought we wouldn't notice that her words were slurred and that some of her responses were odd and delayed, she was kidding herself. I was upset by it too, and I told Mom I'd catch the next flight to London and bring Carrie home.

I immediately called Carrie's hotel room again to let her know I was on my way. The phone rang and rang and rang, with no answer. Mom and I were both picturing another overdose, and I hung up, dialed the hotel, and handed the phone to Mom.

"This is Debbie Reynolds," she told the concierge. "My daughter Carrie Fisher is staying at your hotel, and I know she's in her room, but she isn't answering the phone. I wondered if you could please, please check on her and make sure she's all right."

He refused, explaining that he had no way of knowing she was who she said she was, and there was no convincing him.

As Carrie put it in her book *Wishful Drinking*, "So she did what any normal, concerned mother might do when troubled about her daughter's well-being. She called Ava Gardner."

Mom and Ava were old friends. Mom knew that Ava was in London, and that any woman who could handle Frank Sinatra for six years could make mincemeat out of a hotel concierge. It was about one A.M. in London, but Ava was on the case like Wonder Woman, and minutes later the St. James's Hotel manager and Ava Gardner walked into Carrie's room to find her facedown on the floor, fully dressed including her shoes, either sound asleep or passed out. The TV was blaring, and every window in the suite had been thrown wide open.

Ava called a doctor, who treated Carrie and concluded that while she'd taken too much "medication," she hadn't overdosed.

The next day Carrie was on a plane to L.A., and I met her there. She assured me all the way from LAX to her house on Lookout Mountain that she was fine and that, as always, it would never happen again.

Mom, knowing that Carrie was safe, was able to relax as she and Richard left Miami for their honeymoon cruise. Richard spent the first few days of the cruise on the deck entertaining three lady friends of his from Roanoke who happened to be on the same ship. Mom spent those same days blaming herself for letting her concern for her daughter upstage the attention she should have been paying to her brand-new husband.

Mom and Richard spent a couple of months in Roanoke after their wedding while Richard recovered from a health scare. Mom took care of him after his stay in the hospital and even (kind of) learned to cook. She got to know his friends and family and real estate business associates, and she found them all to be welcoming and unassuming and eager to embrace Richard's new movie star wife. He literally owned the biggest house in town, and the two of them essentially became the king and queen of Roanoke.

One of Richard's oldest friends was a fantastically successful entrepreneur and real estate developer named Elbert Waldron. Mom and Richard thought he would make a fascinating subject for a documentary and hired me to come film it. I recruited my great pal Dusty Ebsen, who happened to be a skilled editor and camera and sound technician, to go with me. Donna had no more interest in being around Mom than Mom had in being around her, and she wasn't about to get on a plane, so she stayed home.

Mom actually cooked an edible dinner during our week or so at Richard's spectacular house. That might have been the headline of that trip if Dusty and I hadn't decided to do some research on our subject, Elbert Waldron, at the Roanoke newspaper office. Since Richard was going to be a part of the documentary, and let's face it, I was curious about my mom's new husband, I researched him too. I found several articles about Richard Hamlett and discovered that, among other things, he'd been charged with bank fraud more than once, and he'd been in some physical fights over finances that led to at least one assault charge. Dusty and I were incredulous.

I showed copies of the articles to Mom. She said she knew all about the trouble he'd had in the past; he'd explained everything to her complete satisfaction; and she and Richard were looking forward, not backward.

Richard, on the other hand, was pissed off that I'd checked him out in the first place and took a "how dare you?" position. As I pointed out to him, this was my mother we were talking about. I had no trouble daring anything when it came to her. Unbeknownst to me at the time, Mom had already been loaning Richard money. But her attorney, David Rudich, my hero, had butted heads with him about it and made him sign notes for every dime he borrowed; and my other hero, CPA David De Salvo, kept impeccable records on every one of those same dimes.

When it was all said and done, though, it was impossible to ignore the fact that Mom was completely smitten with her new husband, and she was happier than she'd been in years. Skeptical as I was, I really, really wanted her to be right about Richard Hamlett.

Then it was back to L.A., back to Donna and The Hiding Place and my friends and an irresistible job offer—a chance to go with a film crew to explore Mount Ararat, the highest mountain in eastern Turkey, in the age-old search for the biblical landing site of Noah's Ark.

I asked Dusty to join the crew as a camera and sound assistant, but his dad Buddy urged him to stay home because of the civil unrest in that part of the world at the time. Dusty ended up passing on the trip, and I went off to Mount Ararat without him.

I'm not sure which was more unforgettable—the trip itself, or what was waiting for me when I came home. I walked through the front door on Cedarbrook Drive to find my wife of four years with none other than my close, trusted pal Dusty.

While I was trying to take this in, I silently scanned the small house. Random stuff of Dusty's was scattered all over the place. He'd obviously been staying there while I was gone. Then they gave me the "we're in love" speech, with added obligatory clichés about being sorry, the old "it just happened" routine, "never meant to hurt you" and a bunch of other bad dialogue. Finally, when the incredulity wore off enough for me to form words again, I said, "What are you guys planning to do, get married or something? Because if you are, for the record, it's fine with me."

I'd come straight home from LAX, and my luggage was still in my car. So I just grabbed a few more of my things from around the house, walked out the door, and headed straight to Carrie's. It took me a while to sort out my thoughts through the numbing haze of the betrayal; but at their core were the facts that I blamed Donna a whole lot more than I blamed Dusty, and my most overwhelming feeling about it wasn't hurt, it was relief.

I'd picked a good time to crash at Carrie's. Carrie's *Star Wars* money was pouring in. *The Blues Brothers* movie she'd done with John Belushi and Dan Aykroyd had been released to a wildly appreciative audience; and she'd completed the *Star Wars* trilogy and loved every minute of it, trusting George Lucas so much by then that she didn't even object to Princess Leia wearing a metal bikini, chained to a giant slug. I'd been too busy with my own life and career to hang around with her more than very briefly on the sets of either *The Empire Strikes Back* or *Return of the Jedi*, and I also didn't want to seem as if I was becoming a *Star Wars* groupie, trying to horn in or insinuate myself into this amazing franchise. I was just proud of her, and so happy for her.

Carrie had bought a great house on Oak Pass, near Mulholland Drive, and she welcomed me and my belongings with open arms. In fact, she was ecstatic that Donna and I were over with and, as she put it, I'd finally come to my senses. She probably threw in "I told you so" twenty or thirty times, and, in the age-old tradition of siblings everywhere, I probably refused to admit that yes, she had. Carrie and Paul Simon were between reconciliations, so the timing of suddenly having me as a roommate was as perfect for her as it was for me, and she was ecstatic about that too. As always, we picked up right where we left off, as confidants, playmates, and siblings—if there's one thing that came naturally to Carrie and me since the day I was born, it was living together.

We'd also been traveling together all our lives, so when Carrie called in the middle of an overseas trip to God knows where a few months after I'd moved to Oak Pass and asked if I'd like to meet her in Singapore, it was the most natural thing in the world. She had a speaking engagement at a university in China, and while we were there we could hang out and do some sightseeing and some shopping, since Christmas was right around the corner. I was packing before we hung up the phone.

Carrie managed to lose her wallet by the time she deplaned in Singapore, so we had that minidrama to deal with at the airport, and all our expenses would be my treat. Luckily, there wasn't a lot of tourism in China in those days and not a lot of money to be spent, so I had more than enough with me to cover us both. The only medications she had with her were her prescribed bipolar meds; either they weren't working or she wasn't taking them. Other than that, she was sober. In fact, we'd just had her one-year AA party at Oak Pass. She was starting to work on her first as-yet-untitled book, ready to Christmas-shop and ready to explore.

That night in our hotel suite we had probably the longest, deepest talk we'd ever had about her bipolar diagnosis and what it was like for her to find her two bipolar "moods," Roy and Pam, taking charge of her no matter what was going on around her. It was scary for her to feel that her emotions were running her rather than the other way around, and even scarier to know that with the right medications, the best she could hope for was that it would be managed, but never cured.

On our first day of sightseeing, Carrie grabbed her boom box and we hopped into the car that was taking us to Tourist Attraction Number One, the Great Wall of China. We were listening to random audiocassettes on her boom box on the way and did a triple take when Paul Simon's song "Something So Right" came on, with lyrics that include the lines "They've got a wall in China / It's a thousand miles long." I mean, seriously, you've got to appreciate the synchronicity when moments like that come along.

I filmed one of Carrie's spontaneous manic episodes on top of the Great Wall of China. She played Christmas music on her boom box, she sang, she danced, and she tried to get the other tourists to join in, most of whom had no idea what the word *Christmas* even meant. It was "Carrie being Carrie," having fun and then some,

With Carrie at the Great Wall of China.

nothing I wasn't used to, nothing I hadn't seen a million times—it just had the name *bipolar* attached to it now.

We stopped at a café for an almost inedible lunch when we'd finished exploring. Carrie had bought a bunch of postcards along the way and started filling them out to send to friends back home, starting each one with "I'm writing to you from the Great Wall of China, sending you a postcard from the edge of the world." And from that came the title of the book she was working on: *Postcards from the Edge*.

We were headed home three weeks later, going through customs at the Honolulu International Airport, when, with no warning, Carrie flipped. The woman at the customs counter seemed to take an instant dislike to Carrie; and as she sorted through the wrapped Christmas gifts in Carrie's luggage we were bringing home from Singapore, she thrust one at Carrie and almost growled, "Open it."

Carrie threw it right back at her and said, "You open it."

The two of them squared off and started yelling at each other. I immediately pictured Carrie and me being escorted off for deep-cavity searches and asked to see the customs agent's supervisor. The whole time I was talking to him, wallet in hand, assuring him that I was perfectly happy to pay whatever duties were owed, I could hear Carrie yelling in the background in a full-blown, aggressive Roy rage. I excused myself, walked over to her, grabbed her coat, pushed her against a column, and said, "Sit! Do not talk!"

Carrie started to argue with me. I moved closer to her face and said, "No! Absolutely not! I said, 'Do not talk!'"

I rejoined the supervisor long enough to get everything settled, and by the time I got back to Carrie, she was in tears. I knelt down beside her. "You know I had to do that," I quietly explained. "You were about to get us in trouble."

She was calm, Pam now, and apologetic. She wasn't crying because I'd torn into her. She was crying because she'd lost control, and she knew it and hated it. I hated it for her and wished for the millionth time that I could do more to help than just keep my promise to never, ever walk away.

A few weeks after Carrie and I got back to L.A., I filed for divorce from Donna. I thought I was pretty generous—I let her stay in the Cedarbrook house while I kept paying the mortgage and expenses until I put it on the market. I also agreed to pay the bills on the American Express card I let her keep "for emergencies only." (Why do people even bother saying that when they give someone a credit card? Have you ever known anyone who didn't go right ahead and use that card whenever they felt like it? Me neither.)

While all that was going on, there was drama going on at another house that seemed to have nothing to do with me at the time—Johnny Rivers and his wife, Christi, whom I knew from The Hiding Place, split up. They were living close by, on Mulholland Drive, and since Johnny had kicked her out, Christi and their three children had no place to live. Donna generously invited them to move into Cedarbrook with her, which was fine with me until I found out that Donna was charging Christi rent to live in a house that wasn't costing her a dime. I wasn't having it, and after some persuasive discussions with me, Donna started paying half the bills (with Christi's rent money).

And then there was the day I stopped by Cedarbrook to retrieve something or other. I knew that Donna and Dusty were still a couple, although they weren't living together. I probably shouldn't have been surprised, but I was, when Donna turned to me and announced, "You know, you and I really do belong together."

She wanted me to move back in. I was incredulous, and more than a little disgusted. I reminded her that last I heard, she wasn't available. "Dusty. My friend," I said. "Remember him?"

"I can't help it," she told me in her trademark victim voice. "I'm torn between the two of you. I love Dusty, but I love you too. You were my hero."

She made those last two comments to my back as I walked to my car and drove away, figuring that was the last such encounter. As with so much about Donna, I was wrong.

I was pleasantly surprised to get a call several weeks later from Ken Copeland, which to me was like getting a call from Billy

Graham. He was at one of his conventions near Los Angeles and wanted to see me. I walked into Ken's hotel suite, genuinely happy to see him. I hadn't seen it coming that Donna would be sitting there too. From the conversation that followed, it became apparent that Donna had called and asked to meet with him, and that she'd been filling him in on her side of the story and her litany of grievances against me.

At some point in my life I'd lost patience with any argument that boils down to "did too/did not." I can't be bothered to defend myself against nonsense. When I'm wrong, I'm wrong, and I'll step up and do my best to make it right. When I'm not, there's nothing for me to say, beyond a calm, simple "Is that so?"

So I listened while Ken, compassionate as always and trying to help, outlined Donna's version of our marriage. I occasionally replied, "That's true"—I would never have nominated myself for Husband of the Year. But for the most part, especially with the luxury of apathy on my side, my only response was "Is that so?"

Donna seemed to have her heart set on high-drama combat that day, but I wasn't about to waste Ken's valuable time. Finally he looked at us both and said, "You two need to stop all this foolishness and get back together."

"Is that so?" I repeated, and with a thank-you nod to Ken, I left.

It didn't happen right away, but Donna and Dusty got married. I thought he was out of his mind, but I stayed out of it, until she charged her wedding shoes on my "for emergencies only" American Express card. I hit the roof over that, called for a meeting at Stan's house (Donna's dad thought she was as out of line as I did), and demanded that she give me back the card. She actually tried to argue about it, but in the end not even she could justify expecting me to pay for the shoes she'd wear when she married the friend of mine she'd cheated with.

Dusty and I are still close friends to this day, by the way, and he and Donna are still living together. I'll leave it at that.

As it turned out, there had been an important development in my life in the weeks after I walked out on Donna and Dusty. I hadn't mentioned it in the meeting with Donna in Ken Copeland's hotel room. It had nothing to do with my complete lack of interest in reconciling with Donna, and it also happened to be none of her business.

I hadn't seen it coming—maybe no one ever does—but to my surprise, over the course of those few short weeks, I learned the difference between infatuation and falling deeply, genuinely, head over heels in love.

I met her at The Hiding Place.

Her name was Rene Russo.

12

WOMAN OF THE YEAR

The three of us at the Thalians Ball.

It started, but didn't, a couple of years into my marriage to Donna. I was in New York with Mom and Carrie, who were both appearing on Broadway—Mom in *Woman of the Year* and Carrie in *Agnes of God*. But of course Donna had opted to stay home on Cedarbrook rather than get on a plane to the East Coast and hang out with two women who didn't like her any more than she liked them.

I answered the phone one day at our hotel to hear, "Todd, this is Rene Russo. I'm sorry to bother you, but if you have time, I could use your help." She sounded upset.

It seems that Rene and the man in her life, a photographer she'd also met at The Hiding Place, were in New York as well, and they were having serious relationship problems. She didn't know what to do, and she needed advice from me, as a trusted elder of her church. After a long phone conversation, I suggested that she and her man and I have dinner.

We did. I sat there for two hours trying to keep an open mind and came away with the opinion that this guy was a complete nut job and she needed to start putting together an exit strategy ASAP.

I was getting ready to head back to L.A. a few days later when Rene called again and asked me to meet her at the *Alice in Wonderland* sculpture in Central Park. We walked around the park while she thanked me for confirming what her heart had already been telling her: it wasn't just her; she really was in a toxic relationship that she had to get out of, no matter how hard it was going to be and how difficult he was likely to make it. She was sad, but she was also at peace for the first time in a long time, because there wasn't a doubt in her mind anymore that it was the right thing to do.

We were in the car saying good-bye when it happened. We were sitting there talking, looking at each other, when all of a sudden to my total shock, and hers too, I'm sure, it was as if a jolt of electricity shot through us. It was light-years beyond physical attraction. Of course I was physically attracted to her. She was Rene Russo. Duh. An acting career wasn't even on her radar back then. She was "just" a supermodel. Just a supermodel with, in fact, nine covers of *Vogue* and countless other magazines to her name. What had happened between us at that moment in that car was a deep, unspoken mutual connection so strong that it was almost tangible. I'd never felt anything like it before, and I was stunned by it.

Neither one of us said or did a thing about it. There was nothing to be said or done. On her way out or not, she was still entangled in a complicated relationship, and I was married. The end. I could hear alarm bells going off all over the place, and my reaction was to run for the hills and make a point of never being alone with her again. It didn't stop me from thinking about her. A lot. But a commitment's a commitment, and a marriage is a marriage.

Then I woke up one day living at Carrie's, with my divorce from Donna well under way, and I reached for the phone. Rene said, "Come on over." She gave me tuberoses when I got there. No woman had ever given me flowers before. It blew me away.

In what seemed like no time at all, Rene and I were in love.

It was a beautiful relationship from the very beginning. We were great friends, compatible in every way, from our senses of humor to our values to our interests to the pace at which we liked to live our lives. We had even been the same age, two years old, when our womanizing fathers walked out on our moms and families. We were both recovering from unhealthy relationships, but we'd both healed enough from them to know we weren't falling into the rebound trap. We just effortlessly "got" each other. She called me "Fishy." As an homage to Mrs. Yang—who woke Carrie and me up every morning of our childhoods with a loving "Callie-fish!" and "Ta-fish!"—I called her "Nay-fish."

Looking back, I'm not sure I had the depth to genuinely fall in love before Rene came along. During my years of The Hiding Place and my marriage to Donna, I did a lot of evolving, asking bigger questions than I ever had about life, meaning, purpose, my own identity, and certainly my own behavior. It wasn't deliberate growth. I wasn't even aware that I needed it. It was more like having grown up perceiving the world through a close-up lens, focused on nothing but whatever was right in front of me, and then slowly being pulled back to a wide shot and saying, "Whoa, what's all this?" Perspective was a novelty for me, and between that and my innate curiosity, I was open to exploring all this new emotional and spiritual territory. It was amazing to find Rene by my side to take the journey with me.

I still remember going to Mom's little house in North Holly-wood to tell her all about it. She'd seen me infatuated many times, but she'd never seen me in love before. She threw her arms around me and said, "I'm so thrilled that you're experiencing this."

So was I.

I was cautiously thrilled for Mom too. There was no doubt about it, she was crazy about her new husband, and he was a big hit with her friends in L.A. He looked great, he was very artic-ulate and socially skilled, and he couldn't have been more atten-tive to Mom. Even Carrie, after her dramatic absence from Mom's third wedding, came to like Richard so much that she convinced me to split the cost of his Christmas present with her, a very ex-pensive briefcase with an engraved brass plate that read *World's Greatest Stepdad*. I still have home movies of him opening that gift on Christmas Day in 1986 at Carrie's Oak Pass house. There we all were, gathered around the usual massive, insanely decorated tree—me, Rene, Carrie, Mom, and Richard, looking like a nor-mal, traditional all-American family celebrating the holiday, if a normal, traditional all-American family happens to include two movie stars and one of the world's most successful high-fashion models.

Mom wanted Richard to experience some of the favorite places we'd visited when Carrie and I were children, so that same normal, traditional all-American family also took lots of overseas vacations together, including Mom's meticulously planned trip through Eu-rope on the Orient Express, with plenty more home movies. The joy of being with Rene was compounded by the joy of finding my-self with a woman who'd not only board an airplane with me but who'd also become great friends with my mother and my sister. Rene even lived with me at Carrie's for a while before we moved into Rene's house on Fareholm Drive in the Hollywood Hills, and the three of us had a ball together.

Not long after we settled into Fareholm, Rene and I decided that we'd get married. There was no question that we both wanted to; it was just a question of where and when.

With Carrie on the Orient Express.

As luck would have it, I was hired to be Carrie's "personal assistant" (read "playmate") while she shot an Agatha Christie movie called *Appointment with Death* in Israel. It was a fantastic trip to a beautiful country. Rene and I stayed in Carrie's hotel suite with her, and when Carrie wasn't filming the three of us shopped, visited the Wailing Wall, shopped, took a private tour of Solomon's Temple and the Dome of the Rock, shopped, and shopped, usually followed by shopping. When Carrie was filming we had a great time hanging out on the set with her and Lauren Bacall and Sir John Gielgud.

When the movie wrapped, Rene and I took an incredible romantic side trip to Jerusalem and Egypt that included riding Arabian horses in the shadow of the Great Pyramids and visiting a sacred site in Jerusalem called the Pool of Bethesda, where Jesus performed one of His miraculous healings.

We were touring the ancient Church of Saint Anne that overlooks the large excavation area of the Pool. It was hallowed, the traditional birthplace of the Virgin Mary. It was magnificent. It was exquisitely peaceful. The acoustics were so incredible that

With Rene Russo on our romantic trip to Egypt.

I burst into an a cappella rendition of "Silent Night" and almost brought myself to tears. It hit us both at the same time—we'd never find a more perfect place to get married.

After a brief talk with a priest, we excitedly went to the hotel, changed into proper clothes, and returned to the Church of Saint Anne, only to be told that we couldn't be married there after all, since it was a requirement that at least one of us have been a baptized Catholic. We were disappointed but not discouraged. We were so sure we'd be getting married sooner or later that we let ourselves get sidetracked by other trips and work and life, and somehow we never got around to it.

Before we knew it we were back in L.A., back to our normal busy lives. Rene's acting career was getting under way. I was working a lot at Mom's DR Studios, which was thriving—everyone from Bette Midler to Madonna to Janet Jackson was rehearsing there. Michael Jackson even rehearsed the video for his *Thriller* album at those clean, comfortable studios, and the tap and hip-hop classes were always filled to capacity, while Mom beamed from the sidelines.

Then Mom and I went on the road, but I came down with a nasty case of the flu, bailed out on the tour a couple of days early, and headed home. I pulled into the garage on Fareholm, started down the hill toward the house, and stopped dead in my tracks when I saw Rene inside with a guy I'd never seen before. They weren't doing anything, and I didn't want to jump to conclusions; but I'd already been blindsided once in my life, by Donna and Dusty, and I wasn't about to go through it again. So instead of taking my chances and strolling on into the house, I called instead, looking right at her through the kitchen window from my vantage point several yards away.

I told Rene I wasn't feeling well and that I was coming home early. Then I casually asked her what she was doing.

She didn't mention anyone being in the house with her.

I asked her again.

She still didn't say a word about the fact that she wasn't alone.

Finally, to put us both out of our misery, I took a long breath and said, "Actually, I'm looking at you right now from the top of the hill."

She panicked. The guy, whoever he was, ran out the door, and I proceeded into the house and confronted her. She couldn't have been more apologetic. She assured me that there was nothing going on between her and that man, he was just a friend, and I believed her.

But then she said something I couldn't get past: "You know, maybe we should date other people."

I suddenly heard, clear as a bell, a piece of advice my mom had drilled into me a thousand times when I first started dating: "Dear, if you ever hear the words 'maybe we should date other people,' run!"

A moving van arrived the next day to pick up my stuff and take it to Carrie's house.

There was none of the relief I'd felt when I left Donna and Dusty at the Cedarbrook house. I loved Rene very much, and it broke my heart to walk away from her, especially when I knew I would never let myself walk back in again, no matter how much I wanted to. We all have our deal-breakers when it comes to relationships, and two of mine had been violated—the "let's date other people" thing, thanks to Mom, and indisputable proof that I couldn't take our conversations at face value anymore. As far as I'm concerned, a relationship without trust is just a mirage. Maybe I learned that from Mom too.

Mom understood, but she was heartbroken. Neither of us ever stopped loving Rene. I'll always be grateful for our time together, I still count her among my close friends, and Mom even remembered her in her will.

Carrie, on the other hand, at least at first, launched right into protective-sister mode the minute I showed up at her house and told her what happened. She was so pissed off, in fact, that she called a friend of hers who worked for one of the tabloids and planted a story. Its title was "Go Fish." Its subtitle was "Carrie Fisher's Brother Dating Michelle Pfeiffer." It was a total lie. I'll go on record right now—I never dated Michelle Pfeiffer. Don't get me wrong, I wouldn't have minded one bit, but I'm pretty sure it's impossible to date someone if you haven't actually ever met them. It was just Carrie's effort at making Rene jealous and sending the message that if you hurt her little brother, you'd find yourself dealing with her, and you wouldn't like it.

In the end, I've never doubted that I did the right thing by leaving. That didn't mean I didn't hate it, but there was nothing left to do but move on.

I put the Cedarbrook house on the market. Donna was still

engaged to Dusty and was still living on Cedarbrook rent-free with her "tenant" Christi Zabel and Christi's three children by her ex-husband Johnny Rivers. I'd gotten to know Christi through The Hiding Place, and as far as I was concerned, Donna had lucked out in the roommate department—Christi was a terrific woman.

One day several weeks after Rene and I broke up, I stopped by Cedarbrook for some reason or other and found Christi gardening on the terraced hillside. We chatted for a while, during which I noticed for the first time that she had a really amazing body. It was more appreciation than lust, just kind of a "Who knew?" about someone I'd known casually for a few years. But I digress. I ended up inviting her to join Carrie and me and several of our friends at an upcoming Super Bowl party at Carrie's house, and she accepted.

I'd never spent relaxed social time with Christi before. I wasn't surprised at how great she was—I already knew she was attractive and likable and funny. I was just kind of fascinated by things about her I'd never noticed before. For example, she was a country girl, generous with attention instead of needing to be the center of it, which is almost unheard-of in this town. She was also much more a grounded, unpretentious mother of three than she was the ex-wife of a rock 'n' roller. She was a brilliant artist and a member of Mensa, but she was grateful about her talent and her intellect rather than arrogant about them, and people were drawn to her humility. I was too, and by the time she left, I wanted to see her again.

I'm saying this literally, not figuratively—my jaw dropped open when I found out that when Christi got home from that Super Bowl party, Donna, aka Dusty's fiancée, announced, and I quote, "I forbid you from dating Todd."

So much for taking orders from Donna. Christi and I started dating anyway.

We fell in love, and we were together for the next twenty years. We were never legally married, but in our eyes and everyone else's, we were a married couple. I embraced the role of stepfather to her

Christi and her three kids, Brandon, Vanessa, and James.

children, although in spite of my upbringing, I skipped the usual stepfather traditions of manicurists, J&B and soda, and gambling us into a financial abyss.

For the most part, it was a happy time, not just for Christi and me but for all of us.

Carrie and I were still pulling for Richard to finally give our mother the loving, successful, secure marriage she deserved. And after Eddie and Harry, let's face it, the bar was set pretty low. Mom went on a multicity tour of Meredith Willson's *The Unsinkable Molly Brown* with Harve Presnell, her costar in the movie. She and Richard coproduced the stage production, and he was delighted to be branching out from real estate. Okay, sure, he replaced the experienced scenic painters with house painters who were cheaper and didn't know what they were doing, and he screwed up on some of the union contracts. But he'd never been a producer before, so it was understandable, and at least he and Mom were together for all those long, tough, exhausting months on the road.

The smash hit movie *When Harry Met Sally* with Meg Ryan and Billy Crystal came out, and Carrie recruited Richard for a cameo role as her character Marie's father, walking her down the aisle at her wedding. (As Mom observed in her book *Unsinkable: A Memoir*, "I guess Eddie Fisher wasn't available." The fact is, Carrie thought Richard looked more like a typical midwestern dad than Eddie did, especially now that Eddie was wading into the unpredictable world of plastic surgery and had started looking oddly Asian for a Jewish boy from Philadelphia.)

In real life, Carrie had met and fallen in love with Bryan Lourd, who'd moved in with her at the Oak Pass house and went on to become a bona fide Hollywood super-agent. Bryan was a great match for Carrie in a lot of ways. He was smart. He was stable. He was a calm, mellow, level-headed guy who didn't let life, or Carrie, shake him up; he just got her better than most. He was also very secure about his own identity—he didn't need Carrie's celebrity to define him, nor was he threatened by it. He was perfectly content being Bryan Lourd, with no desire to evolve into being "Mr. Carrie Fisher." And maybe most of all, he was a great playmate for Carrie. They had fun together. They were fun together. Bryan moved in with Carrie while Rene and I were still living with her, and those were good times for the four of us.

Carrie had also launched a brilliant writing career when her book *Postcards from the Edge* came out. It was promptly optioned by Columbia Pictures, and The Powers That Be were smart enough to hire her to write the screenplay. (Before we get too carried away with the wisdom of The Powers That Be, I should add that Mom asked to read for the role of the mother in *Postcards*, a role that was obviously based on her. She was told she wasn't right for it. Not right to play herself. It's that kind of business sometimes.) *Postcards from the Edge* was Carrie's frank, unapologetic way of "coming out" as a drug addict suffering from bipolar disorder, and we were so proud of the courage it took for her to essentially say, "Here's who I am. Deal with it."

Carrie's first book was a hit. Mom's first book, *Debbie: My Life*, came out shortly after Carrie's. So it apparently made sense in the publishing world to offer me a book deal too. I was excited, my agent Mickey Freiberg was excited, and Christi and I flew to New York for what was a very positive meeting with the publisher. While we were in town we agreed that it would be good form, and the right thing to do, to introduce Christi to my biological father. I hadn't seen Eddie in a few years, and our last face-to-face meeting wasn't exactly heartwarming.

Carrie had wisely invested some of her *Star Wars* money in a New York co-op in the early 1980s, not far from her future husband Paul Simon. One day she was pleasantly surprised by a call from Eddie, telling her he was going to be in New York "on business" and wondering if he could stay with her. She didn't hesitate—he was her dad, after all. Of course he could stay with her.

So Eddie being Eddie, and seeing no distinction between *staying with* and *moving in*, promptly arrived on her doorstep and had himself a high old time (interpret that however you want), taking over Carrie's co-op so completely that she ended up booking herself a hotel room when she was in New York, while Eddie enjoyed the comforts of her home and the liberal use of her many charge accounts.

When his "stay" reached the one-year mark, Mom, knowing that Carrie could never bring herself to kick her father out, took matters into her own hands. She and I hopped on a plane from L.A. to New York, and Eddie answered a firm knock on Carrie's door to find Mom and me standing there glaring at him, Mom with checkbook and pen in hand.

There were no hellos or other pleasantries. Before Eddie could say a word, Mom held up her checkbook and asked, "How much is it going to cost to get you out of here?"

He came up with some very generous figure, Mom wrote him a check, he took it unapologetically and left, and Carrie got to move back into her co-op.

And as usual, just when I thought I couldn't get any angrier at him, he told his version of that story in his shamefully fictional "memoir" a couple of years later and added the comment: "If I'd known she would have paid me to stay away from my daughter all those years, I wouldn't have done it for free."

I was miles past livid when I read that. When I finally got him on the phone I asked him how the hell he could be cruel enough to Carrie to even think such a thing, let alone write it. He didn't write it, he said. It was his ghostwriter, or maybe his editor, or maybe the Tooth Fairy. In other words, he reverted to the motto by which he lived his life: it was anyone's fault but his.

By the time Christi and I were in New York and on our way to introduce her to her new father-in-law (on a biological technicality), Eddie had lucked out and married a sweet, devoted, wealthy Asian woman named Betty Lin. Thanks to her, they were living in a beautiful uptown apartment in Manhattan. Betty and Christi were both too gracious to let the visit go any way but well, in spite of the fact that Eddie was getting more inappropriate and lascivious as the years went by and treated Christi as if she were some woman he was trying to pick up in a singles bar.

During our brief stay, Betty pulled me aside for a quiet, concerned talk. She loved Eddie with all her heart, and she was utterly committed to him no matter what, but he was blasting through her money like a squadron of fighter jets. In an effort to make him happy and keep him that way, she'd given him vast amounts of cash and full access to her credit cards, all of which he'd maxed out countless times. "I give him American Express card, he buy twenty thousand dollars' worth of suits in one day," she told me with tears in her eyes.

Yeah, that sounded just like Eddie. On top of all his other glaring flaws, I knew he was still a drug addict—he'd done drugs with Carrie again not long ago in New York. I may not have had any stones to throw when it came to doing drugs with Carrie, but I'd never done them with her after she'd been through rehab, that's for sure. Nothing Eddie did surprised me anymore; it just disgusted me that he was taking such horrible advantage of yet another kind, decent woman.

Eddie and his fifth wife Betty Lin.

I gave Betty the best advice I could: "Remember that any cash you give him, no matter how much it is, you'll never, ever see it again. Keep all your credit cards away from him and give him one with a thousand-dollar credit limit at most. And do not let him gamble."

She nodded and thanked me. I was sure he'd probably convince her to ignore everything I told her the minute Christi and I walked out the door, but there was nothing I could do about that. She obviously managed to protect at least some of her money from him. When she passed away in 2001 she left him with a trust fund that took care of him until his death in 2010. Without Betty Lin, Eddie Fisher would have died destitute. God bless that woman.

The day after my dubious reunion with dear old Dad, Christi and I flew back to L.A., where I couldn't wait to share the exciting news about my book deal with a major publisher.

Mom was thrilled for me. Carrie, on the other hand, went completely ballistic. Her exact words, at the top of her lungs, were "Can't I ever do something in this family that's just mine? I'm the writer around here, not you! Mom's been trying to compete with me all my life, and now you're doing it too?" To punctuate her explosion, she picked up the phone and pitched a fit to the publisher I'd met with in New York.

Talk about "never saw it coming." I couldn't believe it. I'd heard Carrie accuse Mom of being competitive with her a million times and learned to shrug it off. I knew I'd just be beating my head against a wall if I pointed out the obvious, that actually the opposite was true and it was Carrie, not Mom, with the competitive issues in our family. But now she was accusing me of the same thing? Seriously? At times like that I never knew how much her bipolar disorder might be fueling her tirade, let alone what my "non-enabling" reaction was supposed to be. All I knew was that I was some combination of incredulous and pissed off, and I turned on my heels and walked away.

Few things upset Mom more than Carrie being upset. She rarely stopped to process whether or not Carrie had good reason to be upset. Instead, it was her instinctive knee-jerk reaction to do whatever it took to appease her. The connection between them had been so strong since the day Carrie was born that Mom's world could be peaceful only if Carrie's was too, and there was often no way to predict how, when, or why something might set her off. So sure enough, when I broke it to Mom that Carrie was furious about my getting a publishing deal, she asked me, "Is this deal really that important to you, dear?" In other words, is it really worth upsetting Carrie over?

I gave it a lot of thought, and in the end, I had to admit that if it was going to come down to a choice between writing a book or keeping peace with my mother and sister, it was a no-brainer. I called my agent and told him to cancel the publishing deal. He was astonished. I'm sure the publisher was too. I felt terrible about it, but it seemed like I did it for a worthy cause, and I can't say I regretted it.

Many years later, though, I wrote a script called "813 Greenway Drive"—autobiographical, obviously, and I loved the process, and how gratifying it felt to start it, work through it, and finish it, even when I had to push myself to keep going. I was in the middle of writing it when I told Mom about it, expecting some version of "Good for you!" What I got instead was her immediate concern about how Carrie would react and a gentle, "Maybe you shouldn't do it."

Now it was my turn to go ballistic. "Oh, trust me, I'm doing it, Mom, with or without Carrie's permission."

"Well, dear, you know how your sister is, we have to—"

She was trying to calm me into my usual submission. I wasn't having it. "No, we don't have to. If I want to write or do anything I want creatively, I shouldn't have to drop it because I might be stepping on territory that Carrie has decided is exclusively hers. I did it once, with that publishing deal. I'm not doing it again. Either she grows up and gets over it or she doesn't."

It caught Mom completely off guard—she'd never seen me refuse to do whatever it took to make Carrie okay, and I'm sure she braced herself for another meltdown from her daughter. To some extent, I understood that. Carrie had been through a rough, fragile period—depressed, overweight, and unpredictable—not working and overspending.

But things were turning around for her again, and I was willing to take my chances that she could make it through the "horrible news" that I was writing a script.

After taking a long, deep breath and preparing to dodge the shrapnel, I handed Carrie the rough draft of "813 Greenway Drive," and there wasn't even a whisper of resentment. In fact, she read it, liked it, embraced it, gave me some brilliant notes, and even wrote a few additions to it.

There were times in our lives together when my sister's generosity took my breath away. That was one of those times.

Sadly, some combination of drugs and mental illness destroyed a lot of Carrie's memories. She often talked about having had an unhappy childhood, which Mom and I knew simply wasn't true. I'd recount anecdotes of our adventures together and she'd gape at me, mesmerized, as if she'd never heard of such a thing, let alone lived it. Finally I made a huge memory book for her (and one for Mom, just because I knew she'd love it) full of photos and news clippings and letters and stories, even seemingly trivial scraps of paper, so that even if she couldn't remember everything, she'd still have it on hand to see, touch, and smile about. It fills my heart that she cherished that book.

At the end of the 1980s I started distancing myself from The Hiding Place. Seeing Donna and Dusty every week at The Hiding Place was only a minor annoyance, certainly not a big enough deal to make me walk away from a church that had meant so much to me when Henry and I started it. My problem was that over the years a couple of dynamics seemed to evolve that were the antithesis of what we had in mind in the first place. For one thing, our intention of an organic church based on faith was evolving into a complicated, top-heavy, cliquish infrastructure, more concerned with business operations than with God. For another thing, Henry and I had complained a million times about the fact that traditional Christians always seeming to be asking for money. That was fine as long as the money was going to genuinely worthy causes. But then a movement was started to raise money for a building fund. As if God wanted or needed yet another edifice in His name? As if He cared where we gathered to worship, as long as we gathered to celebrate Him? I was done.

The timing of freeing myself from my Hiding Place obligations actually worked out perfectly.

I finally sold the Cedarbrook house. It seemed right to me, and a smart way to de-escalate the drama and make as clean a break as possible, to give Donna half the proceeds, even though I'd bought the house long before we were married and she wasn't legally entitled to a dime, so that's what I did, over Mom's strenuous vocal, tenacious objections. (And I do mean tenacious—she literally brought it up yet again on the day before she died.) Donna used her half to buy a condo in Santa Monica for her and Dusty. Whatever. I put mine in the bank, with a very specific purpose in mind.

I'd been looking at properties in Malibu and Santa Barbara toward my dream of buying a ranch. I'd become fascinated by a book called *Five Acres and Independence*, about how to transform a small piece of land into a completely self-sustaining environment. While I was living on Cedarbrook I'd spent about a year and a half studying architecture and engineering at the Southern California Institute of Architecture. Maybe some distant childhood memories of building the Western town in our backyard at 813 Greenway Drive were at play in my ranch fantasy, but I was yearning to put my old passions and my architectural skills to good use. The challenge of creating a self-sustaining plot of land sounded like the perfect solution.

Christi wanted to raise her children in a healthy, down-to-earth, safe ranch environment, so she began helping me with a search for exactly the right place, farther and farther north of Los Angeles, where more land could be found for less money. One day we pulled into the secluded driveway of a property for sale near the central California coast. I took one look at the windmill, large pond, and forty beautiful acres of land and made up my mind to buy it on the spot.

And it finally looked as if Mom was realizing one of her dreams, a dream that extended far beyond a perfect museum site for her treasured Hollywood memorabilia collection. She wanted a permanent venue for her stage show, with her husband Richard Hamlett right by her side.

And one day it looked as if that venue was finally within reach.

I was thrilled for her. It almost seemed too good to be true, and you know the old saying: if it seems too good to be true, it probably is.

13

TRUE COLORS

Mom, Carrie, and newborn Billie.

B y April of 1992 Mom was a happily married sixty-year-old woman with a lot of entertaining left to do and a lot of loyalty left to express to her fans. Being on the road forty weeks a year or more was exhausting, but retirement wasn't even a fleeting thought. Grandpaw had peacefully passed away in Palm

Springs, and Mom had bought the house across the street from hers in North Hollywood for Grandma, with an apartment upstairs for Uncle Bill. For a woman whose entire life was motivated by love and family, traveling for months on end just made no sense to Debbie Reynolds anymore, especially with her first grandchild on the way.

We were all thrilled when Carrie and Bryan announced that they were having a baby. It was a natural progression in their successful relationship to have a child together, something they both wanted very much, and getting married wasn't even part of the discussion. Between Eddie Fisher, Harry Karl, Donna Freberg, and Paul Simon, the whole concept of marriage had pretty much lost its charm in our family, not to mention its implied bonuses of stability and commitment. As far as Carrie and Bryan were concerned, what they owed their unborn child wasn't a marriage contract that wasn't necessarily worth the paper it was written on; instead it was a commitment to raise the happiest, healthiest child together that they possibly could.

Mom confided in me more than once during Carrie's pregnancy that yes, she was concerned about Carrie's bipolar disorder, both genetically and when it came to being a solid, responsible, reliable parent. But she'd dreamed of a grandchild from one or both of her children for years, and she was far more hopeful than concerned with Carrie and Bryan's baby on the way. She believed that having a baby would trigger Carrie's maternal instincts and help ground her. Being a mother had given Mom a reason to survive, and to do it with her head held high, when it would have been easier to give up. Maybe a baby would finally give Carrie a reason to get sober and stay that way.

So on July 17, 1992, when Carrie gave birth to Billie Catherine Lourd, that beautiful little girl was a welcome joy to everyone in her family, and Mom had even more motivation to find a permanent place where she could keep entertaining and connecting with her fans and still stay close to home.

Mom adored living next door to her precious granddaughter.

Which is why, when Richard found out that the Paddlewheel Hotel in Las Vegas was going up for auction, it seemed like the answer to a prayer. It was an older hotel on a six-acre lot, halfway between the Vegas Strip and the Convention Center. With renovations, it could house a showroom and a casino, and the 196 hotel rooms could accommodate the inevitable throngs of guests in the number one tourist city in the country. That Mom might also be able to create her Hollywood museum there someday didn't even register at the time—the Paddlewheel could satisfy more than enough dreams for now.

Mom cleaned out her savings for the $200,000 deposit she needed to qualify for the auction, and she won with her bid of $2.1 million. She couldn't have cared less about owning a casino or even a hotel. They just "came with the meal." Her excitement was all about transforming her long, treasured history of performing in Las Vegas into a stable, permanent home base to entertain and connect with her fans, only a one-hour flight from L.A. If a casino and a hotel had her name on them as well, she'd do her damnedest to make them great. But they paled in comparison to the importance of that showroom she'd been yearning for.

Neither Mom nor Richard had mentioned a word of any of this to Carrie and me. Until and unless Mom won the auction, there was nothing to tell. But when they shared the news with us, we were as excited about the possibilities as they were.

I was coproducing a movie called *Twogether,* starring Nick Cassavetes and Brenda Bakke (coincidentally, about an unmarried couple planning to have a child together), when Mom called to say that, minutes earlier, she and Richard had bought the Paddlewheel Hotel in Las Vegas and would be transforming it into the Debbie Reynolds Hotel and Casino.

"I know you're busy with your movie, dear, and I hate to pull you away from it, but I'm hoping you might be willing to design and build my new showroom," she said, as if wild horses could have stopped me.

Mom and Richard were headed to the airport when she called, to go do a show she'd booked in Florida, so we agreed to meet back in Las Vegas in a few days to celebrate and start making plans. But I couldn't wait. The suspense was killing me. I rounded up my *Twogether* crew and filled them in and then jumped in the car and drove to Vegas to have a look at Mom's new acquisition.

I checked in to the Royal Resort and walked down the street to the Paddlewheel. The auction sign was still on the marquee, and the entrance was locked. A security guard in the lobby responded to my taps on the door and let me in, and I immediately noticed that a young man was conducting a tour of the hotel and describing the plans for the property. I quietly blended into the small crowd and followed along, never introducing myself, just listening in.

As we entered the far end of the casino our guide did a *Price Is Right* wave toward a lame little lounge stage where a cheesy animated band was playing. "And this," he proudly announced, "is where the legendary Debbie Reynolds will be performing."

I was still gaping at it as he went on to explain that Debbie Reynolds had been hired by the hotel's new owner, Billy Walters.

What? I'd been around Las Vegas all my life. Anyone who'd

spent more than five minutes there knew the name Billy Walters—
professional gambler/sports betting legend Billy Walters. If Mom
won the Paddlewheel auction, what did Billy Walters have to do
with it?

I slipped away from the group and headed straight for the
county recorder's office.

Sure enough, the property wasn't in Debbie Reynolds's name
or Richard Hamlett's name or the name of some corporation they
might have formed for the purchase.

According to the title, the new owner of the hotel was none
other than Billy Walters.

I raced back to my room and called Mom. It was news to her.
She was sure there must be some perfectly logical explanation, she
said, but I could hear the tension in her voice. I found out later
that immediately after hanging up from my call, she confronted
Richard and asked what the hell was going on. When he refused to
make eye contact with her and mumbled something about a "misunderstanding," she cut straight to the bottom line.

"Today, right now, I want the deed to that hotel in my name,
and only my name, or I'm out," she told him. "You'll be running
the Debbie Reynolds Hotel and Casino without Debbie Reynolds,
and I'm guessing it won't go well."

By the time Mom and Richard got back to Las Vegas a few days
later, the title was in her name where it belonged. The "confusion,"
Richard explained, was due to a short-term loan he'd received
from Billy. No big deal, all taken care of, whatever, let's not talk it
to death.

Mom, relieved that the problem was solved and ready to celebrate, suggested that the three of us go to a lovely dinner that night
at Piero's, her favorite Las Vegas restaurant, so we could start discussing the showroom, which we'd already decided to call the Star
Theater.

The back room of Piero's was crowded with local bigwigs, including county commissioner Thalia Dondero and a few other pol-

iticians in the booth next to ours. We kicked off the evening with a toast to the Debbie Reynolds Hotel and Casino. Then we segued right into the subject of the showroom and Mom's wanting me to design it for her, which seemed to be news to Richard. He sat in silence as I asked Mom, for starters, to name her favorite show-rooms.

"Well," she said, instantly excited, instantly into it, "I love the Desert Inn, as you know. No doubt about it, the Desert Inn is my favorite as a performer. But when it comes to intimacy with the audience, there's no place like Harrah's in Lake Tahoe."

Richard had nothing to contribute to this conversation, so he just sat there looking back and forth between Mom and me as if he were watching a tennis game while we discussed details about those two great showrooms. Finally, tired of being left out, he turned to me and chimed in with what sounded more like a chal-lenge than genuine interest: "What do you know about building a showroom?"

I happily filled him in on the hundreds of venues I'd been to with Mom when she performed, from Vegas to Broadway to the London Palladium to You-Name-It, USA. And oh yes, there were also the years of my mobile sound business with Richard Landers, recording the likes of Stevie Wonder and Leo Sayer and countless artists for Neil Bogart and Richard Perry, not to mention my year and a half of studies at the Southern California Institute of Architecture. When I finally finished, I calmly said, "Okay, your turn, Richard. What do you know about building a showroom?"

He pulled a piece of paper out of his pocket and proudly laid it on the table without a word, obviously thinking it spoke for itself. It did, but not in the way he intended—it was a crude, insipid pie-shaped drawing of what was presumably meant to be modifications to the existing lounge stage. While Mom and Richard had been out of town, I'd been over every inch of the hotel with our building engineer Victor Smith, and I knew what Richard had drawn wasn't just preposterous, it was logistically impossible.

Finally, after a long silence, I managed, "This is your idea of a showroom for my mom? After her four decades of performing, you think she should end up on a lounge stage?"

Mom had tilted her head to see the drawing as well, exactly as disenchanted with it as I was. In the meantime, I saw Richard's face start to redden as he tried unsuccessfully to defend his drawing. That effort hit a brick wall too, when I broke the news that this discussion wasn't about him and his design skills, it was about what Mom wanted and needed and had most certainly earned.

Getting nowhere, he decided to shift the subject a bit, with the proud announcement that, in what he clearly thought was a brilliant business move, he'd bought all the sound equipment from the now-defunct Dunes Hotel, thank you very much.

I let out an involuntary groan. "You're not serious. That equipment is as old as it is worthless, and it sure as hell isn't good enough for Mom." He was glaring at me as I kept going. "You didn't buy this stuff from Al Siniscal, did you? I've known him for years. He used to work for Bill Dilley at Spectra Sonics. I'll get us out of this."

On which, in less than an instant, he exploded. It shocked me, and it shocked Mom. I'd seen him angry before, but I'd never seen him detonate like this. He began ranting at me, so loud and profane that everyone in the restaurant, including Commissioner Dondero and her dinner companions, stopped eating to watch the show. Mom and I looked at each other, and on her silent cue, I opted not to run the risk of escalating his wrath by responding and simply excused myself from the table and left instead.

I was back in my hotel room, deep in thought, wondering if maybe Richard Hamlett wasn't the reformed southern charmer Carrie and I had been hoping he was after all. Maybe he was still the bank-frauding fistfighter I'd read about in the Roanoke newspapers, who'd just been putting on one hell of a smooth act for the pleasure and status of being married to Debbie Reynolds. I didn't want to be right about that, but . . . who was this guy?

There was a knock on the door at one A.M. I answered it to find my tiny mom standing there, apologizing for the way Richard had talked to me, sure that I must be upset. I stopped her and assured her that she didn't owe me an apology, he did; and I would be upset only if I'd been told off by someone I respected. It seems that after I left, she and Richard made a deal—if I'd stay out of his business, he'd stay out of the showroom. DONE!

Mom and I went to the hotel bar and stayed until dawn, having a close, wonderful time planning and designing the Star Theater, the home venue she'd been yearning for and deserved, where she could entertain and be financially secure for the rest of her life.

The Star Theater was scheduled to open the last Saturday in October of 1993. It was an insane deadline, but again, "no such word as *can't*." I was on the phone first thing the next morning recruiting a work crew, starting with Mom's lighting director Joe Bianchi, who was working at the Mirage. It took me less than ten seconds to convince him to join the team, and I had the same luck with every other call I made. Everyone wanted to be part of combining the best of the classic days of Vegas with the best of the current lighting and sound technology to create the finest state-of-the-art theater of its kind in the world.

Once the crew was organized, I paid a visit to Mom's two favorite showrooms, the Desert Inn and the Crystal Room at Harrah's in Lake Tahoe, to measure them and replicate their most attractive features in our space at the Debbie Reynolds Hotel and Casino. My vision was a theater with five hundred seats, to resemble the Rat Pack rooms where both Mom and Eddie had enjoyed performing. There had to be ramps and railings among those five hundred seats, since Mom loved to leave the stage and walk the rails like a tightrope walker, for up-close-and-personal interaction with her audiences. And on the stage itself, a large, beautiful picture frame, in which she'd be the work of art.

As crazy as the showroom deadline was, there was also a hotel, restaurant, and casino that had to be tackled so we wouldn't be opening the Star Theater in the middle of a construction zone. First on the agenda was a trip to the Nevada State Contractors Board to qualify the hotel for a contractor's license so we could do our own renovations. Richard had a general contractor's license from Virginia. I had an electrical contractor's license from California. Victor Smith had a mechanical license from Nevada. All we had to do was combine the licenses and the hotel would be qualified.

So there we sat—Mom, Richard, Victor, and me—with the executives from the contractors board. The executives were eager to help Mom in any and every way they could, and they were pleased to confirm that by combining Victor's license and mine, they could qualify us as the contractors for the hotel. As for Richard's license, they continued with obvious discomfort, they were sorry, but he couldn't be licensed in Nevada, due to his disastrous record in Virginia that included complaints from unpaid subcontractors and suppliers all over the state. We were so focused on the good news that we could officially get to work that we didn't give this latest Richard Hamlett red flag nearly as much attention as it deserved.

Transforming the Paddlewheel was a massive undertaking and an exciting one, and Mom and Victor and I dived right in. Jerry Wunderlich moved from L.A. to do the interior designing, and he recruited Billy Morris, one of his and Mom's old MGM colleagues, to help with the rendering, concept sketches, and installation. Artist Anne Bell painted beautiful collages of movie stars beside the elevators on every floor and accented the décor throughout the hotel with hundreds of paintings of famous faces and film moments.

Of course, as my grandmother used to say, we were working with "champagne taste on a beer budget," so we had to jump at every opportunity to save money wherever we could. The hotel lighting needed to be redone. No problem. Mom brought in huge crystal chandeliers from her MGM collection that had been used in hundreds of films, including *Gone with the Wind*. Uncle Bill restored them, and I hung them in the lobby. We needed booths for the showroom, and tables, chairs, and lamps for the hotel rooms. Again, no problem. As luck and timing would have it, Steve Wynn was auctioning the contents of the Dunes Hotel to make way for his new Bellagio Resort and Casino. We bought every booth, table, chair, and lamp we could get our hands on from the Dunes auction. In fact, we virtually stripped the place—toilets and bathroom stalls, hand railings, the marble *D*s on the main doors, the chandelier outside our showroom, all of them came from the Dunes. With a lot of restoration and reupholstery, they looked like new and saved us a fortune.

Harold Lloyd's legendary Steinway player piano from Mom's collection was installed in the lobby, complete with a wax figure of Mr. Lloyd himself seated on the bench. The giant paddlewheel in front of the hotel was transformed into a giant, spectacular movie reel.

Every day was filled with new ideas, new acquisitions, a lot of hard work, and much excitement. Our goal was to open the hotel rooms by the following June of 1993, and we were determined to achieve that goal for this labor of love or die trying.

I was so busy that it was a breeze to hold up my end of the deal to stay out of Richard's end of things. And he was one busy guy himself.

He spent a lot of his time in meetings behind closed doors. Let's see . . .

He secured a very big deal with the YESCO sign company, with the price inflated to cover his kickback—excuse me, I meant "commission."

He leased the hotel to Joe Ross, a Kansas City hotel owner/operator. Later I'd be asked by the FBI to help them in their investigation of Mr. Ross regarding his alleged connections to mob bosses Harry Tantillo and Joe Valachi.

He brought in Ronald Nitzberg and an attorney named Edward Coleman to arrange the time-share operations on the top floors of the hotel. In theory it was a great idea. The profit margins were amazing, and Debbie's friends and fans could actually own a part of her hotel. Nitzberg and Coleman sold some of the hotel rooms as personal and corporate time-shares; and both of them served on the board of directors, in exchange for generous salaries, time-share commissions, and stock in the venture . . . not to mention Nitzberg's added fees to cover his kickbacks—excuse me, I meant "commissions" again—on the furniture.

Richard leased out the restaurant and the retail space, and he hired a gaming firm called Jackpot Industries to run the casino, since neither he nor Mom had a gaming license yet. The hotel was to get back less than 10 percent of the profits.

Oh, and by the way, he somehow got my mother to personally guarantee all these deals.

When he wasn't wheeling and dealing in his office, Richard was seeing to it that for every step forward we members of the creative/construction team took, he was pushing us two steps back. Mr. In-Charge-of-the-Business/Financing-Team had an overwhelming need to be in charge of everything, whether or not he had a clue what he was doing. On the bright side, though, thanks to his efforts, we learned a lot. For example, did you know that pouring paint stripper down a kitchen grease trap can result in tens of thousands of dollars in environmental protection fines? Or that it's not a good idea to hire work crews who have outstanding felony warrants?

And then there was the great hotel swimming pool renovation. It was a big job, and an important one, and Richard chose to entrust it to the stucco man who'd been in charge of the hotel exterior. When the pool was finally finished, I was given the honor of inaugurating it. I enthusiastically dived in, my foot touched the bottom of the pool, and these ugly gray blobs of something bubbled to the surface. I touched the wall of the pool, and it fell completely apart. It turned out that Richard's guy had lined the pool with wall stucco instead of pool plaster. Another valuable lesson learned, and another $30,000 down the drain. Literally. I brought in Frank Basso, a contractor who'd already done lots of concrete work on the hotel. He did a spectacular job re-renovating the pool, for more than twice what the whole project should have cost in the first place, and in the end, we may have been hemorrhaging money, but hey, at least we could swim.

Somehow, impossibly, by June of 1993, while not all the hotel rooms were ready for guests, we were able to open for the rooms that were. It felt like an amazing accomplishment. Our first tenant was Mom's loyal old friend Rip Taylor. He'd already agreed to be Mom's opening act when the showroom was ready. In the meantime, he and Mom performed in a small first-floor lounge we called Jazz and Jokes. A musical trio made up of pianist Joey Singer, drummer Gerry Genuario, and bass player Bob Badgley performed in that lounge. Jazz and Jokes was a casual, inviting place to hang out for the evening, with no cover charge, and everyone from Steve Wynn to Robert Wagner and Stefanie Powers stopped by. It looked as if the Debbie Reynolds Hotel and Casino was off to a promising start.

But then, despite the fact that our great crew of professional, licensed contractors and I were working hard for long hours every single day, and making real progress, I started getting calls and visits from the Las Vegas Building and Safety Department, accusing me of not complying with codes. Ridiculous. I was pulling every required permit every step of the way. Besides being an ongoing irritant, these repeated unfounded noncompliance suspicions were costing us time we didn't have.

I couldn't figure out what was going on until one day a guy from the code office asked, "By the way, who's Richard Hamlett?"

"He's my mom's husband," I told him. "Why?"

"He the one who's been issuing the complaints about your construction," he said.

Our cement man Frank Basso had hinted at something similar at some point, but with no proof, I kind of shrugged it off. Now I was done shrugging. I confronted Richard, who tried everything

The Debbie Reynolds Hotel and Casino in Las Vegas.

from denying it to claiming he was just looking out for Mom's safety. I didn't have the time or the patience to argue with him. I simply encouraged him, strongly, to knock it off.

Suddenly, according to the calendar, the grand opening of the Star Theater was only forty-eight hours away.

It seemed impossible that it was happening so soon, let alone that the chaos going on around us could be brought to its knees in just a couple more days. I'd hired two crews so we could literally work around the clock. Mom's friends were flying in to lend her money and help in any other way they could, while Mom was doing everything from rehearsing her show in a nearby hotel suite to vacuuming the newly installed carpets. I was Scotch-taping wires together, installing lighting and speakers, and trying to trace the missing main house fiber-optic curtain I'd ordered for the Star Theater stage.

In the middle of all this, Richard suddenly decided that the bar floor in the back of the showroom had to be raised three feet, so that it would be level with the rest of the room, saving the waitresses from having to walk down a few steps to get to the bar. I thought he'd lost his mind. He knew perfectly well what a delay like this would mean. What possible reason could he have for even suggesting something so ridiculous, let alone insisting on it?

I blew up. "Tickets are sold, opening night's been publicized all over the place, and you want to postpone it to tear out the back of the showroom and pour concrete? That's not happening!"

Richard wasn't backing down. Neither was I. We almost came to blows. I finally explained the facts of life to Mom—if she gave in to Richard's harebrained idea, it would be weeks before the Star Theater could open. I reminded her of the deal she'd struck with him, the one where I'd stay out of his business and he'd leave the showroom to me. One hell of a time for him to renege, and now? For this?

She agreed. Vehemently. She overruled Richard, which escalated his rage and increased the backstage tension by a factor of about a billion, but we proceeded as planned.

Opening night arrived. The main house curtain didn't, by the way. My crew and I were scrambling around in the showroom, cleaning up, finishing the wiring in the sound booth and running an hour or two behind schedule. Mom couldn't stand knowing that a lobby full of fans, who'd paid good money for tickets, were being kept waiting, so she personally served them champagne and socialized with them until we could finally throw open the doors and officially introduce the public to Las Vegas's sparkling new hard-won state-of-the-art Star Theater at the Debbie Reynolds Hotel and Casino.

Rip Taylor made the first official entrance on our curtainless stage. He was great, telling jokes and keeping the crowd entertained while my crew and I finished our last-minute details. He was as relieved as I was when I cued him that it was time to introduce Mom.

"Debbie will be here in a minute," he announced to the standing-room-only crowd. "She's been through a lot. Can you believe that Eddie Fisher left her for Elizabeth Taylor?" He paused for the inevitable sympathetic chuckling and then added, "Screw Eddie Fisher."

On which Mom yelled from backstage, "I did. Twice."

Mom entered to gales of laughter and loud cheers. She sang, she joked, she walked the rails to be close to her fans, whom she genuinely thought of as friends, while she thanked them from the bottom of her heart for being her companions on this dream-come-true opening night. She also confided, "I haven't had this much stress since Eddie followed Elizabeth down the Nile," and they roared.

The show was rolling along perfectly and joyfully until about the middle of Mom's act. That's when Richard, who was seated near the front row in the center of the showroom, suddenly stood, strode to the back of the theater, past me in the sound booth, and walked right on out the door. He couldn't have been more conspicuous, partially lit by Mom's spotlight as he headed up the center aisle, and heads turned to watch Debbie Reynolds's husband walk out on her opening night performance. I was too busy to grab him by the lapels and ask where the hell he thought he was going. I could tell Mom was stunned, but she kept going without missing a beat like the seasoned pro she was.

In spite of Richard's inexplicable exit, it was a great evening, and Mom threw a party to thank everyone who made it possible. I was still in the theater cleaning up when our concrete man Frank Basso showed up and asked if I'd seen Richard. When I told him about Richard leaving in the middle of the show, Frank surprised me by breaking into a long, loud laugh. It turned out he knew a whole lot more than I did.

"He was trying to skip out on me, exactly like I knew he would," he explained. "Too bad for him I blocked his car with my truck, and I was sitting there waiting for him when he hurried into the parking lot."

I couldn't imagine what he was talking about. "Why would Richard try to skip out on you?"

Frank had a big grin on his face. "Because he bet me ten thousand dollars that the Star Theater wouldn't be ready in time to open tonight."

Stunned isn't a strong enough word. I thought back on all those noncompliance complaints to the Building and Safety Department, and Richard's idiotic demand about raising the floor in the back of the showroom. Suddenly it all made perfect, horrible sense—Richard had bet ten thousand dollars against my mom, against his own wife. I was building toward a serious redline.

"Where is he, Frank?"

He shrugged. "Beats me. We got into a fight, but I don't think I hurt him too badly. Last time I saw him he was pretty pissed off and ten thousand dollars poorer, but I'm sure he's okay." He couldn't resist adding, "He's not much of a fighter."

Richard was a no-show at Mom's celebration party. He was a no-show all night, in fact, and all the next day and all the next evening for Mom's spectacular second performance at the Star Theater. He was obviously off somewhere licking his wounds, and thanks to a lot of rumors I'd heard that Mom couldn't let herself believe, I had a pretty good idea where he might be. Richard had allegedly flown a mistress named Jane from Roanoke to Las Vegas and put her up at the Stardust Hotel, to keep himself entertained while Mom was working her ass off getting herself and the showroom ready for opening night.

The official debut of the Star Theater was a huge night for Mom, and it was a huge night for me too. My commitment to her and to the hotel was that I'd stay long enough to get the showroom successfully opened. Then I'd head back home to my wife and stepkids at the ranch, and back to L.A. to resume my producing career.

I was ready to get out of there. As proud as I was of an achievement that felt like nothing short of miraculous, I was exhausted. I needed sleep. I needed peace and quiet. I needed a break from watching my back every minute and wondering what fresh hell Richard was up to.

I started packing.

Mom, in the meantime, was at her Vegas condo, settled in after her second show with a bottle of white zinfandel. She was in an inebriated rage by the time Richard came wandering in at four o'clock in the morning, and the confrontation between them turned so ugly that she ended up hiding from him, afraid of him, until she finally heard him leave. She then called security and instructed them to never, ever let him into the garage or the building again.

I was finishing packing the next day, unaware of any of that, when our hotel comptroller Shawna tracked me down, in tears, carrying a huge armload of files.

"I'm resigning," she said, "and I wanted you to have all this information before I leave."

I was shocked. She'd been a good, trusted employee, and I knew Mom would hate to lose her.

"Why, Shawna? What's wrong?"

"See for yourself," she told me as she set down the files and started flipping through them. "Double leases, kickback deals, money being secretly wired out of the country—you name it, it's in here."

I was glancing through the reams of paperwork while she pointed out document after convoluted document that didn't add up. Some of them I understood. Most of them were far beyond me. The only thing I could tell with absolute certainty was that the hotel was in a potentially fatal amount of trouble, and my heart sank.

I gathered up the files, headed straight to Mom, and filled her in. She was devastated. She was overwhelmed. And she was very angry. So angry that she didn't tell me, yet, about the nightmare Richard had put her through in that condo several hours earlier. (In fact, I only learned the disturbing details of that nightmare many years later, when she described it in her book *Unsinkable*.)

Instead, she picked up the phone and called her accountant, David De Salvo. Richard had managed to get rid of Mom's loyal, vigilant attorney David Rudich with the same argument he used to get rid of anyone else who asked questions he didn't like: "I just can't work with him, Debbie." But David De Salvo stayed on, keeping meticulous records of every bit of groundwork David Rudich had laid, untangling one seemingly impossible financial ball of yarn after another. If anyone could make sense of this twisted mess our comptroller had handed me, it was David De Salvo.

I didn't stick around to listen to Mom's conversation with David. I knew he'd take good care of her, and I had business to take care of at the hotel.

I found Richard in his small office. He was busy boxing it all up and cleaning it out, and he wasn't happy to see me. I asked if he was going somewhere. He growled at me to get out. I took another step or two toward him.

"I told you this on your wedding day, but apparently you didn't listen, so I'll say it again," I said. "Do not fuck with my mother!"

He jumped to his feet and came at me, yelling and cursing at the top of his lungs while I stood my ground. He was several inches taller than I am, which didn't matter to me. I was redlining and ready to take him on.

I have no idea what would have happened if Mom hadn't suddenly appeared behind me. She grabbed the back of my shirt and started pulling me out of the room. I kept telling her to let me handle this, and she kept pulling until finally I gave in and stormed away. What's the old saying? "Don't do the crime if you can't do the time," right? And he wasn't worth it.

I went back to my room, called Christi to bring her up-to-date on what was happening, and then began unpacking. As much as I wanted to go home and get away from this disaster, there was no way I could leave my mom to fend for herself.

Two nights later Mom called Richard in his mistress Jane's room at the Stardust and asked him to meet her at the coffee shop in her hotel. She wasn't about to be alone with him again. Not ever. She also never let me anywhere near him again, which was a good thing. From what she told me later that night, I might have been led out in handcuffs.

According to Mom, Richard informed her during that conversation that he was in it for the money, that she'd never get rid of him because everything was in his name, and that he didn't love her, he loved Jane. Then he kissed her hand and walked away.

What a guy, huh?

And that, boys and girls, is the story of why Debbie Reynolds, after her third divorce, looked back on Eddie Fisher as the best of her three husbands.

And we were still a long way from being finished with Richard Hamlett.

14

WANDERING IN THE DESERT

Smiling onstage for our Las Vegas shareholders.

ith Richard gone, Mom was again faced with the
prospect of being left alone. I wasn't about to let that
happen. I headed back to my room to finish unpacking, and she and I began trying to sort through the tangled, overwhelming chaos the hotel and her life had become.

The new road to salvation seemed to be the idea, already in motion, of taking the Debbie Reynolds Hotel and Casino public, merging it into a shell corporation, and selling the stock. We'd be able to pay off all the debt and bad leases. We could pay off hotel operator Joe Ross and send him back to Kansas City, and we could also pay off our restaurant operator and reclaim the restaurant for ourselves.

Mom and I knew nothing about the ins and outs of going public, so we left it to ex–hockey player Joe Kowal and a couple of his associates to handle it for us. A whole new addition to the hotel complex was conceived that would make Mom's dream even more complete: we'd build a museum to finally show off her collection, and I'd be brought onstage to make the announcement at the upcoming shareholders meeting in the Star Theater. To preview the announcement, we held a fashion show outside the entrance to the theater, where models glided through the crowd in treasures like the Marilyn Monroe "subway dress" that hadn't been seen since Marilyn spectacularly wore it in *The Seven Year Itch*, and the incredible Barbra Streisand gold gown from *Hello, Dolly!*

The fashion show and the meeting that followed were even more successful than we'd hoped, and for the first time in much too long, we were sure we were getting a glimpse of a distant light at the end of the tunnel . . . which, as we all know, sometimes signals the approach of an oncoming train.

Mom put me in charge of designing and building the museum, and my head immediately started spinning with ideas. Among them was a memory of the Carousel Theater at Disneyland, in which the audience revolved around a succession of tableaux on stages, and from that memory evolved the concept of a 125-seat theater featuring revolving 35 mm screens on stages. Mom had saved every Academy Award–winning and –nominated movie, from the silent era to contemporary films, so we'd project clips of the original films in which the costumes or props in the collection appeared on those revolving screens. As the clips ran, pools of light would come up on those same costumes or props around the theater. You'd be watching a clip of Claudette Colbert in the 1934 film *Cleopatra*, for example, when the exact costume she was wearing would materialize several feet away and be transformed from an ensemble on a mannequin to a living, breathing piece of cinematic history. With the help of Sony's Patrick Gilbert, we had access to the latest state-of-the-art equipment and created one of the first high-definition theaters in the world, and certainly the only theater in the world with revolving displays of priceless Hollywood artifacts.

While I was immersed in getting the museum construction under way, the public company team was busy looking for a president who'd be bankable to prospective shareholders. They found and hired Henry Ricci from the Sahara Hotel. He was a very nice man, but frankly, it came to appear as if he'd been chosen because they could manipulate him without ever letting him know what was really going on. Unfortunately, Henry was too naive, and so were we, to understand what was happening—the offering money was starting to roll in, but only a fraction of it was going to the hotel and its debts. The rest was being funneled straight into the pockets of the men who took the Debbie Reynolds Hotel and Casino public in the first place.

The museum was only half completed when once again we were left holding the bag.

We were facing the probability of having to close the hotel immediately when we were contacted by Bennett Funding, who was holding the mortgage on the property and handling all the timeshare paper. Mom and I were summoned to Bennett headquarters in Syracuse, New York, for a summit conference with their president and CEO, who dropped a bombshell: They would stay in the deal only if I took over as the CEO of the Debbie Reynolds Hotel and Casino.

We were stunned. I knew exactly as much about being CEO of a hotel as I knew about performing brain surgery. We decided to get a second opinion from Steve Wynn, the superstar of hotel operators, who'd been nothing but supportive since the minute Mom bought the Paddlewheel. He'd said more than once that if we ever needed his help, all we had to do was call.

We called. Immediately.

We met in Steve's office on the top floor of the Mirage, and Mom told him the whole story, from Richard's deceptions, to the variety of troubles we'd had with management, to our need for a loan to keep the hotel open, to the help we needed with getting a gaming license. To her embarrassment, she was crying by the time she'd finished.

He was kind but firm as he reminded her that there was no place for tears in the business world. Then he turned to me and asked how old I was.

"I'm thirty-four," I told him.

He turned back to Mom and said, "He should take over. You need to throw all these people out. Get rid of all these players."

"I don't have any experience running a hotel," I pointed out.

He didn't bat an eye. "So what? Neither did I when I started. You're old enough, and you won't rip off your mom like everyone else apparently has."

Mom and I were still trying to take this in when Steve called the head of the Nevada Gaming Commission, whose name, believe it or not, was Chairman Bible, to see about getting us a license for the hotel. The catch-22 was that we couldn't get a gaming license when we were undercapitalized. By the time we left Steve's office, even after a talk between no less than Steve Wynn and Chairman Bible, we still had no gaming license, and I was officially the new CEO of the Debbie Reynolds Hotel and Casino.

Now that we'd satisfied their condition that I be named CEO, Bennett Management came through with the loan, so it was off to finish transforming a seven-thousand-square-foot space into a spectacular museum worthy of the collection it would house— and, as Steve advised, to start getting rid of all the foxes in the henhouse.

The new, reluctant CEO of the Debbie Reynolds Hotel and Casino.

I'm still not sure which job was more of a challenge.

When I took over the hotel, the restaurant and bar were losing $75,000 a month, thanks, it turned out, to employees who were looting the booze and food lockers. The sheriff's department informed me that some members of our kitchen staff were dealing crack cocaine out the back door of the hotel. The *National Enquirer* reported that a few of our employees were having

In Central Park in New York City at a photo shoot in 1973 with Mom and Carrie.

With Carrie at East 74th Street in 1973.

Carrie's birthday in 1975.

Carrie and
Dan Aykroyd,
1982.

Carrie and
Paul Simon,
1983.

Uncle Bill and me at Carrie and Paul's wedding, 1983.

Carrie and Bryan Lourd, 1992.

Carrie and Billie at Carrie's house.

Carrie and Billie at my office, 1995.

Mom, Carrie, and Billie in 1997.

With Billie at Carrie's house, 1998.

In Venice at Paul Allen's birthday, 1997.

Carrie and Billie in Venice, 1997.

Debbie and Carrie at the Oak Pass Road house.

With Carrie at my birthday in 1991.

Carrie at the Oak Pass house.

Four generations: Carrie, Grandma, Billie, and Mom.

Carrie and me in Singapore at Raffles drinking Singapore Slings. Carrie's was a virgin drink. 1985.

Carrie and Mom in the dining car on the Orient Express.

Rene Russo, Carrie, and me on the Orient Express, 1986.

With Christi,
1988.

With Christi in
Ouray, Colorado,
1988.

With Eddie and Carrie at Carrie and Penny Marshall's birthday party, 1996.

With Mom at the Star Theater, 1994.

The Debbie Reynolds Museum, 1994. This is the Marilyn Monroe, "subway dress," *The Seven Year Itch* display.

The Marilyn Monroe costume collection at the Paley Center Auction, 2011.

The Paley Center Auction, 2011.

With Cat at Freedom Farms, 2010.

BELOW: With Mom and Cat at the South Point Hotel in 2012.

Debbie and Eddie's honeymoon at the Greenbrier Resort in West Virginia, 1955. Me and Cat re-creating Mom and Dad's honeymoon photo on our anniversary sixty-four years later. *(Mike Wyatt/Greenbrier Photography)*

Mom's last performance, South Point Hotel, 2014.

Mom and Carrie, London Palladium, 1974.

Carrie and Billie, South Point Hotel, 2014.

sex in our unbooked hotel rooms (to which I responded, "Well, at least someone's getting use out of those rooms"). Even some of our most trusted employees were caught red-handed stealing money from cash registers and helping themselves to anything that wasn't nailed down. In an effort to stop an alarming number of thefts from our meat locker, I gave the only key to that locker to our chief of security, who was promptly caught on tape heading out the back door taking a tray of meat to his car. Bartenders, waiters and waitresses, cleaning staff, you name it—it turned out we were essentially operating a high-end giveaway for people we were paying to steal from us, many of them hired by and undoubtedly inspired by their former fearless leader Richard Hamlett.

It was amazing what a difference it made when I dramatically increased the number of surveillance cameras, installed them in strategic locations without telling the employees where they were, and let human nature take its course. Sometimes, as with the great meat locker caper, I'd catch the perpetrators on tape. Other times, when the cameras happened to miss something I'd heard was going on, I'd call the suspect(s) into my office, hold up a tape that for all I knew could have been blank and ask, "Do I really need to play this for you?" I was astonished at how many of them would simply hang their heads, say no, and confess to crimes I could never have proved if they'd kept their mouths shut. When the dust settled and my first couple of months as CEO had passed, I'd fired about two hundred employees.

Some of the original time-share executives were also asked to leave, when their background checks turned out to be less than favorable. The time-share operation was actually very profitable, and it was critical to our relationship with the Bennetts. We eventually got it cleaned up and back on track with the help of a man named David Crabtree, one of the few people we kept from the Hamlett regime and one of the few who was with us to the very end.

If Richard Hamlett had just ridden off into the sunset with his mistress Jane and been out of our lives once and for all, it might have been easier for Mom to pick up the pieces and move on. But she'd been deeply in love with him, because she didn't know how to love any other way, and she was still struggling with the difference between grieving the loss of the man she thought she'd married and grieving the loss of the man he was. It didn't help that from time to time he would call to tell her he wasn't really happy without her.

Fortunately (or not), many more calls were coming in to remind her that she couldn't believe a word that came out of his mouth. A man sued her for breaching what he claimed was his brokerage agreement for all the time-share players he'd brought in. Mom won the suit, but only after spending more money, time, and energy than she had to spare. A few Caesars Palace executives showed up one day to try to collect Richard's overdue debts at the casino. Mom explained, firmly, that they wouldn't be getting any money from her that was owed by Mr. Hamlett.

Every week brought new evidence of the terrible deals Richard had made on behalf of Mom and the hotel, and of the distinct probability that he was juggling their assets so she'd come out on the short end of their divorce. They owned more properties together than Mom even knew about, and to further complicate things, he called one day to tell her he was going into a clinic in San Diego for prostate surgery.

Richard was one of those people who conduct their lives under the assumption that people never talk to each other. While he was supposedly in San Diego undergoing prostate surgery, Mom heard from friends of hers in Roanoke that he'd bought a new Lincoln for himself and a new Jaguar for Jane; that he and Jane were enjoying popular watering holes all over Roanoke on Mom's credit cards; and that the happy couple was about to take a two-week vacation in Europe, scheduled to leave on May 24, 1994. It seems they'd be boarding the Orient Express and re-creating, stop for stop, the trip that Mom had so brilliantly orchestrated for herself, Richard,

Rene, Carrie, and me years earlier, when he was still masquerading as her adoring, devoted husband.

So while Mom was drowning in lawsuits and debts she knew nothing about, and working herself to exhaustion in the Star Theater night after night, and we were desperately scrambling to save ourselves and our massive financial and emotional investment in Las Vegas, Richard and Jane were embarking on a two-week European vacation . . . how? On what money, or whose? It was time to find out what was going on and how bad things really were.

On May 29, 1994, while Richard and Jane were probably letting Mom treat them to a lovely night on the town in Paris or Rome, we boarded a plane in Las Vegas after Mom's show for what we came to call the Raid on Roanoke—me, Mom, Fred Pierson, Margie Duncan, and Margie's son Mark. We got a few hours' sleep on the plane before Mom's first friend in Roanoke, Bootie Bell Chewning, picked us up at the airport and took us straight to Richard's house, the house he and Mom had shared so many times during their marriage. It came as no surprise to any of us that the locks had been changed.

As we walked around the outside of the house looking for any door or window that might have been left unlocked, a few neighbors came out of their houses, leaving for work or wherever. They were delighted to spot Mom, whom they hadn't seen in quite some time, and waved over at her. "Debbie! Nice to see you!"

She didn't miss a beat. "Nice to see you too!" she waved back with that iconic smile. "I'm here to surprise Richard for our anniversary!"

We had no luck finding an unsecured door or window, so I finally took a window off its track, climbed in, and opened the front door to let Mom and the gang inside. As far as Mom and I were concerned, her divorce from Richard wasn't finalized yet, and she'd more than paid for that house, whether she'd meant to or not. If someone called the cops to report a break-in, we were more than ready to take them on.

The five of us immediately split up and started searching the house. We thought we were prepared for whatever we might unearth. We were wrong.

Mom's good china was in crates, and there were huge containers of costumes from her *Molly Brown* tour that she and Richard produced. Her cosmetics and hair appliances were scattered all over the floor of her closet, where another woman's clothes, presumably Jane's, were neatly hanging. We found and boxed up enough of Mom's belongings to warrant renting a truck to haul it all back to Las Vegas.

Nothing, though, remotely compared to the shock that was waiting for Mom in one of Richard's nightstand drawers. I'll never forget the painful disbelief on her face when she came almost stumbling out of his bedroom and handed me a small stack of photos she'd found there—of Richard, Jane, and a young child. We didn't need a calculator to piece together the most stunning betrayal of all. While Richard was pretending to be my mother's doting, attentive, adoring husband, he wasn't just living a double life, he might actually have fathered a child with his mistress. Those pictures were like a particularly vicious gut punch that sent us both reeling.

To be perfectly honest, Mom and I took one look at those photos and immediately assumed the child was Richard's. Carrie, who was fascinated by the Raid on Roanoke and had demanded updates every step of the way, was the one who asked the obvious question when I called her with that late-breaking news: "How do we know that's Richard's child?" Of course, the answer is, we didn't know. Carrie certainly wasn't defending Richard when she asked that question—she was as disappointed as I was in who he'd turned out to be. She was just giving Mom and me a reminder from back in L.A., a few thousand miles away from the drama we were swept up in, not to leap to an obvious conclusion, especially when we had more than enough other complaints about him to start organizing a lynch mob.

Once Mom and I finally got our bearings again, it was on to

Richard's office. His bookkeeper let us in, and we dived in to the task of copying files and a hard drive full of backdated deeds to properties that supposedly belonged to Mom but had been transferred to everyone from Jane to various relatives of hers and Richard's.

Richard's property manager stopped by while we were there, but Mom easily deflected him with the "here to surprise my husband for our anniversary" line. He just smiled without saying a word, probably well aware that Mom's husband was in Europe with his girlfriend and preferring to stay out of it.

There were more surprises waiting for us at the county treasurer's office. Richard had been threatening Mom with foreclosure on a Roanoke property she'd paid for in full in 1984. "Expenses and taxes," he explained. Richard's first wife was suing Jane over her loss of that same property, in paperwork dated 1992 which indicated that the property had been put in Jane's name and then in Richard's brother's name. "Deed roulette" was obviously a specialty in Richard Hamlett's repertoire, and we hoped against hope that Mom's lawyers could manage to unravel the tangled mess of photocopies we'd be handing them.

Before we left the office, the treasurer showed us notices to Richard from Roanoke County for $31,183.10 in overdue taxes—every dime of which Mom had given him money to pay when the taxes were due, and every dime of which he'd apparently pocketed. The hits just kept on coming.

We'd left Las Vegas for Roanoke on Sunday night. Mark drove the rental truck full of Mom's belongings and files to Las Vegas, while the rest of us flew back and arrived late Tuesday afternoon, exhausted, heads spinning and glad we went. Mom hit the stage at the Star Theater right on time that night. Not once did she ever let Richard Hamlett or anyone else cause her to disappoint her fans.

While Mom's divorce lawyers were busy slogging through the mind-numbing rabbit holes of Richard's business transactions, we focused all our energy on the hotel again. We needed money, and we needed employees we could trust now that we'd weeded out so many we couldn't. As a stroke of luck, I happened to think of Henry Cutrona and called him up. I'd heard he was on sabbatical from The Hiding Place, and all of L.A. was still recovering from the devastating Northridge earthquake a few months earlier, so he might be ready for a little change of scenery.

Sure enough, he was more than ready. He'd been bled dry by people at The Hiding Place for years, to the point where he'd gone from his usual healthy tan to kind of an ash white. He barely even had enough strength to wave hello when I pulled up to his house in L.A. to move him and his stuff to the hotel, where he took over as general manager. It was fantastic for both Mom and me to have him by our side again; and it freed me up, with the help of loans from some generous friends who were eager to do anything they could to help Mom, to finally finish the museum.

The private grand opening of the Hollywood Motion Picture Museum at the Debbie Reynolds Hotel and Casino took place on Mom's sixty-third birthday, April 1, 1995. It could easily have been mistaken for a smaller, more intimate version of the Academy Awards, but a lot more relaxed and a lot more fun. Celebrities from all over the country arrived in classic cars and were greeted by Turner Classic Movies's Robert Osborne, who hosted the event, while multiple cameras captured every glittering, star-studded moment. Mom's collection and the museum itself inspired unanimous raves, bordering on awe. In fact, actor and Academy board member Roddy McDowall, who was known to be a very tough critic, declared it "impeccable."

After experiencing the museum, everyone gathered in the Star Theater, where Mom took the stage for a special performance, which evolved into a spectacular, champagne-fueled party. As festive as it all was, it was also emotional for Mom and me to look around from time to time and realize that we finally did it, that we were actually witnessing the successful result of all those decades of dreaming and struggling.

Christi created beautiful art for the Hollywood Motion Picture Museum.

It was one of the happiest nights of her life, which made it one of the happiest nights of my life too, until a few friends started asking me, casually at first, where my wife Christi had wandered off to, and it occurred to me that I hadn't seen her in the last hour or two. In the moment, I pushed it out of my mind, which, as I would learn later, was a mistake.

For now, the bottom line was that with the showroom in full swing, the museum running fourteen shows a day, every hour on the hour, to sold-out crowds; the hotel averaging an occupancy of five hundred guests per night; and the time-share operation turning a nice profit, we were enjoying occasional glimmers of optimism. Sadly, those brief glimmers couldn't overcome the dark clouds of debt, the perpetual lawsuits, and the trail of incomprehensible leases Richard Hamlett had left in his wake.

It still kills me—if he'd chosen to be the man he presented himself to be instead of the scoundrel he was, Mom could have lived out the rest of her life as a happily married wife, mother, and grandmother, with a safe, secure home where she could entertain and share her memorabilia treasures with the fans she loved so much. Adding to her pain was the fact that she always blamed herself for her bad choices more than she ever blamed the people who deceived her into making those choices. She was a fighter, not a victim, and she always took full responsibility for her part in everything that ever happened to her.

In sharp contrast, according to a lot of press, including an article in *Vanity Fair*, Richard Hamlett blamed me for the destruction of his marriage to my mother. I'd love to take a deep, proud bow for that, but I can't help but wonder—isn't Richard's position a little like blaming a speeding ticket on the cop who busted you?

So there was Mom, ready to work her way through another nervous breakdown with her six shows a week at the Star Theater, when Carrie and Billie came to visit the Debbie Reynolds Hotel and Casino. I'd been calling Carrie from time to time to fill her in on current affairs in Vegas, but for the most part I kept her separate from it. Business and finance weren't exactly right up her alley, there was nothing she could do about any of it anyway, and she was very busy with motherhood, her career, her life, and her campaign to stay sober.

It was the first time Carrie had been to the hotel since the museum opened, and I can still see the look on her face as she walked slowly through it, mesmerized, blown away, not saying a word, obviously thinking, "So this is what Mom has been fantasizing about for all these years." Suddenly, finally, Mom's collection wasn't just racks and boxes and piles of "stuff" we'd been stepping over and making room for since the late 1960s. It was a breathtaking history of our business, one beautifully displayed treasure after another that our mother hoped would be thought of someday as her most lasting achievement on this earth for countless generations to come. It deeply touched me to witness how deeply it touched Carrie.

When Carrie had finished her long, almost reverential tour of the museum, she and Billie and I retired to my office. Carrie had something she needed to discuss with me in private. I had a life-size cardboard replica of Princess Leia there that Billie, age three, thought was a great big hilarious picture of her mommy in a funny dress and funny hair. She and I were busy playing with that when Carrie pulled a script out of her bag, handed it to me, and said, "You need to help me convince Mom to do this."

The script was called "Mother." It was written by Carrie's friend Albert Brooks, and he'd agreed to meet with Mom as a possibility for the title role.

My knee-jerk reaction was "No way." But the more Carrie and I talked about it, the more we agreed that it might be just what Mom needed at that point in time, and after all, it was her decision to make, not mine. So we handed her the script, explained where it came from and why she should read it, and left the rest to her.

Mom had met Albert Brooks with Carrie socially a few times, but she couldn't really connect a face to the name. She loved Albert's screenplay, though, so she made an appointment—reluctantly—to audition for him. Mom had lost her enthusiasm for auditions in the 1980s, when she was asked to audition for a sitcom in a room full of twenty-somethings. Before she began reading the scenes, they asked her what acting experience she had. It speaks volumes about her grace under fire that she didn't just walk out.

But again, she thought Albert's script was brilliant, and Albert was a friend of Carrie's, so Mom showed up, read a couple of scenes with him, and was in total disbelief when he hired her on the spot, without even having to consult with a bunch of "suits" before he officially told her the part was hers.

Carrie and I were thrilled for her, but also worried about her. It had been twenty years since Mom had played a major role in a movie, and she deserved to be showcased, especially with an incredibly gifted costar/writer/director like Albert Brooks. On the other hand, she was under an ungodly amount of pressure, trying to keep the hotel going while dealing with the massive financial problems that were threatening to bury us. When she wasn't performing in the showroom she was performing at every one-nighter she could book to make every dime she could. Adding the responsibility of a title role in *Mother* could be a joy for her, and/or create more anxiety than even Debbie Reynolds could handle.

With great difficulty, Mom decided to say yes to Albert. Her great friends Annie Russell and Lillian Burns Sidney flew in to work on her role with her, and she was getting excited about playing Albert's passive-aggressive perfectionist mother.

But then, three weeks before filming began, she started having such excruciating stomach pains that she checked herself into the emergency room at St. Joseph's Medical Center in Burbank, where X-rays showed that her stomach had completely burned through. The cause: severe stress. She was hospitalized for a week, on an IV and no solid food, while, at her insistence, Annie and Lillian came every day to keep right on coaching and running lines with her. Because it was the right thing to do, she called Albert from the hospital to tell him what was going on. He was kind enough to tell her not to worry, just to focus on getting well, without even hinting at how concerned he must have been about this potential delay in the start date of his movie. In the end, *Mother* started right on time, and Albert was every bit as kind throughout the filming. At one point toward the end of the shoot, Mom finally buckled under the pressure, and he shot around her for a couple of days so she could rest and "recharge her batteries."

We obviously couldn't let the Star Theater go dark for the duration of Mom's absence, so I decided to put together and produce a live show, revue style, consisting of tributes to the greatest movie musical dance numbers of all time. With permission from Mom's old friend Jack Haley Jr., it was called *That's Entertainment Live*. We recruited a fantastic cast of singers and dancers from all over the country, duplicated the choreography and arrangements from the original numbers, and even copied the original costumes, many of which were in Mom's collection. (The replica costumes were so well done, in fact, that on opening night some guy yelled at me for my "unconscionable" decision to compromise fragile vintage legendary costumes by using them in a live show. I didn't have the energy or the desire to correct him, so I just said, "Well, you got to do what you got to do when you have bills to pay," and walked away.) We all worked our asses off on that show, including our live narrator Rip Taylor; and local critics were as impressed with it as Mom was when she finally got to see it. We ended up continuing it every day in conjunction with the museum showings after Mom came back to the Star Theater, so that three times a day you could buy a ticket to the museum and then head straight to the showroom to see *That's Entertainment Live*.

No doubt about it, stress or no stress, exhaustion or no exhaustion, Mom made exactly the right decision when she said yes to Albert. She came to think of *Mother* as one of her best films. The audience at the Los Angeles premiere gave the cast a standing ovation. Critic Andrew Sarris called it the best film of 1996. And Albert's script won awards from both the National Society of Film Critics and the New York Film Critics Circle.

God bless you, Albert Brooks, for your great talent, your kind, compassionate heart, and for giving Mom a triumph in her life at a time when she desperately needed it. And God bless Carrie for putting Mom and Albert together in the first place, while she was dealing with so many challenges of her own.

Several weeks before Carrie and Billie came to Las Vegas to see Mom's museum, I'd walked into Carrie's house on Oak Pass to find her on her bed, sobbing uncontrollably. I asked what was wrong, and she finally got the words out.

"Bryan is leaving me . . . for a man."

I couldn't believe it. I didn't believe it, and asked, "How do you know that?"

"He told me," she said.

Okay. End of discussion. In that case, I had to believe it, but I couldn't have been more shocked. There wasn't a thing about Bryan, or about his and Carrie's relationship, that had given even the slightest hint that this might be coming. Many years later Carrie made a lot of jokes in public about her magical power to turn men gay; but the truth is, in private, when it happened, it was devastatingly painful for her, and for Mom and me as well. No one in their right mind would ever call either of us homophobic, so the

Billie Lourd, the great love of Carrie's and Bryan's lives.

"leaving me for a man" part was just an unexpected twist and, in the end, beside the point. We'd loved Carrie and Bryan together. We'd loved how she thrived when she was with him. And we'd had much higher hopes for Billie than to be raised by two parents who weren't together, no matter how much both of her parents loved her.

But I have to say, it's a tribute to both Carrie and Bryan that after they split up they managed to keep the majority of their relationship focused on coparenting Billie, the daughter they both cherished. There were many times when, for a variety of reasons, Carrie was unable to be the kind of loving, reliable mother Billie deserved, and Bryan was always happy to take over as her loving, reliable father.

Of course, Carrie was very open about her pattern of rehab, relapses, and countless AA meetings. Our old friend Connie Freiberg, who started babysitting for Carrie and me when Mom was still married to Eddie, was one of Carrie's great AA champions. Carrie also found her way to a great sponsor, a guy named Clancy, who helped her get sober many times. But between battling drugs and battling mental illness, not even her profound love for Billie could always give her the strength to keep winning.

Billie was safe and sound with Bryan in the summer of 1997 when Carrie went through a serious manic episode and stayed awake for six days. Her doctors diagnosed it as a bad interaction of her medications and hospitalized her at Cedars-Sinai for a supervised "medication vacation," as they called it.

Six straight days of not sleeping had left Carrie psychotic, as it would anyone. One of the ways her psychosis manifested itself was that she thought everything on television was about her, and bear in mind, she was a self-proclaimed TV junkie. She was watching a lot of CNN at the time, and its live nonstop coverage of the Gianni Versace murder and the intensive manhunt for his killer, Andrew Cunanan. Carrie wasn't just riveted to it—as she described it, thanks to her mania and sleep deprivation, "I was Gianni Versace, Andrew Cunanan, and the police."

I was at the hotel when I got the call from Cedars-Sinai telling me that Carrie had gone off the rails. I told them I was on my way, recruited Henry to go with me, and we rushed off to L.A.

We could hear Carrie ranting and yelling every profanity in her extensive vocabulary the minute we stepped off the elevator and into the hallway outside her room. It was amazing and heartbreaking—they'd given her enough medication to sedate an elephant, and she was still wide awake. She was so out of control that when a doctor joined us in her room shortly after Henry and I arrived, she greeted him with a cheerful "Finally, here's someone who can tell us what it's like to get his cock sucked."

A few hours later we got her checked into the Thalians Mental Health Center at Cedars-Sinai, which ultimately led to my escorting her to the Silver Hill Hospital in Connecticut for their thirty-day inpatient program. This isn't a complaint, it's just a fact—for a guy who never had a drug or alcohol problem, I was becoming a virtual expert on rehab facilities. It had been years since Carrie had been to rehab or a clinic, but somehow, no matter how much time passes, and how much you hope the danger has passed once and for all, that phone call is more of a disappointment than a surprise.

At any rate, with my sister in the safe, qualified care of psychiatric and addiction specialists . . .

. . . my estranged stepfather three thousand miles away with his mistress and, possibly, their child . . .

. . . and my mother busy with her team of lawyers and accountants, preparing to do battle to save her hotel and her memorabilia collection from a husband who was planning to take her down any way he could . . .

. . . it was time to shift my focus to my wife and stepchildren . . . or, to put it another way—

Meanwhile, back at the ranch . . .

15

DOUBLE LIFE

Billie and Mom in costume at Paul Allen's birthday party.

From the day we moved to the ranch, long before the phone call from Mom announcing that she'd bought a hotel in Las Vegas, Christi had invested her heart, soul, and tireless energy into those forty beautiful acres. She was a strong, amazing woman who'd spent her salt-of-the-earth childhood in the High Sierras, and she was as gifted at farming as she was at art. She planted trees and crops. She milked our cows and tended to our horses and made her own butter. She drove our shiny new John Deere tractor as if she'd grown up on it. The kids were happily enrolled in school in the small nearby town of Creston, where Christi taught art classes.

I was in my element as much as she was, hard at work creating a self-sustaining, alternative-energy, environmentally responsible property and loving every sweaty, exhausting minute of it. Progress at the ranch was well under way by the time Mom invited me to design and build the Star Theater at the Debbie Reynolds Hotel and Casino.

It's a six-and-a-half-hour commute each way from Creston, California, to Las Vegas, Nevada. I made the trip as often as I could while the hotel and showroom were under construction. I'd hired Fred Pierson, the associate producer on *Twogether*, to be my assistant at the hotel, and he rode shotgun on those long drives back and forth to the ranch—he and caffeine were in charge of keeping me from falling asleep on the road. There were times when Christi would come to Vegas with me to help decorate the hotel with her artwork, but for the most part she and the caretakers were in charge of the ranch and the kids while I was trying to save Mom from Richard Hamlett and his merry band of crooks.

When I became CEO of hotel and casino operations, we started work on the museum, and I was essentially holding down two very stressful full-time jobs, I saw no way around moving Christi and the kids to Las Vegas and letting our caretakers handle the ranch. Mom was completely alone, with sharks circling around her, and leaving her even occasionally to deal with it by herself was out of the question. Carrie certainly wasn't an option to take my place, for obvious reasons. Like it or not, ready or not, it was me or nobody.

I bought a small house on the old Sahara golf course in Vegas. The house had an interesting history: Sonny Liston had lived there and had either died or been killed there, depending on whose account you believe. It was just big enough for each of my stepchildren to have their own bedroom, and I hired Christi to be head of the hotel and museum art department. She did a magnificent job on museum backdrops and other projects around the hotel, but from the very beginning it was obvious that she was becoming unraveled and starting to drink more than she should. As much as she loved the ranch, the stress of being in charge of it and the kids without me had already been taking its toll on her. Moving to Las Vegas just exacerbated her anxiety and her drinking; she hated it there from the minute we crossed into the city limits. But she was a huge part of getting the museum ready for our grand, private, invitation-only premiere on Mom's birthday, and I couldn't have been more proud of her and her stunning contributions to that perfect evening.

I was too busy at the premiere greeting friends and celebrities from all over the country, partying, talking to the press, and doing interviews with Mom to keep track of Christi; so I didn't think much about it at first when people started casually asking me where she was. When I finally began noticing that it had been a while since I'd seen her and asked the security team to keep an eye out for her, I still wasn't especially alarmed. The alarm didn't set in until one of our security guys rushed up to me and told me they'd found her. I left the party and followed him to the engineering room in the basement.

Christi was lying on the floor, passed out. A half-empty gallon bottle of vodka was lying beside her. She had glass shards in her hair, and she looked as if she'd been beaten up. She was completely hammered, but when she was finally able to answer my frantic questions about what the hell had happened to her, she slurred out that she'd been mugged and raped.

We managed to discreetly get her out of there and off to the hospital. The police met us in the emergency room to investigate the alleged mugging and rape. The rape kit established that no rape had taken place, which made it pretty unlikely that Christi had been mugged either. It was much more likely that the shards of glass and Christi's injuries were the result of her own drunken stumbling. She was too drunk to coherently answer any questions, and with nothing credible to investigate, the police left. Once they were gone, the doctor arrived with her test results. He told me that in his twenty years of practice he'd never seen an alcohol level as high as hers, and it was a miracle she was still alive.

It's an understatement to say I was completely blindsided by all this. I'd seen Christi drink socially before, never to excess, and I'd never had any reason to give it a moment's thought. When she finally sobered up enough to have a rational conversation, I asked her why she'd wandered off in the first place. Everyone at the museum premiere, and at the show and the party that followed, had been blown away by her artwork and wanted to meet her and congratulate her. So instead of being surrounded by a room full of new fans, she thought it would be a great idea to throw back half a gallon of vodka, get literally falling-down drunk, and pass out on the basement floor. What possible sense did that make?

She agreed that it made no sense at all. Her only explanation was that it was too much for her and she just couldn't handle it. She was so sorry and embarrassed, it was impossible to be angry with her.

At her insistence I left her at the hospital to sleep it off while I headed back to the hotel. It was almost dawn, and I knew the party would still be going on—no self-respecting Debbie Reynolds celebration ended without greeting the sun, and God help you if you yawned or glanced at your watch before then. Sure enough, there was Mom, surrounded by close, loving friends, having the time of her life, her spectacularly successful museum premiere and her birthday combined to give her the most fun, and the most hope, she'd had in a long time. She'd been so busy entertaining and being entertained that she didn't even ask where I'd been for the last several hours, and I wasn't about to tell her. It was her night, and it was going to stay that way.

If that had been the last of the drama with Christi, I would have gone right on keeping it from Mom. Unfortunately, that wasn't the case. Not even close.

It was just a couple of days later. I was at the house, taking a break from the hotel, sitting on the bed in the master bedroom listening to Christi vent about how much she hated Las Vegas and hated our lives there. I told her what I'd already told her many times before, and what I still believe to this day: I couldn't and wouldn't leave my mother alone and unprotected in that hotel, in that business, in that city, fragile and in over her head, when, for all either one of us knew at that point, I was the only person around that she could trust anymore.

I'm not sure when Christi slipped into the bathroom and closed the door. All I know is that suddenly, from inside the bathroom, two deafening gunshots rang out. I leapt up, scared to death, and raced to that door. She hadn't just closed it, she'd locked it, so I kicked it in and found her standing there in the hazy, smoky, acrid air, holding my 9 mm gun, sobbing hysterically. One bullet had gone through the vanity. The other one had shattered part of the bathtub. She never did tell me if she'd had even a passing thought of killing herself and lost her nerve, or if she'd simply snapped and started shooting. Either way, I was furious with her. It was bad enough that she'd fired a gun in the house at all, but the kids happened to be home at the time, for god's sake! She handed over the gun. I immediately unloaded it and left her to go find the kids and assure them that everything was okay, whether I believed it or not.

At that point in time, even though I didn't know it was possible, Mom and I had grown closer than ever. We were like two soldiers sharing a foxhole, fighting to survive while one battle after another raged around us. Since the Richard Hamlett days, we'd developed a ritual in which I'd sit on the floor of her dressing room at the hotel while she'd get ready for that night's show and share the headlines of the day.

The night of the shooting I filled her in on what had been going on with Christi. She liked Christi in general, but Mom had her limits when it came to anyone who might be a potential threat to her son or his happiness. I found out much later that, after that particular debriefing session in her dressing room, she pulled Christi aside and said, from the core of her soul, "If you ever hurt Todd with a gun, either on purpose or accidentally, I will kill you." Like Warren Beatty all those years ago, when Mom warned him that if he laid a hand on Carrie she would take out a hit on him, Christi didn't doubt her for a second.

Again, Christi was deeply remorseful, begging me and her children and God for forgiveness. She agonized over it, and again, it was impossible not to forgive her.

Several nights later, at about one A.M., I was at work at the hotel when I got a call from the Las Vegas police, telling me to get to a truck stop on the outskirts of town ASAP. "We have your wife," they said. Not a call you ever want to get, trust me.

I floored it to the truck stop, and sure enough, there in the parking lot were two cops and Christi, who was three sheets to the wind and yelling at the cops. She was about to get arrested, so I stepped in front of her, pushed her into my car, closed the door, and asked the cops to fill me in.

The short version of the story went like this:

Christi was at the truck stop (your guess is as good as mine), drunk as hell.

There was some kind of domestic disturbance between a man and a woman.

Christi jumped out of her car and got in an actual fistfight with the man. Apparently it wasn't going well for her, because she ran back to her car, reached in, grabbed my gun, and aimed it at the man.

The man managed to get the gun away from her, and the cops arrived.

There was a half-empty bottle of Jack Daniel's in Christi's car, and bullets scattered around all over the floor and the passenger seat. She'd obviously grabbed a handful of bullets on her way out the door of our house; and if there was any good news in this ridiculous situation, it was the fact that she'd grabbed the wrong bullets for that particular gun.

The cops and I talked and I showed them my concealed weapons permit. In the end they said, "Get her out of here," and I did, gladly.

I was livid, and really not receptive to hearing Christi's apologies, remorse, and empty promises anymore. It had been about eight days since her meltdown at the museum opening and three days since she fired a gun in our bathroom, and now this? Seriously? The kids deserved better. I deserved better, and Christi deserved better. She obviously needed help, as in immediately, or we weren't going to make it.

After about a week of serious conversations, a lot of tears, much research, and a bunch of arrangements, she reluctantly checked into the Betty Ford Center in Rancho Mirage, California. And to her great credit, once she got there, she really embraced it. Again, by then I was pretty damned familiar with rehab facilities, and as far as I'm concerned, the Betty Ford Center was the most effective. I went to family functions at the facility, which were very enlightening. By the time Christi checked out again, she was the sober, healthy, clearheaded woman I'd fallen in love with in the first place; and she stayed that way for the next six years.

There was no way I was going to reward her hard-won sobriety by dragging her back to Las Vegas, where she'd been so miserable. Instead, she went from Betty Ford straight back to the kids and the ranch, and I resigned myself to resuming the unavoidable four-hundred-mile commute. Rather than let it kill me, as I'd been thinking it might, on top of everything else that was going on, I bought a small plane and cut the trip from Vegas to the ranch from a six-and-a-half-hour drive to a much more manageable two-hour flight.

It was worth the investment. There was no way I was leaving Mom until she was safe and secure and everything at the hotel was settled one way or another, and we still had a long way to go, not to mention some unfinished business with Richard Hamlett.

Mom's divorce from Richard was final on May 14, 1996. As part of the divorce decree, Mom was awarded her hotel and her share of the properties she'd bought in Virginia. Richard was ordered to pay Mom's attorney fees and to repay every dime he'd "borrowed" from everything of hers he could hijack. The grand total: just under $9 million.

Mom and I celebrated, but not for long. Predictably, Richard filed an appeal and managed to get the venue moved from Las Vegas to a Virginia court, because of his "busy schedule." Mom spent much of 1997 paying a fortune to fly her legal teams back and forth to collect the money Richard had been ordered to pay her.

Apparently he was counting on her getting tired of the fight and giving up. What he forgot is that he was dealing with Debbie Reynolds, and it was frustrating the hell out of him. He called her one night in a rage and said, "If you keep trying to get this money, I'll do whatever it takes to bring down the people around you."

Shortly after that phone call, he declared bankruptcy. The one thing I'll always give Richard Hamlett credit for—he was absolutely brilliant at manipulating the system.

Mom's back was almost flat against the wall when the movie business surprised her with another brief, much-needed ray of sunshine. Scott Rudin, one of the producers of *Mother*, offered her a role in a Kevin Kline film called *In & Out*. It was shot back east, giving her a refreshing change of scenery, and she loved working with everyone in the cast.

By the time she got back to Las Vegas, she was reenergized, with a whole new perspective. We had a good, long talk and came to the conclusion that it didn't make sense anymore to keep throwing good money after bad. The Virginia bankruptcy court obviously wasn't going to hold Richard Hamlett accountable. Why go on chasing him for properties back east that weren't worth all that much to begin with? Why not just cut our losses and move on?

So when Richard's lawyer called Mom's attorney and offered to settle with her for the flat fee of $300,000 for those properties—i.e., $30,000 more than what she'd paid Richard for his share in the hotel—she took the deal. She hated it, but she took it, and neither of us ever doubted that it was exactly the right thing to do.

In fact, we tallied the whole thing up for Mom's book *Unsinkable*:

AMOUNT I WAS AWARDED BY DIVORCE COURT:

$8.9 MILLION

TOTAL OF LEGAL BILLS TO CHASE MY EX:

$1.4 MILLION

MONEY COLLECTED FROM HUSBAND NUMBER THREE:

NEXT TO NOTHING

FEELING I HAD GETTING RID OF THAT

DEVIL WITH THE KILLER BLUE EYES:

PRICELESS

Now all we had to do was try to save the Debbie Reynolds Hotel and Casino, if it was still even possible.

By the summer of 1997, everything Mom owned was mortgaged to the hilt. Let's face it, when you have to start borrowing against your life insurance, you know you're in trouble. All the creditors were tired of waiting. They'd all filed lawsuits. We couldn't hold them off any longer; and apparently they couldn't believe—even the judges couldn't believe—that Debbie Reynolds of all people couldn't find a way to come up with more money. I'd spent over a year looking for backers and chasing down prospective deals. An offer from a worm farmer didn't pan out. A potential investor we called Yellow Socks fell through. We spent a Christmas in Sedona, Arizona, at Los Abrigados, compliments of its owner Joe Martori of ILX Resorts, who seemed so interested that we shot a commercial about the impending merger between ILX and the Debbie Reynolds Resort and Casino; but in the end he decided the risk was too high and walked away.

Finally, sadly, we had to cave to the inevitable—both Mom and the hotel declared bankruptcy. Then, about six months before the bankruptcies were finalized, hope arrived in the form of a man named David Siegel. David was king of the time-share business, and we had a very viable time-share operation in place, with six acres available for potential expansion. He was also a private company who could merge into our public company. David Crabtree and I flew to Florida to hear what he had in mind. We were blown away—he made the extraordinary offer of buying 92.5 percent of the hotel stock, in a merger deal between David Siegel's company, Westgate Resorts, and the Debbie Reynolds Resort and Casino, a deal that was valued at $22 million. Westgate Resorts would manage the hotel and time-share operations, and Mom and I would manage the gaming and entertainment. We could have paid off the creditors and stockholders, and the hotel could have stayed in business.

Unfortunately, our greedy unsecured creditors seemed to be unfamiliar with the concept of "a bird in the hand" and decided they could do even better than that if the hotel was auctioned off, and in June of 1998 they took us to court to block David Siegel's offer.

In the end, to our utter incredulity, the judge agreed with the creditors. He blocked David Siegel's offer with a cavalier "I'm a poker player."

And I involuntarily burst out so everyone could hear, "A poker player with our shareholders' money."

The auction for the hotel was scheduled for August 5, 1998, or, as we called it from then on, Black Wednesday. By the time it was over, the hotel belonged to the World Wrestling Federation, and we were out of business.

Needless to say, it was painful to see Mom so devastated and having to start over. Again. She was sixty-six. No one worked harder, tried harder, and loved harder than she did. She deserved all the happiness, joy, and security in this world; but she kept getting deceived and robbed blind by men she cared for so much, deeply trusted, and treated with nothing but kindness and respect until the truth of who they really were became unavoidable. It's easy to say I wish she'd been less trusting and more skeptical, more cynical, when guys like Harry and Richard came along, and sent them packing before they got within ten miles of her. But that would mean wishing away a whole lot of what made my mom so special—her inherent purity, her lifelong habit of always assuming the best in people, her fierce loyalty when she'd given her heart to someone, and the fact that because she didn't have a duplicitous bone in her body, it wasn't part of her makeup to sense duplicity in anyone else.

Not for a second did this latest disaster dim my faith in her. In fact, it only made me even more in awe of her, because, as always,

Me and Mom, closer than ever after her third divorce.

after a few weeks of grieving and regrouping, she summoned her strength and returned to the fighter she was. There was a line in *The Unsinkable Molly Brown* she never forgot, that she'd quote when she began to feel as if she didn't have what it took to fight one more time: "Nobody wants me down as much as I want me up! I ain't down yet."

And no, she most certainly wasn't. Instead of giving in to the defeat she was feeling in every area of her life, she turned to her most reliable way of handling a crisis—she went back to work.

First she hit the road, in Atlantic City, on cruises, in nightclubs, everywhere she could connect with the fans whose energy and appreciation brought her such joy.

And then, an unexpected answer to a prayer came along, when she was offered the recurring role of Bobbi Adler, Debra Messing's mother, on the hit series *Will & Grace*. The first episode she taped was called "The Unsinkable Mommy Adler," and she got to sing a chorus of "Good Morning," one of the iconic songs from *Singin' in the Rain*. She was so flattered that not only was she offered the job, but the part was designed specifically for her.

She shot a total of twelve episodes of *Will & Grace* between 1999 and 2006, scheduling her appearances on the road between tapings. She loved every minute of working on that series, and Megan Mullally became a good friend of both hers and Carrie's over the years.

Carrie's life had taken a turn for the better too, since her stay in the psych ward and Silver Hill and the hard work and sobriety that followed. Billie was living with her again, in an eclectic gated house she'd bought with Bryan right after the Northridge earthquake in 1994. Cary Grant once owned that house, and between husbands, Elizabeth Taylor frequently stayed in one of the guest rooms when her friend Edith Head lived there. Carrie swore she'd occasionally see Edith Head's spirit wandering the property in a yellow nightgown. She wasn't nearly as surprised by Edith Head's presence as she was by the fact that the most legendary wardrobe designer in

Carrie's house on Coldwater Canyon.

the business wouldn't choose to waft around in something a little more chic.

In one of those seemingly "meant to be" developments, there was a caretaker's house by the gate to Carrie's acreage that came up for sale. Carrie called Mom and encouraged her to buy it. The days when Carrie couldn't get far enough away from Mom were over, and she wanted Mom to be a part of Billie's life, especially now that she and Bryan were living separately. So after Uncle Bill and I finished some renovations, Mom happily became Carrie and Billie's close neighbor. It would have been a disaster if it had been Mom's idea instead of Carrie's, or if Mom hadn't known her daughter well enough to give her plenty of space. In fact, after Mom moved in, sometimes as much as a week would go by when Carrie and Mom didn't even see each other. Mom would fight the temptation to stick her head out the door to say hello when she heard Carrie's car in the driveway, or to make up an excuse to knock on Carrie's door. But they made it work. Mom got to live within easy walking distance of her daughter and granddaughter, and gently, gradually the historic occasional ice between her and Carrie began to thaw.

Carrie's writing career had really taken off after the success of the book and the movie of *Postcards from the Edge*. She wrote for the Academy Awards and other specials, and she'd become a sought-after script doctor. And then she wrote a TV movie that was fun and campy and gutsy as hell, about three aging movie stars and their high-powered agent. It was called *These Old Broads*. The movie stars were played by Mom, Shirley MacLaine, and Joan Collins, and the agent was played by Elizabeth Taylor.

Elizabeth's health was failing by then. Among other problems, she had arthritis in her spine, and she was in relentless pain. Her doctors were opposed to her doing *These Old Broads*, but she insisted on taking the job. She and Carrie had become friends over the years, and she and Mom had long since rebuilt their relationship from the foundation of their teenage years together as two of MGM's up-and-coming actresses.

In fact, as luck would have it, *These Old Broads* was shot on the back lot at MGM. It wasn't just a nostalgic experience for Mom and Elizabeth, it was a nostalgic experience for Carrie and me as well. I was cast in a small part in that movie, and Carrie was almost always on the set. She and I spent long hours between scenes together, walking that back lot, reliving our childhood, pointing out where the Western town used to be, where we shot our war movies, where Mom's dressing room used to be, where she'd park her custom-made green Rolls-Royce, where life seemed like just one big, happy adventure after another. It seemed like yesterday and a million years ago at the same time, and it was such a twist of fate that she and I and Mom and Elizabeth were all there shooting a movie together so many decades later.

There was an ironic scene in Carrie's *These Old Broads* script about Elizabeth's character stealing Mom's character's husband during an alcoholic blackout. Before they shot the scene, Elizabeth asked Mom to come to her dressing room. Mom sat down beside her, and Elizabeth got right to the point, with tears in her eyes.

"Debbie," she said, "I'm so sorry for what I did to you with Eddie."

It caught Mom off guard that Elizabeth was still so emotional about it, and she pointed out, meaning it, "That was another lifetime. You and I made up years ago."

Elizabeth's voice broke. "I just feel so awful when I think of how I hurt you and your children."

Mom's voice broke too, when she told me about that conversation. She and Elizabeth spent some nice quiet time together during the filming of *These Old Broads*—they even spent an evening sitting in Elizabeth's bed watching a movie and eating a pumpkin pie Mom brought for the occasion. Mom always marveled that it was Carrie's script that made those moments possible for two women who, despite being at the center of the greatest, most painful tabloid scandal of the 1950s, never really stopped loving each other.

Ten years later, when Elizabeth was close to death, Mom called her.

"Getting old is really shitty," Mom said. Elizabeth laughed and agreed. Mom encouraged her to be strong and hang in there, knowing how much pain her friend was in.

"I'm really trying," Elizabeth whispered, but Mom could tell she was tired of the fight. She was relieved and happy for her when she passed away and found peace.

Elizabeth remembered Mom in her will, with a pair of spectacular sapphire earrings and a matching bracelet and necklace. It reminded Mom of Elizabeth's generosity years earlier, when one of Richard Burton's *Cleopatra* costumes was being auctioned. Mom desperately wanted it for her collection, but she couldn't afford to bid on it, so she called Elizabeth to ask for help.

Elizabeth didn't hesitate. She wanted Mom to have it, and she told her to go right ahead and buy it.

Mom won the auction. She now owned Richard's costume from the movie that famously brought Elizabeth Taylor and Richard Burton together and ended the marriage of Elizabeth Taylor and Eddie Fisher.

Mom called Elizabeth to share the news.

"How much was your winning bid?" Elizabeth asked.

Mom took a breath and answered, "Sixteen thousand dollars."

Elizabeth sent Mom a $16,000 check the next day.

Needless to say, Richard Burton's *Cleopatra* costume became one of the pieces of Mom's incredible memorabilia collection she cherished most—a piece that almost single-handedly reignited her determination to find a forever home for the treasures that meant the world to her.

16

EXODUS

Carrie and me watching war movies during her London rehab.

S adly, inevitably, it was time to vacate the Debbie Reynolds Hotel and Casino.

During the hotel bankruptcy we'd moved the bulk of Mom's collection to a warehouse in Las Vegas. We'd kept the costumes for years at the DR Studios, but some of them were starting to show their age; and it was obvious that I needed to do some research on the best way to preserve them. So off they went, in a convoy of six huge trucks, to the newly constructed six-thousand-square-foot addition to the shop building at the ranch, and off I went to London to educate myself on the proper care of these irreplaceable costumes.

The curators of the Victoria and Albert Museum were the best of the best, and happy to help. The textiles in their collection, that, for example, Henry VIII had worn four hundred years earlier were impeccably preserved, while some of the gowns and other clothing in Mom's collection that were less than a hundred years old were falling apart on their hangers. I had a lot to learn. For starters, the costumes didn't belong on hangers. They had to be wrapped in acid-free tissue and laid flat. The labels used by MGM and 20th Century Fox contained acid that could burn through the fabric. Those labels had to be removed and replaced. Last but certainly not least, the costumes had to be stored at a steady, controlled temperature, which meant a major overhaul of my warehouse and, as a result, a quadrupled electricity bill. Not for one second did I wonder, even to myself, if it was worth it.

While I was building the museum at the hotel, I'd also started

Costume storage at the warehouse in Las Vegas.

building a database of every costume and prop in the collection—every bit of information about them, from the films and scenes they appeared in to the actors who wore or used them. It was a massive project, and it took years to complete. It also underscored something we'd known for over a decade: a whole lot of items in Mom's collection were missing.

We hadn't originally noticed that some pieces were mysteriously disappearing until, on January 2, 1980, the Burbank Police Department served a search warrant on the Debbie Reynolds Studios in North Hollywood, where we were already housing the vast majority of Mom's memorabilia.

The cops weren't after Mom. They were after John Lebold.

John Lebold was the trusted friend who'd helped my buddies and me haul countless items to Greenway Drive when Mom bought them at the MGM auction. He'd helped Mary pack up everything in my room when I moved to New York in my teens to be with Mom and Carrie. He was so close to Mom that she'd put him in charge of organizing her collection and becoming her curator when we first started talking about opening a Hollywood museum.

We had no idea that, in the process, he was helping himself to anything and everything he thought he could get away with.

So in 1980 he was charged with larceny, for allegedly stealing costumes and props from the Burbank Studios. John had been given free access to their wardrobe department's storage areas, claiming to be doing research for Mom's museum. The police confiscated 667 items from DR Studios. Twenty-six of them were returned to John after a trial and a hung jury. The rest were given back to the Burbank Studios, and the larceny charges were dropped.

As Mom explained years later to the *Los Angeles Times*, "[John] walked up to me [during the MGM auction] and said, 'We have the same dream.' I took him on at that time to help me to preserve my costumes. Somehow along the way he lost his dream of a Hollywood museum and it became a business. I have never lost my dream. I firmly believe we will have our museum."

Mom severed her ties with John after that trial in the 1980s, and we all went on with our lives. Then, well over a decade later, there I was, hard at work on the hotel museum, when a friend tracked me down with a brochure in his hand.

"Have you seen this big Hollywood display at a museum in Boston?" he asked. "You think some of these costumes might be your mom's?"

He handed me the brochure from the John Lebold Collection. Hours later I was on a plane to Boston to confirm the photos I'd seen in the brochure. Sure enough, a lot of Mom's costumes were right there in front of me.

I called Mom, and I hired a lawyer. We managed to get an injunction so that nothing could leave the museum until the matter was settled. In the meantime, we discovered, as did Warner Bros. Studios, that John was holding an Internet auction for 1,178 pieces of Hollywood memorabilia, including Julie Andrews's jumper and guitar from *The Sound of Music*, the stone tablets Charlton Heston carried in *The Ten Commandments*, Judy Garland's blue gingham dress from *The Wizard of Oz*, and a pair of jeans and a T-shirt worn by James Dean in *Giant*.

Both Warner Bros. and Mom filed lawsuits against John Lebold.

By the time we went to court in 2000, we'd moved the museum's part of the collection to the warehouse at the ranch. I flew to Boston for the trial, where the judge essentially told John, "Settle with the studio and with Ms. Reynolds and give them back their items, or you'll be facing criminal charges."

John was very sheepish and contrite with me after the hearing. I still remember looking at him when he approached me outside the courtroom and saying, "Make this right." I wasn't just referring to the court case, or his unconscionable betrayal of Mom's trust in him. I was also thinking I wouldn't want to be in his shoes when Judgment Day comes.

Thank God things were going much more smoothly at the ranch, and it was good to be home. Christi was sober again, and she and the kids were happy and healthy. She was creating spectacular artwork that ended up in homes of the likes of Robert Redford

Our fantasy house at the ranch.

and Ted Turner. Years earlier she'd gone away for a week to an artists' retreat with her dad, my great old friend Larry Zabel; and while she was at the retreat I'd added a second story to the barn and built an art studio for her there.

There were two side-by-side windows with a space between them in Christi's studio that overlooked our little farmhouse. She filled that space with a beautiful painting of her fantasy house It became my fantasy house too, so when I was back from the hotel to stay and was able to borrow enough money, I decided to build it.

I started by telling everyone at the ranch they had an hour to get all their belongings out of the farmhouse. Once that was done, based on something very cool I'd seen on TV when I was a boy and fantasized about ever since (it's a guy thing), I drove a bull-dozer right through the middle of that house and demolished it.

Then, with the help of Armando Garbada, an amazing Italian carpenter and craftsman I recruited from the hotel to be our ranch manager, I designed and built the house in Christi's painting, with one major adjustment: inspired by Molly Brown's fondest wishes in *The Unsinkable Molly Brown*, I added a room especially for Mom, with "a lookin'-out window over the valley" and "a big brass bed." I didn't breathe a word to her about it until it was finished. I then invited her to the ranch and had the joy of watching the look on her face when she stepped into that room for the first time. She burst into tears of awe—no one had ever built her a room before. She'd spent her life doing that kind of thing for everyone else, so a room designed just for her that she hadn't even asked for was long overdue as far as I was concerned. She loved coming there to visit and decompress, and to decorate her room with lots of memorabilia from *The Unsinkable Molly Brown*.

Then, when the house was finished, Christi completed our animal family at the ranch, for the time being. In addition to our horses and cows and chickens and geese and ducks and deer, she presented me with Yippi, an Australian shepherd mix puppy who was the best birthday present, sidekick, and traveling companion I could ever have asked for.

And while so many dreams were coming true at the ranch, it

The *Molly Brown* room at the ranch, designed just for Mom.

looked as if they might finally be coming true for Mom in Holly-wood, too . . . again . . .

A company called TrizecHahn was developing a theater and shopping complex at the corner of Hollywood Boulevard and Highland Avenue, in the heart of Hollywood, surrounding Grau-man's Chinese Theatre and a whole array of other entertainment industry attractions. And what did they think would be a perfect addition to their complex? A Hollywood memorabilia museum!

We were put in touch with the Royal Bank of Canada, who would fund our entire project with a bond offering. The Com-munity Redevelopment Agency for the City of Los Angeles had agreed to issue a cover letter that guaranteed the bonds. We were ecstatic. We signed a lease with TrizecHahn for a generous space on the fourth floor of the Hollywood & Highland Center, and in June 2001, a groundbreaking ceremony was held for our Holly-wood Motion Picture Museum. Mom, Carrie, Uncle Bill, and I posed for about a thousand pictures, every bit as excited and happy as we looked; and Johnny Grant, the honorary mayor of Holly-wood, was on hand to present Mom with a $50,000 check.

I hired renowned architect Dianna Wong to design the space for us, and we started construction immediately. Unfortunately, so did the other tenants of the Hollywood & Highland Center, who couldn't have been more disruptive if they'd tried. The restau-rant directly beneath our space, for example, decided to run their ventilation shafts right up into the middle of our museum's film theater, and hardly a day went by when we didn't find ourselves working around other tenants' pipes, columns, and wiring. It was insane and apparently unavoidable, so much so that the president of TrizecHahn moved us to the glass-enclosed "nose" of the build-ing, a ten-thousand-square-foot multilevel space with an incredi-ble view of the city.

So we took a long, deep breath, signed a new lease, and started over. Dianna began redesigning the larger, differently configured space while we dismantled and hauled everything we'd already installed from our fourth-floor site to our relocated, much more expensive dream come true.

There was nothing for Mom to do but wait and worry, so Carrie and I urged her to go to New York for an event she'd had her heart set on attending—a Michael Jackson concert at Madison Square Garden, to celebrate the thirtieth anniversary of his show business career. Mom and Michael had become friends while he was rehearsing his "Thriller" and "Beat It" videos at her dance studio, and she'd been yearning for a chance to see him perform live. The timing was perfect. She'd leave L.A. on Sunday, go to Michael's sold-out concert on Monday night, and be back in plenty of time for her sold-out concert near San Diego the following Saturday afternoon. A break from the relentless stress she'd been under would do her good, and in the meantime, with luck, we could finish moving the museum to its newest new home while she was gone.

Before he took the stage at Madison Square Garden, Michael escorted his dear friend Elizabeth Taylor to her seat near Mom's. She and Mom waved to each other, and the concert began—as magical, brilliant, and electrifying as the crowd expected, so thrilling that Mom was still too revved up from it to sleep when she got back to her midtown hotel that night, September 10, 2001.

It was early morning, a couple of hours after she finally dozed off, when she was awakened by a horrible acrid burning smell. She was sure that the hotel must be on fire and put in a frightened call to the front desk. No, they told her, it wasn't the hotel, there had been "a crash downtown," and she should stay in her room until further notice.

Alarmed, Mom turned on the TV. On the one channel that was still functioning she, like the rest of the country, watched in gut-wrenching disbelief as footage ran over and over again of planes crashing into the World Trade Center, the Twin Towers collapsing, and a third plane hitting the Pentagon. She kept pacing from the TV to the window in the hope of finding something to look at, somewhere, that made sense.

The phone rang. It startled her, and she grabbed it instantly.

It was Tim Mendelson, Elizabeth Taylor's assistant. "Debbie," he said, "Elizabeth heard that you were here alone, and she'd like you to come stay with us at the Pierre."

It was like someone—not just someone, but Elizabeth Taylor—had thrown Mom a life jacket. She quickly packed and hurried into the car Elizabeth sent for her, and she and Elizabeth held each other and sobbed the instant she stepped into Elizabeth's suite. The two of them, along with Elizabeth's assistant, her doctor, her masseur, and her butler, gathered in front of the TV, unable to turn away from the unfolding horror and doing their best to comfort one another through the unreal reality.

Every American knows exactly where they were and what they were doing on that awful morning. What Carrie and I were doing was trying desperately to find our mother in a city under attack three thousand miles away. When Mom finally got through to us and assured us that she was safe with Elizabeth, we were overwhelmed with relief and endless gratitude to Elizabeth.

Mom knew exactly how lucky she was compared to the hell countless other people were going through. She was stranded in New York at a five-star hotel with Elizabeth Taylor and her entourage, and she wasn't about to feel sorry for herself. But on the Friday after that obscene Tuesday, she broke, with a whole other reason for her tears. Her show near San Diego, a show that had been sold out for months, was scheduled for the next day; but by government order, the airlines were grounded. There was obviously no way around it, she was going to have to cancel that show, and there was nothing she hated more than letting down her fans.

Elizabeth listened, put a reassuring hand on Mom's shoulder, and said, "Maybe John can help." She disappeared into her bedroom to make some phone calls and emerged several minutes later to announce, "We have a plane, Debbie. We're leaving tomorrow morning."

"John" was Elizabeth's ex-husband, Senator John Warner of Virginia. True to his word, Senator Warner had a private plane waiting for Mom, Elizabeth, and Elizabeth's entourage first thing the next morning at Teterboro Airport. I made some calls on this end, and by the time that plane landed at Van Nuys Airport, Bob Petersen's helicopter was waiting to fly Mom straight on to the theater a hundred miles south of L.A. She arrived at 1:35 P.M. for her 2:00 P.M. curtain.

The crowd had been warned that she might not make it and why, so when she walked onstage at exactly 2:00 P.M., they jumped to their feet and cheered. There wasn't a dry eye in the house, including Mom's. She cut through the raw emotion in the room by giving Elizabeth Taylor all the credit for seeing to it that she hadn't spent the past few nightmarish days alone in New York, and for her being there with them, safe and sound, on that Saturday afternoon, ending the story with "I guess that makes up for the Eddie thing."

She sang and danced and joked her heart out for the next hour and a half. Then she ended her performance with "God Bless America" while the crowd accepted her invitation to stand and sing it with her, a theater full of new friends united in grief for the countless tragedies of 9/11 and in gratitude for the brave heroes and survivors. It was a show Mom remembered and was especially moved by for the rest of her life.

Picking up the pieces and moving on from September 11 was a challenge, and progress was unavoidably slow on the museum. Unbeknownst to us, the development was in the process of going under. Mom was having trouble underwriting the huge amount of extra work necessary for our move to the "nose" of complex, and we missed the November opening of the Hollywood & Highland Center. Then we missed our projected February opening. It was time to rally the troops one more time.

In the summer of 2002 I called Greg Orman in Kansas City. He'd lent us money for the Debbie Reynolds Hotel and Casino, and he'd guaranteed $1 million to David Siegel on the day of the hotel auction if David wanted to bid. Greg immediately jumped on a plane to L.A., and Mom and I gave him a tour of the complex. He was impressed enough to give us an unsecured bridge loan of $1.5 million at an interest rate of 10 percent, which allowed us to hire more workers to finally complete the museum. In exchange, we assured him with absolute certainty that this would be a short-term loan, just to tide us over until the promised bond money came through.

Then, immediately after Greg gave us the loan, the Los Angeles Community Redevelopment Agency ambushed us. Despite their promise to guarantee bonds to cover the development of the complex, they pulled their backing of the bonds, because of the money trouble the city of Los Angeles was having after 9/11. Our banker at the Royal Bank of Canada was stunned—he'd presold the bonds with assurance from L.A. that the bonds were valid. In the blink of an eye, with one terse, dispassionate letter from the redevelopment agency to the lawyers and tenants at Hollywood & Highland, our deal was dead. Mom's dream of a Hollywood museum vanished into thin air, again, along with the $1 million plus she'd spent on plans, construction, and rent. We had no choice but to abandon our lease and walk away from a massive amount of blood, sweat, labor, and hope.

It was almost ironic when Debbie Reynolds, who couldn't for the life of her find a home for her world-class collection of costumes, was awarded the Costume Designers Guild President's Award.

It was almost as ironic that they'd asked Carrie to present her with the award. Until her visit to the museum in Las Vegas, Carrie had pretty much thought of the collection as some stubborn fixation of Mom's, except for a few costumes and props, like Brando's Désirée bed, that she got a kick out of having around. She trivialized the collection so much, in fact, that once, when she was trying to think of something unique to give George Lucas for his birthday, she asked Mom if she could give him the *Wizard of Oz* ruby slippers—who wouldn't like to have those, right? If you look up the word *incredulous* in the dictionary, you'll find a picture of Mom's response to that question.

But by the time Carrie and I were sitting on her bed, working on her speech for Mom's Costume Designers Guild award, talking about the historic value of those costumes and reliving that day at the Vegas museum, it was clear that she got it, and got it to her core.

The awards ceremony began with a montage of clips of some of the most extraordinary costumes in the history of film—about 90 percent of which were part of Mom's collection. That fact registered with Carrie, and I watched from the wings when she took the stage to deliver her speech and introduce Mom. She was brilliant and passionate. "These costumes are the tangibles," she told guild members, the tangibles that remain from the legendary films they represented, like the paintbrushes and palettes Renoir or Picasso used to create their masterpieces, and it's our honor and our duty to preserve them for ourselves and for every generation still to come.

She concluded her brief, powerful remarks, presented Mom with the President's Award, came offstage, and collapsed into my arms, completely spent, having more than made up for all those years of dismissiveness by pouring her heart out in defense of our mother's dream. It was extraordinary and incredibly touching, and I'll always be glad I was there that night to film it.

Mom was doing an amazing job of keeping that Debbie Reynolds smile on her face through all the press surrounding the Costume Designers award and even a Lifetime Achievement Award from the Hollywood Chamber of Commerce. But behind the scenes it was feeling as if we couldn't get a break. Adding to the debacle of the Hollywood & Highland Center, along came a lawsuit from TrizecHahn, who was trying to sue us for breaking our lease at the complex. The suit was dismissed, but the legal fees it took to fight it drove us even further into the deep, deep hole we were already in.

So I was in no mood for jokes when an envelope arrived from a company called BIV Retail in Pigeon Forge, Tennessee. BIV Retail? Never heard of it. Pigeon Forge, Tennessee? Never heard of it. Just what I needed—more junk mail. Mom had received an identical envelope and had exactly the same reaction I did: Who are these people, and are they suing us too?

Purely going through the motions, I tore open the envelope. According to the letter and the attached proposal, BIV Retail was interested in building a museum in Pigeon Forge, Tennessee, as a permanent home for Mom's collection. See what I mean? Does that sound as unlikely to you as it did to us? What did pique my interest a little in the proposal, though, was the proud "as we're sure you already know" revelation that Pigeon Forge, Tennessee, happens to be the home of Dolly Parton's wildly popular Dollywood. Okay, I kept reading—I most certainly had heard of Dollywood. I called Mom and filled her in.

Then a developer named Glen Bilbo, of BIV Retail, called to ask if I'd received the proposal and offered to fly me to Tennessee to see this place for myself. Mom and I were still skeptical; but if this was a legitimate offer from a legitimate company, it was worth checking out, maybe even a Godsend. So I hopped on a plane and flew to Tennessee to meet with BIV Retail and take a tour of Dollywood.

Pigeon Forge, population about seven thousand or so, turned out to be a charming picture postcard town, sitting right in the heart of the Great Smoky Mountains, and even more of a tourist attraction than the other mega popular midwestern entertainment center, Branson, Missouri. Dollywood was fun everywhere you turned, filled with theaters, theme park rides, a water park, live entertainment, a resort, and dozens of other features that attract literally millions of visitors per year. In no time at all I went from "never heard of it" to "love everything about it."

The proposed plan was that the Debbie Reynolds Hollywood Museum would be built as part of Pigeon Forge's upcoming Belle Island Village, a spectacular twenty-three-acre family destination on an actual island in the Little Pigeon River. BIV Retail was genuinely excited about Mom and her collection, and it was a refreshing change of pace to be on the receiving end of all that enthusiasm. To sweeten the deal, they offered to pay for everything and retire the Greg Orman loan. By the time I flew back to L.A. to sit down with Mom, outline BIV Retail's offer, and show her the million photos I took of her memorabilia's potential new home, I was genuinely excited too.

She was intrigued, no doubt about it, especially when I pointed out a feature of Pigeon Forge, Tennessee, I knew would carry a lot of weight with her.

"These are your people," I told her. "These people are 'home.'" Movie star Debbie Reynolds was always, at her core, Mary Frances Reynolds from El Paso, Texas, Ray and Maxene Reynolds's daughter, Uncle Bill's little sister. All the fame, wealth, and glamour in the world never diminished that down-to-earth essence in Mom that audiences related to from the first moment she set foot on a sound stage. She'd feel as at home in Pigeon Forge as she had ever felt in the heart of Beverly Hills, and the more we talked about it, the more her eyes lit up.

She wanted time to weigh her options. She wasn't about to dismiss the Belle Island Village offer, she just had to give Hollywood another chance to make the museum a reality. Every item in her collection had been created there, after all, and was part of the history, the legacy, and the fabric of the film industry that made Hollywood the world-renowned mecca it was. We'd been disappointed time after time, year after year, decade after decade. But "no such word as *can't*." If Mom was up for giving her museum in Hollywood one more big push, I'd be right by her side.

Mom had dinner with Roger Mayer, the treasurer of the Academy of Motion Picture Arts and Sciences. He confirmed that the Academy had bought land for a museum, and that they were putting together big money to build one. But the board of directors said thanks, but no thanks—they weren't interested in Mom's collection. Why? "We don't see the relevance of costumes to a Hollywood museum."

What?

Carrie arranged a meeting for her and me with Steven Spielberg and his associate Andy Spahn. Carrie and Steven had known each other for years, and the minute we stepped in the door of his office she ran over and jumped into his lap like a three-year-old. He loved it. They were adorable together, and I was thinking this meeting was already going even better than I'd hoped. We gave our presentation, and Steven and Andy listened attentively. But Steven was already very involved in the United States Holocaust Memorial Museum and its Steven Spielberg Film and Video Archive, so he was essentially "already spoken for" by a museum very near and dear to his heart. In other words, again, thanks, but no thanks.

Carrie talked to her good friend, studio executive, business magnate, producer, and philanthropist David Geffen. Not only did he take the "thanks, but no thanks" position, he also tossed in a bit of discouragement that I'm sure was meant to be helpful: "Why don't you just sell that stuff?" Never mind, David.

And then there was George Lucas. George is a collector of film memorabilia, and Mom's collection even included one of the cameras he'd used to shoot the first *Star Wars* movie. He was kind. He was gracious. He also wasn't exactly a fan of the industry, and he felt Mom's museum should be the industry's responsibility, not his—a polite way of saying he couldn't have been less interested.

Dream or no dream, sooner or later, a point comes when it's time to let some reality creep in and stop beating your head against a brick wall.

The reality was, Hollywood should have cared, but it didn't.

So in March of 2004, Mom officially announced the relocation of her collection to Belle Island Village in Pigeon Forge, Tennessee.

17

WHAT'S A
PIGEON FORGE?

Escorting Carrie to the *Wishful Drinking* premier after-party.

Pigeon Forge, Tennessee, was great to us. The people were
warm and gracious and welcomed us with open arms, and
the proposed museum site in the upcoming Belle Island Village complex was spectacular. We'd be surrounded by retail shops,
restaurants, carnival rides, and other great tourist attractions like
the Darrell Waltrip Racing Experience and a sanctuary full of
thriving river otters called Otter Cove.

The developers obviously believed in the museum as much as we did and backed up that belief with a $12 million investment. Mom and I immediately started collaborating on the design right down to the last detail and had an incredible time doing it. Glen Bilbo and BIV Retail were projecting a potential profit in the millions in our first year, and we weren't about to let them down.

The museum's new home would be a ten-story, sixty-thousand-square-foot building with an exterior replicating the riverboat from the MGM musical *Show Boat*. The entrance would be an homage to Hollywood's great old movie palaces, similar to the entrance we created in Las Vegas but on a much larger scale. Mom's *Gone with the Wind* chandeliers would frame massive grand staircases, and there would be twelve themed pavilions, one for each film genre, from the Silent Era to Sci-Fi to Horror to Musicals to Animation. There would be two two-hundred-seat theaters with thirty-foot screens for film clips, and revolving carousels for the costumes featured in those clips. At any given time the Las Vegas museum had housed about 10 percent of Mom's collection. Our facility on Belle Island would easily accommodate about 80 percent.

It was a huge, exciting undertaking, and we couldn't have asked for a more skilled, hardworking set of architects, engineers, designers, and an amazing crew from Killian Construction. I can't begin to count the number of round trips I made between the ranch, L.A., and Belle Island. I parked my motorhome on Belle Island and lived in it with Yippi for weeks at a time, falling more and more in love with it and the project with every visit. Mom loved traveling to Belle Island too. Sure enough, these were "her people," and she couldn't wait to get to know them and entertain them when this latest incarnation of her dream came true.

I don't know whether to call it luck or fate or divine intervention that I "just happened to be" on an L.A. leg of all those round trips, I just know that I was exactly where I needed to be when I got a frantic, hysterical, terrified call from Carrie and was able to get to her within minutes.

The Belle Island Hollywood museum under construction.

On the morning of February 26, 2005, Carrie woke up to find Republican media advisor Greg Stevens lying next to her, dead in her bed. (Billie was living with Bryan at the time, thank God.) Greg was gay, Carrie's friend, not a lover, sharing her bed for a spontaneous slumber party where, she told me, they'd stayed up all night snorting OxyContin; and he'd been loaded but seemed fine when she fell asleep a few hours earlier. By the time I got to the house, Greg's body had already been taken away by the coroner's office, and Carrie was completely off the rails—frantic, sobbing hysterically, and talking a mile a minute, almost incoherent, at a time when she really needed to shut up.

The press was understandably all over it. I mean, how often does a bona fide movie star/celebrity (and card-carrying Democrat, by the way) find a popular, well-known Republican political operative dead in her bed, from what the coroner called a combination of OxyContin use and sleep apnea? And Carrie was in no shape to handle it. I managed to get her out of there, and after a lot of urgent phone calls making a lot of arrangements, Mom, her assistant Jen, and I were on a plane with her, en route to a private outpatient rehab clinic in the English countryside.

I stayed in England with Carrie for several weeks while her doctors and I weaned her off of OxyContin. She was already a dual-diagnosis bipolar. Now Greg's sudden, shocking death had added post-traumatic stress disorder to the mix, and she was really struggling and freaking out. She recognized the ridiculous illogic of wanting to take drugs to help her through a friend's fatal overdose, but she couldn't imagine ever recovering from it, with drugs or without them. She was Pam while we were there—very small, withdrawn, depressed, frightened, trying desperately to understand why, when she'd been doing exactly what Greg had been doing, she was still here and he wasn't. It took 100 percent of my focus just to get her through it, and I literally never left her side.

To give her hope that yes, she could recover, she had to recover, if not for herself, for her daughter, her family, her career, her life, I told her story after story I'd learned from my lifelong passion for war movies, stories of the millions of people who've survived unspeakable violence, fear, and the loss of friends and comrades. She said, "Show me," and we started watching war movies together. She was hooked immediately and never lost her fascination with war movies and documentaries. A line of dialogue from *Heartbreak Ridge*, one of the movies we watched in England together, was "Adapt! Overcome! Persevere!" Those words made such a deep impression on her that she had them painted over her bed when we got home, where they stayed for the rest of her time on this planet.

With her doctors' help, Carrie had weaned herself down to a quarter of an OxyContin pill per day by the time we were back in Los Angeles. She was holding on by a thread, very hard to handle, angry and unpredictable, Roy again, and when she returned to L.A., she continued her treatment with a psychiatrist at the Thalians Mental Health Center at Cedars-Sinai. Rather than have Carrie meet him in his office, he'd meet with her in my motorhome in the Cedars parking lot; and in addition to continuing to wean her off OxyContin, he also put her on a program involving a fairly new opioid addiction treatment called Suboxone.

Needless to say, Carrie's healing was slow. She had a lot to process, from the trauma she'd been through with Greg's death to her ongoing struggles with addiction and bipolar disorder to her growing awareness that a whole lot of other people were struggling with their own issues just as she was to the fact that it wasn't just her anymore—she had a daughter she was responsible for and responsible to. If courage, a sense of humor, and love for her daughter had been enough to overcome pretty much anything, Carrie would have sailed right through, no doubt about that. But as she fought her way back to her definition of "normal," with the words "Adapt! Overcome! Persevere!" as her mantra, she turned to a way to download her feelings and let the voices in her head express themselves that had helped to calm her all her life: she picked up a pen and a legal pad and started writing.

The result was a one-woman show, and eventual book, called *Wishful Drinking*. It was honest, cathartic, and funny as hell, and it had evolved over many years. Long before Greg Stevens died, Carrie had decided to "come out" about her bipolar disorder on national television, in an *ABC Primetime* interview with Diane Sawyer in 2000, motivated partly by the responsibility she felt as a celebrity, partly by her frequent comment about our family wearing our underwear on the outside of our clothes, and probably most of all, by becoming Billie's mom.

As she said to Diane Sawyer during that interview, "Prior to having a child, I really did feel, it's my business if I wanted to stop my medications. I no longer feel that's so. It's a much easier decision if you have a child. You really don't want to be the person putting that look into anyone's eyes after a while."

It was the Diane Sawyer interview that led to Carrie's becoming a spokeswoman for those who suffer from bipolar disorder and other mental illnesses. Because she was Carrie, she even found a way to be hilarious about it and help Mom and me laugh out loud

about something that honestly scared us both for her, in her book
Wishful Drinking:

> I now get awards all the time for being mentally ill. I'm apparently
> very good at it and am honored for it regularly. Probably one of the
> reasons I'm such a shoo-in is that there's no swimsuit portion of the
> competition.
>
> Hey, look, it's better than being bad at being mentally ill, right?
> How tragic would it be to be runner-up for Bipolar Woman of the
> Year?

But even after all the psychiatrists, mental health facilities, AA
meetings, and rehabs she'd been to, she still couldn't find her way
to a peaceful mind. She relapsed again, now calling OxyContin
an attempt to "mute the large sound of Greg Stevens' fallen tree."
She started gaining a lot of weight, which depressed the hell out
of her, which only led to more OxyContin. One day, high as a
kite, she drove Billie and a few of Billie's friends to a nearby mall
for a good old over-the-top shopping fix; and a couple of Carrie's
closest allies did exactly what they should have done. They called
Bryan and told him that Carrie was using heavily again and had
even gotten behind the wheel with Billie in the car.

Bryan did exactly what he should have done. He hired a lawyer
and a world-class psychiatrist in an effort to protect Billie.

I admit it, I wasn't always a fan of Bryan's, for the simple reason
that he deeply hurt one of My Girls when he left Carrie. But over
the years I became aware that Carrie had put Bryan through a lot,
through no fault of his own (or really hers either, for that matter),
and that he was a great, protective, rock-solid coparent to Billie
without ever trying to demonize Carrie. I was and am grateful to
Bryan Lourd, on Carrie's behalf and Billie's.

So when Bryan, in the wake of hearing that Carrie was in no
shape to be trusted with their daughter, started arranging for her to
see a psychiatrist he'd chosen, Mom and I couldn't say we blamed
him; but we also jumped into protective mode and realized that

if we let that happen, Carrie might permanently lose custody of Billie. Carrie was extremely remorseful about her drug-fueled irresponsibility with Billie, and she'd also completely lost track of her "edit button." She wasn't thinking logically, there was no telling what might come flying out of her mouth at any given moment, and it was more likely than not that if she started talking to a skilled psychiatrist, it would take her five minutes or less to throw herself under the bus.

Mom's conclusion: "We've got to get her out of here." And I couldn't have agreed more. We packed Carrie up, and I took her to the ranch and settled her into Mom's room for a few months. We went antiquing a lot, which she loved; we watched a lot of war movies; and mostly, she tapered off OxyContin again, enough to be stabilized again, at least for the time being.

I drove her back to L.A., and we checked her into another rehab. She lasted a few days and then left. I tracked her down and took her to a Baskin-Robbins, where in the past we'd discussed an endless variety of subjects while we were growing up—our little movies, Harry's farting, how funny it is when you get water in your belly button, you name it. Now there we were, decades later, discussing Carrie's mental illness and drug addiction—what we could do about them that we hadn't already tried. The more we talked, the more we kept coming back to the fact that it seemed almost absurd to keep putting her in rehabs. There was nothing they could tell her that she hadn't already heard a million times, and no treatment plan they could come up with that she hadn't already tried. She was such an expert at rehab by then that she could have opened one of her own and taught there, but it still wouldn't have changed the bottom line. She was never going to stop, not completely. She was going to keep right on self-medicating and trying to stabilize herself, she'd just do it quietly and privately and do her damnedest to stay "sober enough" that not even the supportive friends at her AA meetings would notice she was still using—in small quantities, but using is using.

Mom and I had a long, painful talk that night about that bottom line. It was hard for both of us to resolve the distinction between giving up on rehab and giving up on Carrie. Of course, neither of us would ever give up on Carrie, not in this lifetime, not on this planet. But there was no answer to the question "How many rehabs can she go to?" There was no argument against the timeworn definition of insanity—doing the same thing over and over again and expecting a different result. Finally, sadly, Mom resigned herself to the same conclusion I'd come to with Carrie that afternoon and agreed that whatever ride Carrie signed up for, we'd be there to take it with her, but it was time for us to just let her be.

And there was no doubt about it, Carrie wasn't about to give up, not when at the top of her priority list was trying to earn her way back into Billie's life and become the kind of mother Billie deserved. She had a few sessions with a child psychologist to, as she put it, "help me help Billie through this." Carrie was convinced at that point that Billie hated her and would never be able to forgive her, probably because at that point Carrie hated and couldn't forgive herself. She was ready and willing to do anything to be worthy of being Billie Lourd's mom again, even when "anything" turned out to be taking a doctor's suggestion to give electroconvulsive therapy a try. Or, to put it more simply, that's when Carrie signed up for shock treatments.

She'd seen shock treatments in lots of movies. So had Mom and I. You probably have too. And just the thought of some evil, sadistic doctor delivering jolts of electricity into Carrie's head while she thrashed helplessly around on a gurney terrified us. As if the imagery wasn't bad enough, when I asked one of her doctors to show me research on the long-term effects of what they kept euphemistically referring to as electroconvulsive therapy, he replied, "There isn't any." No research to tell us if we could look forward to Carrie becoming a turnip a few years down the line. Thanks a lot. That's very confidence-inspiring.

But Carrie was so determined to heal that she signed up for shock treatments anyway; and we were relieved to hear that they'd been extremely overdramatized in movies, and/or that science had come a long way. There was no thrashing, thanks to an anti-convulsant; she slept through the ten-minute procedure, thanks to a short-term anesthetic; and the only side effect she complained about was memory loss, which she claimed diminished a bit over time. In the long run, after a series of shock treatments that went on for weeks, she gave them credit for rescuing her from her deep depression and doing for her what she'd counted on drugs to do.

Maybe Mom and I would have been more impressed if drugs hadn't crept back into her life.

There's a phrase I must have heard a thousand times in a thousand "family member of an addict" meetings—that addiction is a disease that's "resistant to treatment." I heard it, I understood the words, but I'm not sure it ever really sank in how dependent successful recovery is on the addict's "default." If addicts don't believe to their core that their life will be better if they're clean and sober, no therapist or rehab or shock treatment in the world is going to work forever.

Sadly, if Carrie hadn't led me to that conclusion, I'm sure I would have found my way there through Christi.

I still remember how I scoffed when the team at the Betty Ford Center kept warning Christi and their other alcoholic patients, "If you take another drink, you're going to die." I thought it was some kind of melodramatic scare tactic, a little too over-the-top to be believed. I was wrong.

Very slowly but surely since she had "graduated" from Betty Ford, especially when she'd see our friends have a glass of wine or two with dinner, Christi started wondering out loud why she couldn't have a glass or two right along with them. Her six years of sobriety proved she may have had a problem once upon a time, but she didn't anymore, right? If our friends could have a harmless drink every once in a while, why couldn't she? No reason at all, as far as she was concerned; and with all the time I was spending commuting to Belle Island and trying to help Carrie fight her way back to "her version of normal," I wasn't at the ranch often enough to encourage her not to risk it. Even if I had been there, I might have spoken up, but I'm not sure it would have been in me to put my foot down and forbid her from drinking. I'm the first to admit, for all the addiction I'd seen in my life, I never could relate to it, but I'd definitely learned that a simple "Stop it!" was useless.

Sure enough, the drink or two Christi started enjoying "socially"/"every once in a while"/"a few times a week at most" was exactly the slippery slope the Betty Ford Center predicted. By 2007 she was drinking heavily again. I had my theories about what was behind it, but so what? The bottom line was, I hated it. So did she—enough to be remorseful about it, just not enough to quit.

To her credit, she never let drinking interfere with her productivity, either as an artist or around the ranch. There wasn't ever a trace of laziness in her, and no work was beneath her or too tough for her to tackle. She never ceased to amaze our ranch hands and me. Whether we were building the house, repairing fences, or cleaning up after our menagerie of animals, Christi was right there, working shoulder to shoulder with us, no matter how sober, drunk, or hungover she was.

One of our neighbors was aware of all the alternative energy measures we'd implemented at the ranch, and he asked me to design and install a similar extensive system at his vineyard in Creston. I took the job, happily, and Christi, our ranch crew, and I got to work. She was driving the trencher one day when she started complaining about a severe pain in her shoulder. When it didn't get better, I took her to the doctor for X-rays.

Christi and I waited in his office for the results, more inconvenienced than nervous. She had no patience with the idea of being laid up for days, let alone weeks. We were busy hoping it was just a sprain but bracing ourselves for words like *broken* and *surgery* and *cast* when the doctor walked back in, and nothing could have prepared us for the diagnosis he gave us instead.

Christi had inoperable stage four cancer.

The impact of those words is indescribable, maybe like being hit in the stomach with a baseball bat but a hundred times worse. She was immediately, understandably terrified. I wasn't ready to take one doctor's word for it and drove her to L.A. for more opinions. Doctor after doctor told us the same thing—the cancer had started in her esophagus and spread throughout her body. There weren't that many treatment options, but there were some, any of which Christi was willing to try. The most hopeful doctor we saw was a homeopath who pointed out what great physical shape she was in and added, "I've seen people pull through this, but you've got to stop drinking."

We were headed from that appointment to Carrie's, where we were spending the night, when I told Christi what I truly believed, what I felt to the depth of my soul: "I think if you stop drinking and we follow this doctor's orders, you can beat this."

She agreed wholeheartedly. She believed it too.

Then that same night, in Carrie's guesthouse, she got completely and totally hammered.

I stormed out, with a furious "No way! I'm leaving! I won't watch you kill yourself!" and marched straight to my car. I was pulling out when I saw her standing on the balcony, looking down at the driveway. It took me about two seconds to realize that there was no way I could leave her in the middle of everything she was going through. Whatever was ahead of us, I'd be there or never forgive myself.

Christi went through every possible treatment over the next several months. She never did stop drinking, but she put up an amazing fight; and I'll always wonder if those treatments extended her life or just tortured her through the time she had left. With her doctors' approval, we set up a fully equipped hospital room for her at the house, where we were surrounded by an endless supply of love and support. The kids were there, of course. Mom was there, right by our side every minute. Carrie checked in every day or two. Christi's dad, her sister, her nephew, and a steady stream of friends and our amazing ranch "family" were there, and I was so grateful.

As hard as I tried not to let Christi see it, I was devastated watching the strongest woman I'd ever known deteriorate to the point where I had to carry her to the bathroom and to a little pool we had outside that seemed to soothe her.

And then, I don't know how to explain it, but on the morning of August 17, 2008, Yippi and I were sitting beside Christi on her bed when I had the most overwhelming, peaceful feeling that she was ready to go Home. I quietly rounded up everyone in the house to hurry to her bedside, whispered to her, "If you need to leave, you leave. Everything is taken care of here," and within five minutes, in a room full of love and gratitude and admiration, she was gone.

We held a memorial service for Christi on the sound stage at the ranch a month later—a sound stage that Christi helped build during her chemotherapy. Four hundred people were there to celebrate the life of that amazing mother, wife, artist, and friend. The room was filled with her paintings, including several we borrowed back from her buyers for the occasion. Carrie was back east filming a movie called *Sorority Row*, but she sent a beautiful Mary Oliver poem titled "When Death Comes" and included a personal message to Christi that she wrote, and that Henry read:

> Christi didn't just visit this world—she filled it with her humor and her own particular spirit. And she hasn't left this world yet, nor is she likely to.
>
> We have lost her in one way, but in knowing her we gained in so many others. . . .
>
> I'll love you, Christi, as long as I'm alive. . . . And that love will keep you living in all of us for the duration of our particular forever.

It was exactly the send-off she would have wanted and exactly the send-off I wanted her to have, to thank her for our two amazing decades together. It wasn't always easy, for either one of us, but we came through it loving each other. If you've ever been through the death of a loved one after a long, torturous, irreversible illness, you know that seeing them slip away, seeing their suffering finally end, seeing them at peace for the first time in far too long brings a certain sense of peace and relief for you too. As hard as it is to say good-bye, it's unthinkable to wish them another minute of another hour of another day in all that pain, especially when you believe, as I do, that next time you see them—and there will be a next time—they'll be healthy and blissfully happy again.

Maybe it was the old show business tradition that "the show must go on," or maybe it was because Mom's dream and her whole future were at stake; but somehow, in the midst of all that, we didn't miss a beat on the Belle Island museum project. She and I were there with the great people of Pigeon Forge on May 27, 2008, for an amazing party and "topping-off ceremony," where we signed a massive steel beam and then watched as a crane set it in place on top of that huge, jaw-dropping building.

Mom was hopeful . . . again.

Then the impossible happened . . . again.

Our underwriter for the museum was Countrywide Financial. That name might sound familiar—Countrywide Financial got a lot of press in 2008, when it went down in flames with the rest

With Mom outside the Belle Island museum at the "topping-off ceremony."

of the economy. And we went down right along with it. Bank of America took over but didn't honor the loans Countrywide had in place. Funding for the developers' loan vanished into thin air, and the whole Belle Island Village project headed into foreclosure.

The building was 90 percent finished. Eighty percent of the beautiful new complex was rented out. Two thousand jobs were on the line. The developer appealed to the county, asking them to guarantee a bond offering to finish Belle Island Village. The county said no. They'd "decided to go with another project." It made no more sense to Mom and me than our decades of hearing that Hollywood couldn't care less about building a Hollywood museum.

A very smart, very savvy, very heartfelt bond proposal was submitted to the state. The state passed.

I put in a call to the governor of Tennessee, Phil Bredesen. So did Mom. He never called back.

Shattered isn't a strong enough word. Once again, for reasons far beyond our control, Mom's dream had crashed and burned. We were devastated for ourselves, for Glen Bilbo and BIV Retail, for all the workers and prospective tenants of Belle Island Village, and for the people of Pigeon Forge, who'd been so gracious to us and so supportive of the village complex every step of the way.

Mom reacted the way she had so many times before; and sadly, she'd had a lot of practice at it by now: she worked her way through another nervous breakdown. She went on the road, including an exhausting three week, fifteen-city tour in England and Wales, and she said yes to every TV and voice-over job that came long.

In the meantime, I was trying unsuccessfully to avert yet another lawsuit. Our $1.5 million loan from Greg Orman had gone on for more than five years. It was in default, and the longer we went without repaying the loan or the interest, the more the interest rate kept rising. I tried several times to negotiate a settlement with him. He was asking for $9 million. We offered $3 million, which would have almost doubled his investment. He said no, and a court date was scheduled for September 8, 2010.

Even after this latest devastation in Pigeon Forge, Tennessee, there was still "no such word as *can't*," and we decided to throw our shoulders one more time into finding a home for Mom's collection. Carrie arranged a meeting for me with her friend Paul Allen, philanthropist and cofounder of Microsoft. I gave him and his sister Jo Lynn Allen a presentation that included the idea of merging the collection with their EMP Museum in Seattle, a combined music and science fiction museum. They were incredibly gracious. They listened intently. And they passed.

Mom had four separate meetings with the Motion Picture Academy. They weren't interested in helping her save the costumes, but they were willing to let her donate her posters to the academy. Gee, thanks.

Perhaps our most significant meeting, for a completely unexpected reason, was the time we spent with Warren Buffett.

Mom had performed with the Omaha Symphony in Nebraska in April of 2006. Warren and a group of friends came backstage to meet her after the show, and he invited her to a dinner party at his home with his then-girlfriend and two other couples. They exchanged autographed photos of each other, he played the ukulele and sang for her, and he just enchanted the hell out of her in general. It was an easy leap to the conclusion that he might be just the man to understand the potential of a museum to house Mom's collection.

We flew to Omaha, and Warren was kind enough, in the middle of his insane schedule, to listen to what we'd been through and the broad scope of what we were trying to accomplish. Once we finished, he looked at Mom with a genuinely sympathetic smile and said, "Debbie, don't sell the farm."

Mom asked him what he meant.

"You mustn't indebt yourself," he told her, "and you mustn't sell the farm."

We talked about it all the way home. Mom interpreted Warren's advice to mean that her forty-year dream was clouding her judgment, and it could end up costing her everything. The only real savings she had, the only security she could fall back on after a lifetime of hard, hard work, was her collection. She was seventy-eight years old. If she kept putting that security on the line for a building to house it, there was no guarantee that she would ever earn back what she spent.

She took it in. So did I. The added weight of Warren Buffett's voice gave it even more gravity. And we still had the anxiety of the Greg Orman trial ahead of us.

Carrie and I finally sat Mom down for what we knew was the last talk she wanted to have. We encouraged her to sell her collection.

We kept it as positive as possible, even pointing out that sometimes "no such word as *can't*" might even apply to her mantra, "I can't give up my dream." She heard us, and she didn't say, "Absolutely not." What she did say was that she'd let the outcome of the Orman trial make the decision for her. If the judge would rule in our favor for the $3 million settlement we'd offered, we might be okay. Anything more than that and she'd have no choice.

The good news: The judge denied Greg's request for $9 million.

The bad news: She also denied our $3 million offer.

Greg Orman was awarded $5.3 million, to be paid within the next few months.

And just like that, the dream was over.

Mom took the hit without moving a muscle. She just stared at the judge through tear-filled eyes while I reached over and held her hand. It was devastating, but it was also a relief—a sad one, but a relief. No one could ever accuse us of not trying hard enough to get Mom's museum built, or of leaving a stone unturned, or of failing to follow up on a possibility. We'd never have to agonize again over a decision about the museum. The decision had been made for us.

It was time to auction off Mom's treasured, beloved collection.

18

THE END OF THE
RAINBOW

Mom hiding her heartbreak at the Paley Center auction.

W
e were selling Mom's collection. It seemed surreal, but we'd been left with no choice. Now all we had to do was make this the most incredible auction Hollywood had ever seen.

After a lot of meetings with a lot of auction houses, we chose a company called Profiles in History. They had a five-star reputation, they were known to be very knowledgeable and classy, and

Mom and I both had some interesting (pardon the expression) history with their CEO, Joe Maddalena. Joe had been so interested in Mom's collection over the years that he once bid $5,000 to have lunch with her and pitch Profiles in History in case she ever decided to sell. She liked him, and his $5,000 check for a lunch date definitely made an impression.

My Joe Maddalena experience was more complicated than that. In fact, it took a few years to play out. But it was more than worth the wait, for so many reasons.

Back in the Hollywood & Highland Center days, while we were hard at work on can't-miss museum site 2, Planet Hollywood held a movie memorabilia auction. Naturally, we were interested, and we raised some money for the auction in case some great items came along. One item I was drawn to like a heat-seeking missile was the suit Rex Harrison wore to the Royal Ascot horse race in *My Fair Lady*. I thought Mom had lost her mind when I excitedly told her about it and she said she wasn't interested.

I was incredulous. "*My Fair Lady,* Mom! Eight Academy Awards in 1964! Best Picture! Rex Harrison, Best Actor! Best Costume Design! What do you mean, you're not interested?!"

She reminded me of something that was common knowledge among collectors— the Audrey Hepburn costumes from *My Fair Lady,* including her unforgettable Ascot dress, had been stolen from Warner Bros. years earlier and had never been seen again. "I'll never have a chance to own that dress or any of Audrey's other pieces."

As far as I was concerned, that made the Rex Harrison Ascot suit even more important. As far as she was concerned, it would be meaningless without Audrey Hepburn's Ascot dress to go with it.

I bought it anyway. For $8,000.

Not only did Mom blow up at me for not listening to her when she told me not to buy it, she kept bringing up that Rex Harrison suit at least once a month for years, especially when she'd had a glass of white zinfandel or two. It became an ongoing thing, both of us absolutely sure we were right and neither of us willing to back down.

And then one day, there on the cover of a Profiles in History catalogue for an upcoming auction, was a photo of Audrey Hepburn in the Ascot dress! I couldn't believe it, and I immediately grabbed the phone and called a friend at Warner Bros. to ask what was going on. They'd been told by their legal department that they had no recourse to recover it, and if they wanted it, they'd have to buy it. They weren't about to buy back their own costume, so the Ascot dress was being auctioned by Profiles in History.

I went to Audrey Hepburn's son Sean Hepburn Ferrer, and we partnered to bid on that dress. We didn't win it. The $100,000 winning bid was too rich for our blood. It was disappointing, obviously, but it validated the decision I'd made when the Ascot dress first resurfaced—I didn't tell Mom a thing about it, including the fact that Sean and I were bidding on it. Much better that she knew nothing, especially since it would have triggered yet another lecture about what an idiot I was for buying that damned Rex Harrison suit.

It was four days later when I got a very unexpected call from Joe Maddalena at Profiles in History. It seems the winning bidder of the Ascot dress had backed out, and since mine was the next highest bid, I could buy it if I was still interested. For $100,000? Not a chance. Joe and I went back and forth on the price for a while, until finally he said, "Okay, I'll tell you what. You give me a couple of costumes from your mom's collection, plus another $10,000, and I'll give you the dress."

Sold! I put $10,000 on my American Express card, gave Joe a couple of Mom's less important costumes, and picked up the miraculously reincarnated Audrey Hepburn Ascot dress.

Still not a word to Mom. Instead, I took the dress to the ranch, laid it across the bed in Mom's room, put the Rex Harrison suit on a mannequin beside it, and then called Mom and made up some story about needing her to come to the ranch for a couple of days.

I wish I had a picture of the look on her face when I opened the door to her room for her and she saw that dress and that suit there together. It's a look that probably hasn't been seen on this earth since Moses first laid eyes on the burning bush. Let's just say she was literally moved to tears at finding Henry Higgins and Eliza Doolittle together again, where they belonged, in her care, where they belonged, and I never had to sit through another scolding about buying Rex Harrison's suit.

Needless to say, after all that, there was no one Mom and I would have entrusted more with the Debbie Reynolds Hollywood Motion Picture auction than Joe Maddalena and Profiles in History. We signed with them in December of 2010—another significant headline in an otherwise memorable year.

Three months earlier, on September 22, 2010, Eddie Fisher died, of complications following hip surgery. And thank God, the one thing Carrie had spent her life yearning for—mattering to her father—happened before he left.

By 2008 Carrie had done some leveling out emotionally. She and Billie were finding peace together again, and Carrie had finally kicked off her *Wishful Drinking* tour, setting box office records at the Berkeley Repertory Theatre.

Eddie was living alone in a penthouse apartment in San Francisco in 2008. Betty Lin had bought the apartment ten years earlier, and she and Eddie enjoyed spending much of their time there together until she passed away from lung cancer in 2001. When Carrie arrived in Berkeley and discovered that Eddie's next-door neighbor was routinely stealing from him, she immediately relocated Eddie to a little house in the Berkeley Hills. I helped with the manual labor, but all credit goes to Carrie for everything else about that move; and it was nothing short of mesmerizing to see the deep joy it gave her just to be with him and help his caregivers look after him and feel needed by him. He'd sit in his wheelchair all day, or lie in his bed, watching CNN and smoking one joint after another, prompting her to give him the fond new nickname "Puff Daddy." As she marveled to me more than once, she finally got what she'd always wanted from him by giving that exact thing to him—in the end, she was a great parent to Eddie Fisher.

She was even responsible for seeing to it that our once-upon-a-

Carrie on tour with her one-woman show, *Wishful Drinking*.

time teen idol father got just one more standing ovation. Eddie's nurses took him to the Berkeley Rep one night to see Carrie's show, and she brought him onstage. He was in his wheelchair, slightly hunched over. She knelt beside him, he held her hand, and they gazed into each other's eyes and sang a song they'd sung together when she was a little girl—"If I Loved You," from the musical *Carousel*. The audience leapt to its feet when the last note faded away, and when they stood up, so did Eddie. Slowly, but he did it, as if singing with his daughter and the long ovation that followed had miraculously healed him as much as it healed Carrie.

I went to Carrie's show in Berkeley a few times, and I always spent a couple of hours with her and Eddie at his house while I was there. He actually looked as if he was in fairly good shape. He certainly wasn't overweight, and he was eating well and seemed very "present." The last time I saw him he was in his wheelchair, in the living room of his little house, enjoying a joint, surrounded by Carrie and his capable, unbelievably patient nurses. I don't remember my last words to him, or his last words to me.

Carrie took it very, very hard when Eddie died, but those months they spent together, getting to really know and love each other, gave her a peace about him she'd yearned for all her life, so that she could finally smile through her tears when she talked about him. Mom was matter-of-fact about it—nothing more, understandably. This isn't easy to say, but I didn't shed a tear. I'm still kind of conflicted about that. On one hand, Eddie Fisher deeply, deeply hurt both my girls; and I spent my life learning not to let him hurt me, and learning it well. On the other hand, if it weren't for Eddie Fisher, I wouldn't exist. The commandment says, "Honor thy father and mother," but what if they're not honorable?

I guess, in the end, I'm fine leaving it at a simple "Thanks, Eddie."

No doubt about it, though, the biggest headline in my life by the time 2010 came to an end was the fact that I was no longer single.

After Christi's death, the last thing on my mind was finding a new relationship. Between ongoing work on the ranch, Belle Island, the Greg Orman lawsuit, and eighty or ninety thousand other priorities, I was busy, probably even burying myself in busyness to keep my mind off the grief of losing her. A year later her clothes were still in her closet. Her daughter, Vanessa, had finished college and moved to Santa Barbara, and her sons, James and Brandon, were still living at the ranch. Life looked just familiar enough, so why change it?

Finally Carrie, aka my big sister, aka the woman who once planted a tabloid lie about me and Michelle Pfeiffer to make Rene Russo jealous, decided a year was enough recovery time for me.

"How much longer are you going to sit up at that ranch and not get on with your life?" she demanded on the phone one day. I told her I didn't know. I might have even told her to butt out. I wasn't ready to admit to her or to myself that it was a damned good question.

A few days after that phone call, on an impulse, I jumped into the motorhome with Yippi and we took off to go skiing in Mammoth, just the two of us, so I could try to regain some sense of control in my life, rather than that sinking feeling that life was controlling me and I was only a passenger. Among the countless things I thought about was how I felt, how I really felt, about the idea of being alone. I was surprised at how quickly and clearly it hit me that it wasn't what I wanted. Not at all.

I called Carrie. "You're right," I admitted, "it's time to move on."

She didn't even take a breath. "What about Beverly?"

I knew she was referring to Beverly D'Angelo, one of her best friends. It just jolted me a little. I'd obviously known Beverly for years, and I certainly liked her, but I'd never even considered dating her. I decided Carrie must have had at least some indication that Beverly would be good with this or she wouldn't have brought her up in the first place; so sure, great, I called Beverly and suggested we get together.

She and I had several long phone conversations about some turmoil that was going on in her life, and she wondered out loud more than once how I'd feel about rescuing her. As a joke I sent her a life jacket. When I went to pick her up for our first official dinner date, she greeted me in that life jacket. It was cute of her, and it pretty much set the tone for our whole brief relationship. We had fun. We appreciated the familiarity of hanging out together. We also discovered that it's not easy for two people with fairly complicated lives to be adept at an uncomplicated relationship; and we ultimately agreed that, no matter how enchanted Carrie was with her matchmaking skills, we'd be fools to mess up a perfectly good friendship by trying to turn it into something more.

My time with Beverly was anything but a waste. Again, it was fun, and it also opened my eyes to the realization that I'd been lonelier than I let myself acknowledge since Christi died, and that I very much preferred "not alone," if and only if exactly the right woman came along.

And did she ever, in the most amazing way.

Henry Cutrona, my great old friend/sidekick/hotel manager/ Hiding Place cofounder, had settled into a nice, quiet residential neighborhood in Las Vegas. We'd always stayed in close touch, and in the fall of 2009 he started mentioning that he'd been hanging out a lot with a woman named Cat (Catherine) Hickland, who'd moved to a house just a couple of streets away.

She was a Hiding Place alumnus, he told me, but the name didn't ring a bell.

It turned out Henry and Cat had even more history than the Hiding Place. Cat was an actress, currently one of the stars of a New York soap opera called *One Life to Live*. But long before then, she'd played David Hasselhoff's love interest on the series *Knight Rider*. She and David got married both on the series and in real life ("for about five minutes," she would want me to add), and Henry had officiated at both the on-screen and offscreen weddings. She'd also appeared on Broadway as Fantine in *Les Misérables*; she was a published author; she was a motivational public speaker; and she had her own cosmetics company. She'd been divorced from her second husband, an actor named Michael Knight, for a few years, although they were still the best of friends. Now, in addition to commuting to New York for her soap job, she'd gotten her certificate as a master hypnotist and was in Las Vegas developing a career in stage hypnosis, as well as conducting weekend seminars she called "Get Your Fire Back."

I was obviously pretty impressed with that list of accomplishments. But there was one thing he said, one simple comment, that overshadowed her résumé as far as I was concerned: "She's one of us." I'd never heard Henry say that about anyone, ever. I had to get to know this woman.

Cat and I corresponded on Facebook and talked on the phone for three months before I finally insisted on meeting her. She tried to put me off—she'd fractured her foot and was wearing a walking boot, which wasn't exactly the look she was hoping for when we officially met for the first time. "Can't we just wait until this thing is off my foot?" she asked.

Of course, I couldn't have cared less about the boot, but I wasn't about to push. "Look," I said, "I'm coming to Las Vegas in my motorhome. It'll be parked in front of Henry's, and I'll be there whether you want to meet me or not."

I admit it, I was nervous when Yippi and I pulled up to Henry's house in the motorhome in January of 2010. I honestly had no idea whether Cat would be there or not, but I really hoped she would. She admitted later that she'd been a little scared to come. It had been a year and a half since she'd been involved with anyone, and she was perfectly comfortable without a man in her life, other than her 110-pound pit bull Noss. She wasn't afraid we wouldn't like each other, she was afraid we would, and then what?

But sure enough, there she was, in Henry's front yard, in her walking boot, with this incredible smile that turned out to be as inherent to her as her height and eye color. She was blond, she was beautiful, and she exuded happiness. I couldn't believe I'd never noticed her at The Hiding Place all those years ago. Henry cooked dinner for us, and I remember thinking she and I were perfect for each other when we both took our raw diced tomatoes off our pasta before we dived in—I love tomatoes in pasta sauce, but I hate raw tomatoes. So does she. I mean, seriously, what are the odds? (I'm kidding, but not.) I'm not even sure I would call it love at first sight. It seemed bigger than that, as if our being together from that night on was simply an already established fact, just waiting for both of us to be ready.

We went back to my RV after dinner, talked for hours, and spent the night together. I'd never believed in soul mates before. That night I changed my mind. I'd brought a necklace with me from the ranch, a gold and jade fish pendant that Carrie had given me years earlier, on the outside chance that Cat and I might really, really connect. I pulled it out of a drawer in the motorhome, presented it to her the next morning, and asked if she would accept it as a "going steady" symbol. She said, "Yes, I will," and I proudly, happily put it on her.

From that moment on, we were inseparable.

Yippi and I stayed at Cat's for the next couple of weeks. I immersed myself to the point where I turned off my cell phone and didn't make or take a single call. Nobody could reach me, and it was a luxury. Of course, "nobody" included Mom, who wasn't accustomed to not being able to get in touch with me for days at a time.

I finally returned her several calls and told her all about Cat. Then I put Cat on the phone with her. Again, Cat is a happy woman. It's her default setting, and it comes from the inside out. She lives it, she breathes it, she wears it, and it rides on her voice when she talks (until and unless you cross her or someone she loves, but that's a whole other story). She greeted Mom with this great, friendly enthusiasm. Mom said hello back with the guarded, tepid, arm's-length tone she used to warn newcomers that if they were even thinking about trying to get close to her or her children, they were going to earn their way there. And in the meantime, she'd already been down the "benefit of the doubt" road many times, it hadn't gone well, and she wasn't falling for it again.

It was a brief conversation, with Cat telling Mom how much she was looking forward to meeting her and other friendly introductory noises. Mom's response was a simple polite and very firm, "Please, whatever you do, don't hurt my son. He's been through so much."

It turned out that my theory about using the motorhome as a yardstick for the potential of a relationship was exactly correct—if you can get along together in a motorhome for any length of time, the two of you have a future together. Very soon after Cat and I met, we took a three-month RV trip from Las Vegas to Florida so that I could meet her mother, and we both loved every minute of it. Cat had flown across the country thousands of times, but she'd never experienced the incredible beauty of the sights and the people of the "fly-over states." She got it. In fact, she didn't just get it, she lived it and inhaled it and made it hers. She embraced every part of my life, from the motorhome to the ranch to, and especially, every animal that lived there, while never missing a beat in her own busy life. We were off to an incredible start. Unfortunately, she and Mom and Carrie weren't.

For one thing, Cat seemed like such an alien to them that they were almost expecting her to sprout antennae. I mean, who's that upbeat, warm, and positive all the time? No one, right? Alcohol problem? No way. Drug problem? Not a chance. If this wasn't some artificially induced high, there was only one other possible explanation: It wasn't real. It was an act, to lure me in. Then once she had me hooked, Cat was bound to drop this ray-of-sunshine facade and expose herself for the shallow, opportunistic phony who was lurking beneath the surface. Cat sensed their distrust, and she'd heard enough stories from me to understand it. She was also smart enough not to force herself on them. She just went about her business, went right on being who she was, and let things play themselves out.

We'd been together for several months when Mom called Cat to say she was coming to Las Vegas and she'd like to take Cat to dinner. I happened to be at the ranch, while Cat was in Vegas working with a couple of hypnosis colleagues, so it would be just the two of them, alone together for the first time.

Mom took Cat to Piero's, her favorite restaurant. They ended up talking nonstop for three hours, at the end of which Mom smiled at Cat and said, from the bottom of her heart, "You're a good girl."

They were thick as thieves from that night on, in a relationship they both cherished, a relationship that ended the way it began when, years later, in her final days on earth, Mom smiled up at Cat from bed and spoke her last words to her: "You're a good girl."

By the time Mom and I signed the auction contract with Profiles in History in December of 2010, we had the added luxury of having Cat by our side, and an incredible amount of work to do between then and June 18, 2011, when the actual auction would be held.

Most of the activity centered around the ranch, where the Hollywood Motion Picture Museum part of the collection was housed

Mom and Cat, loving in-laws and best of friends.
(courtesy of Amy Preston Wedding Photography)

in the climate-controlled warehouse. Other parts of the collection were trucked in from Las Vegas and L.A. Mom's assistants Jenny Aiavolasiti and Donald Light came up from L.A. to stay for the duration. The entire Profiles team, including Joe Maddalena, were there to put all the costumes on mannequins to be photographed for the catalogue and the website. We used the ranch sound stage and the salvaged revolving stages from the Debbie Reynolds Hotel and Casino to display the mannequins so we could shoot the costumes at a full 360 degrees. A command center full of computers ran the film clips I'd put together for the Las Vegas museum to verify every costume and every prop.

While all that was going on, Profiles in History hired an incredible, unparalleled press agent named Nancy Seltzer, who kept Mom busy with interviews and appearances all over the country. Carrie and Mom did a spectacular couple of segments together on *The Oprah Winfrey Show*, where they debuted some of the costumes to be sold. Mom told a story about the collection's signature piece, the Marilyn Monroe "subway dress" from *The Seven Year Itch*—it seems that Marilyn's husband at the time, Joe DiMaggio, was very upset about the scene in the movie in which a gust of air blew up through the sidewalk grate she was standing on, because when the skirt billowed up around her it allowed audiences to see Marilyn's panties. And there wasn't a dry eye on Oprah's set or in her audience when, for the first time on television, Mom and Carrie sang together. "Happy Days Are Here Again." Indeed.

From *The View* to *Today* to *Extra* and *The Wall Street Journal*, Mom publicized the auction while all of us at the ranch worked our way through sleep deprivation without a single complaint. The fantastic Paley Center for Media in Beverly Hills generously offered their three-story white-stone-and-glass space for the event, including a two-week exhibit prior to the auction. Profiles in History and I filled all three stories with props and costumes on mannequins, beautifully lit, with a monitor beside each display showing the classic film clips that featured them. The Marilyn Monroe "subway dress" rotated dramatically in the plexiglass display case from the hotel in the spacious lobby beside a poster-sized black-and-white photo of Marilyn in that same dress, at the iconic moment when the skirt billowed up and Marilyn laughed.

We felt grateful and vindicated when literally thousands of people showed up at the Paley Center during the two-week previews. Mom went several times to chat with her fans and the ever-present media, and she was great as always, that Debbie Reynolds smile hiding her profound heartbreak over the death of her dream for her fans and the knowledge that very soon her cherished treasures would be scattered to the highest bidders and the four winds. I lost count of the number of times Mom was asked some version of "Why didn't you have someone in Hollywood create a museum for your collection?" I know, there was no way for them to know what we'd been through for all these years, but honestly, it was all Mom and I could do not to shoot back with a sarcastic "Gee, why didn't we think of that?"

The night before the auction Cat and I sat with Mom on her porch, trying to talk her down from her panic and her severe case of the what-ifs. What if no one shows up? What if people show up but no one bids? What if they bid, but not enough to cover the Greg Orman settlement, and I lose all these treasures and still end up buried in debt? What if . . . ? What if . . . ?

We promised her it was going to be a spectacular auction and a massive success. "I know how bittersweet this is for you," I told her, "but just remember, if you find yourself starting to cry, you'll be able to dry your eyes with hundred-dollar bills."

She smiled at that, and Cat and I held her hands, painfully aware that she was dreading the next day and looking forward to having it over with at the same time. She was privately praying that some wealthy investor would swoop in and buy the whole collection so her treasures wouldn't be scattered all over the world and somehow, somewhere, her beloved fans would still have a place where they could go to see them and love them as much as she did.

It felt to her like a death in the family—she was being forced to participate in an event she'd hoped to God would never happen.

*   *   *

The morning of the auction arrived. Saturday, June 18, 2011.

Fans, friends, prospective buyers, and of course, the press started crowding around the Paley long before the doors opened at 10:00 A.M. We took it as a good omen that Carrie and Billie were going to be there after all. They were scheduled to be on a plane to London, but thanks to a computer glitch with the airlines, their flight "just happened to be" delayed until the next day.

By the time my camera crew greeted Mom at the Paley's back entrance and filmed her as she joined Cat, Yippi, and me inside, the 150-seat theater was completely filled, as was the overflow-seating area in the lobby. Carrie, Billie, and Beverly D'Angelo were already seated in the packed auditorium. Manned computers were lined up for Internet bidding, and the words DEB-BIE REYNOLDS—THE AUCTION were projected on both sides of the large screen where photographs of each item would be displayed as its turn came up.

Every eye in the auditorium followed Mom as Cat, Yippi, and I escorted her to her seat next to Carrie. Mom cheerfully waved at them like the perfect hostess she was. The air was so thick with anticipation that it was hard to breathe.

Joe Maddalena took the stage and introduced Mom, and the crowd cheered and yelled, "Bravo!" as she made her way to the microphone to talk about her beloved hard-won collection for the last time.

She thanked everyone for being there and then acknowledged what a sad day it was for her.

"I've been collecting these treasures for forty-five years," she said, "and I'm only forty." She waited for the laughter and cheers to die down. Then she summed up, briefly but eloquently, what had been the driving force behind her passion since the day she bought her first treasure at the MGM auction forty-five years earlier: "These precious items, really, I just pray that you who obtain these pieces will love and care for them as much as we do for our future generations."

Mom kicking off the Debbie Reynolds Studios auction.

Her voice choked with tears for a second before she thanked Profiles in History, decorator Philip Hoffman, me, and Carrie. She proudly added, "And my granddaughter, we even have another child. Her name is Billie Catherine, she's right over there."

She waved to Billie. Mom's dear friend Rose Marie, of *The Dick Van Dyke Show* and *Hollywood Squares* fame, happened to be sitting right in front of us, and she seized the opportunity to wave at

Mom, on which Mom got roars of laughter by responding, "Rose Marie, stop that. You're not my granddaughter!"

She concluded, "I know you love everything as much as I do. I'm so thrilled that I was around to save it because I was so stubborn, I wouldn't give up. Thanks for being here."

She never showed it, but as I took her back to her seat I could feel how much it took out of her to put everyone at ease while her heart was breaking. Once she was settled in again, the auctioneer walked to the podium and announced the first item while a picture of it appeared on the screen—a Bell & Howell movie camera from 1915. The reserve opening bid was set at $10,000. In a matter of moments, it sold for $30,000.

Next came the "Suit of Lights" matador outfit Rudolph Valentino wore in *Blood and Sand*. Reserve opening bid: $60,000. Winning bid: $210,000.

Charlie Chaplin's iconic bowler hat: $110,000.

Marilyn Monroe's 1952 MG-TD roadster from the movie *Monkey Business*: $210,000.

Julie Andrews's signed guitar from *The Sound of Music*: $140,000. Her jumper from that same scene in that same movie: $550,000.

It was overwhelming, it was thrilling, and we were just getting started. The signature piece, the "subway dress," was Lot 354, so we still had a long way to go.

Mom was taking a break in the green room with Margie Duncan and other friends, watching on the monitor when Lot 111 came up—the original ruby slippers designed for Judy Garland in *The Wizard of Oz*, before director Victor Fleming decided he wanted something more 1939-fashionable. They sold for $510,000. Judy's blue-and-white gingham *Wizard of Oz* dress: $910,000.

Hours later, Mom was back in her seat in the auditorium, watching in a dazed fog when the Audrey Hepburn Ascot dress from *My Fair Lady* came along. You remember, the dress I bought from Joe Maddalena for $10,000 and a couple of costumes from Mom's collection. The Rex Harrison Ascot suit that cost me $8,000 had

The guitar from *The Sound of Music. (courtesy of Lou Bustamonte/ Profiles in History)*

already sold for $11,000. The winning bid on the Audrey Hepburn dress? $3.8 million.

Mom's reaction? A whispered "Holy shit."

The Audrey Hepburn Royal Ascot dress from
My Fair Lady. (courtesy of Lou Bustamonte/Profiles in History)

Finally, when evening had set in, the already incredible intensity in the room ratcheted up by a factor of about a zillion, the audience began whistling, gasping, and applauding as Lot 354, the Marilyn Monroe dress, appeared on the screen.

The auctioneer hadn't even announced it yet when one of the

Bidding underway at the Debbie Reynolds Studios auction.

men at the computers relayed the news that his anonymous Inter-net bidder had already spoken up.

"I have an opening bid of . . ."

The auctioneer cut him off with a cheerful "I'm not ready for you yet." Then he turned to the breathless audience to tell them what they already knew: "Lot 354 is the Marilyn Monroe ivory pleated subway dress from *The Seven Year Itch*. Let's start the bidding at . . ."

He gestured to the man representing the Internet bidder, who took the cue and called out, "One million dollars."

The crowd went crazy.

The bids kept coming fast and furious, increasing by $100,000 increments. A pause at the $2,300,000 mark prompted the auc-tioneer to start "Going once . . ." before he was cut off by another bidder.

"Three million dollars!"

That was immediately upstaged by "Four million!"

The audience was as blown away as we were, and I wondered if they knew the same thing we knew—at four million dollars, the Marilyn Monroe dress had just broken the record for the highest price ever paid for a motion picture costume.

There were only two bidders left by the time the dress hit the $4.5 million mark. The auctioneer scanned the room.

"Do I hear four million six hundred thousand?"

Yes, he did.

There was a long pause. You could have heard a pin drop in that room. Finally the auctioneer broke the silence.

"Anybody else? Four million six hundred thousand, and . . . sold!"

With the addition of the 20 percent auction house premium, the Marilyn Monroe dress had just been won by its new owner for $5,520,000.

The audience leapt to its feet, whooping and whistling and applauding with excitement. We were so stunned that it took us a few seconds to join them, and the crowd went even wilder when they saw Mom stand up. Carrie threw her arms around her, partly out of sheer joy and partly to make sure she wasn't so overwhelmed she'd collapse.

When the auction ended and we did the math, we must have stared at the total sales figure for five minutes without blinking. In that one ten-hour period, Mom's collection—actually, only part of it, since we'd already agreed with Profiles in History that there would still be two more auctions to come—brought in a gross profit of $22.8 million.

Mom's wish that one wealthy investor would buy all those treasures and keep them together in one glorious edifice hadn't come true; and based on the locations of many of the winning bidders, we had good reason to believe there are some spectacular Hollywood museums to be found in South Korea and Dubai. Good for them, and shame on Hollywood.

But far more to the point . . . Greg Orman? Paid in full. Every other debt that had been weighing Mom down for decades? Paid in full. And there was more than enough left over to give her comfort and security for as long as she lived.

As the reality slowly sank in, she let out what was probably her first real exhale since she divorced Harry Karl a few lifetimes earlier. She summed it up perfectly, with grateful tears in her eyes:

She'd saved the collection against all odds. She'd saved the collection in spite of everyone who shrugged it off with a polite "Not interested" or told her she was crazy to keep hanging on to it.

And now, in return, the collection had saved her.

19

BRIGHT LIGHTS

With Mom, Carrie, and Billie at the South Point Casino.

B y the time 2012 rolled around, we were on a general family high.

The second auction at the Paley Center, on December 3, 2011, was another triumph. We'd broken movie memorabilia sales and attendance records at the first auction six months earlier. The Paley was so appreciative that they let us put the items for the sec-

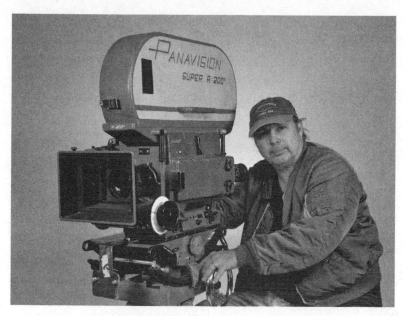

With the Panavision PSR 35 mm camera George Lucas
used to film the original *Star Wars*.

ond auction on display months ahead of time; and lines literally
formed around the block to see these latest treasures from Mom's
collection, while she was celebrating being debt-free, appreciated,
and vindicated. We broke another record that day, when the Panavision PSR 35 mm camera George Lucas used to film the original *Star Wars* sold for $520,000, making it the most expensive
piece of science fiction memorabilia ever sold. Total sales at the
second auction: approximately $5 million.

Cat and I combined our resources and bought a great house in
Las Vegas. Escrow closed on January 16, 2012, and by February
we were busy doing extensive renovations, including rebuilding a
casita on the property to transform it into a guesthouse for Mom,
at Mom's insistence—she wanted to spend a lot of time with us, but
she didn't want to be underfoot. (She was also a fervent believer in
the old Benjamin Franklin observation that fish and houseguests
begin to stink after three days.) Mom and Cat were incredibly
close by then. Cat would lie in Mom's bed with her and they'd

watch movies together, talk about me behind my back (the good and the bad, I'm sure), and have very deep conversations about anything and everything. It was almost uncanny how much they had in common. They shared beliefs in God and spirituality, and they were both tenacious self-made, self-motivated women who spent a good deal of time on the road, Mom as an entertainer and Cat as the world's only celebrity stage hypnotist. It was a joy to watch them together.

Carrie, in the meantime, had become a spokeswoman for Jenny Craig and was losing a lot of weight, pulling out of her PTSD and depression over Eddie's death and traveling all over the world doing personal appearances and promoting her new book *Shock-aholic*. She was always surrounded by friends; and "friends" and assistants came and went fairly often. She was mystified by that, and when yet another assistant we all liked was non-negotiably on his way out the door, she asked me why she couldn't seem to hang on to them for more than maybe a year or two at a time. It was one of those "do you really want me to answer that?" conversations. For one thing, I told her, and it was no news to her, she was a complicated person, not always a breeze to predict or deal with. For another thing, sadly, it's a common phenomenon in Hollywood—assistants who try to be vigilant and protective and are willing to say no to their employers, especially when it comes to monitoring their drug use, tend not to last long, while those who always say yes, even at the expense of their employers' well-being, end up with a lot more job security. Needless to say, I got along beautifully with some of Carrie's assistants and not nearly as well with others.

Cat caught on fairly quickly to Carrie's complexities, and to Carrie's unspoken signals that she didn't particularly appreciate or trust Cat's closeness to Mom at that point in time. But rather than get in each other's faces about it and cause Mom and me any unnecessary stress, they pretty much went on about their lives and kept a drama-free distance from each other.

In fact, it was at Carrie's house that Cat and I got married, on

December 22, 2012. It was casual and perfect, exactly the way we wanted it, with about a hundred friends there to celebrate with us. Carrie and Yippi were my "best men," Carrie puffing on her vape pen throughout the ceremony. Henry officiated. We livestreamed it so that Cat's mom and sister could "be there" without making the trip from Florida.

A couple of unexpected highlights happened when it was time for me to present Cat with her ring. Henry was leading us in a combined Christian and American Indian prayer, and all heads were bowed, when Carrie reached into her pocket to retrieve the ring and promptly dropped it. Henry peripherally noticed but went right on with the prayer while Carrie hit the ground to look for the ring, and she was beaming with pride when she found it, stood, and handed it to me.

Then Henry explained to the guests that Mom had given the ring to me to give to Cat—it was actually Mom's wedding ring. On which Mom turned to the guests from her seat in the front row and announced, "I'll bet you're all wondering which one!"

They were, actually, and the answer is, it was Mom's wedding ring from Eddie. A few people asked Mom later if she didn't think that might be kind of a negative way for me and Cat to start our marriage. But as Mom explained, regardless of what happened a few years down the line, on the day Eddie gave her that ring, they were deeply, joyfully, gorgeously in love. There was no negativity about it, and that's exactly what she was wishing for us. In fact, Mom even surprised us that night by booking Cat and Yippi and me into the same bungalow at the Beverly Hills Hotel where she and Eddie spent their honeymoon night.

And then, at the end of the ceremony, in keeping with the Native American influence in Henry's prayer, Carrie passed her vape pen for each of us to take a hit, since there was no peace pipe available.

I doubt if any of our guests noticed, but Mom was fairly subdued on the day Cat and I got married. She was so happy for us and so happy that Cat was now officially part of the family. Physically, though, she wasn't well, and all things considered, it wasn't

Carrie triumphantly rescued the ring at my wedding to Cat.
(courtesy of Amy Preston Wedding Photography)

surprising, after several months that would have been a challenge for most women half her age.

In the spring of 2012, shortly after Mom turned eighty, she had been offered a part that was very near and dear to her heart—she played the mother of her old friend Liberace in an HBO movie called *Behind the Candelabra*.

Mom and Lee, as those close to Liberace called him, knew and admired each other forever from their decades as headliners at the biggest, best showrooms in Las Vegas. She was close to him and his family, especially his mother Frances, who lived next door to him and was addicted to the slot machine Lee had installed in her living room. Mom, a brilliantly observant impersonator all her life, knew every mannerism, every nuance of Frances's behavior, and she couldn't wait to do her justice onscreen. She used some of Grandma Reynolds's dresses as part of her wardrobe, and her makeup was as astonishing and unglamorous as it gets. I still remember getting a text one day—no words, just a close-up of an elderly, ordinary-looking woman staring impassively into the camera. I was completely stumped and even ran around showing it to people and asking, "Who the hell would be sending me a picture of some random old lady?", before I realized it was Mom, just sharing her Frances Liberace look with me from her makeup chair.

Mom loved to brag that she taught Lee to fly. When he was performing at the Hilton, he'd enter by flying from the back of the showroom over the audience to the stage. The problem was, his feet kept lagging behind him while he was in the air, and he kept landing on his face. Mom had mounted so many shows that she was considered an expert among the Vegas crowd when it came to technical glitches. All it took was adjusting his rigging so that it stopped pitching him forward, and Lee nailed every landing from then on, thanks to Mom.

She was devastated when Lee died of pneumonia due to complications from AIDS in February of 1987, and she was honored to be part of a respectful, compassionate movie about him, surrounded by a brilliant cast and an equally brilliant director—Michael Douglas was spectacular as Liberace, Matt Damon was equally spectacular as Liberace's lover Scott Thorson, and Steve Soderbergh directed the whole magnificent production. Mom, as Frances Liberace, outdid herself and took everyone's breath away, and everyone from Tom Hanks to Clint Eastwood went out of their way to rave about her when *Behind the Candelabra* was shown at the Telluride Film Festival. It went on to win countless awards, including two Golden Globes and eleven prime-time Emmys. She was proud of that movie to the day she left this earth.

Rather than heading home from *Behind the Candelabra* and getting some well-deserved rest, Mom decided, because she was Debbie Reynolds, that it would be a great idea to hit the road again, this time to do her show in Branson, Missouri, in September of 2012. While she was there she discovered that she was allergic to a new pill she was taking; and by the time she got home, her feet were very swollen, she was having trouble breathing, and she was thoroughly exhausted.

We checked her into the hospital, where they discovered that her kidneys had almost failed. Her doctors released her a week later only on the condition that she cancel all her appearances for the rest of the year. She did. In fact, she dutifully obeyed every order from every one of her doctors; and all of us, including Mom, assumed she'd be back to normal before long.

Then one day, with no warning, she was suddenly incoherent. She would talk, and she seemed to understand what we were saying to her, but she was making no sense whatsoever, as if the connection between her brain and her mouth had shorted out. She was aware of it too, because she was obviously frightened by it, and needless to say, so were we.

We raced back to the hospital, where her doctors quickly diagnosed the problem as a TIA, a transient ischemic attack, which is commonly thought of as a ministroke. In Mom's case it was caused by alarmingly high blood pressure, they put her on more medication, and thank God, she slowly came back into focus.

Mom had been suffering from chronic back pain for a few years. Doctor after doctor tried to figure out what was causing it. When they failed at that, they settled for trying control it with pain medication. It helped some, but it certainly didn't make the pain go away; and with just a few limitations here and there, she refused to let it stop her. Carrie and I hated that she was in pain, but it didn't scare us. The TIA did, a lot. It was the first time we'd seen her disoriented and disconnected, and probably the first time it had occurred to us that our unsinkable, inextinguishable, indestructible mom might actually be mortal.

And yet, there she was, less than three months after a close call with kidney failure and a TIA, beaming and joking and looking beautiful in a million pictures with Cat and me and our friends at the wedding, so maybe this mortality thing was negotiable after all, if you were someone as special as Debbie Reynolds.

I'm not sure anything terrified Carrie more than the thought of losing Mom. That one glimpse of the possibility hit her hard, and she started talking about the idea of doing a documentary about her, a "legacy piece," as she called it, "while we still can."

I was all for it, but there was a big problem: Mom would want nothing to do with a "legacy piece," or a "puff piece," as she used to call them, about her amazing life, her amazing career, and, she would have added, "blah, blah, and blah." Giving herself accolades, blowing her own horn, being part of anything that would essentially send the message "Look at me! I'm Debbie Reynolds! Aren't I fantastic?" was out of the question. She didn't even like watching her own movies. The trick wouldn't be getting this documentary made. The trick would be coming up with a way to sell it to Mom that she might actually go for.

Slowly but surely over the next several months we kept refining the concept for a project that came to be known as *Bright Lights*. Mom had been asked a thousand times in a thousand interviews what she was most proud of, what she considered to be her greatest accomplishment. She always gave the same answer: "My children." If we pitched the idea to her as a documentary about our family, about our lives and the love story among the three of us, no "legacy piece," no cloying homage, maybe we'd get a yes out of her.

It worked. She said yes.

Carrie talked to producer Charlie Wessler, a childhood friend of ours who happened to be living in her guesthouse at the time. Charlie loved the idea and suggested we talk to Academy Award–winning producer/director Fisher Stevens and his partner, producer/director Alexis Bloom. They were on board in the blink of an eye, and we were thrilled to have them.

One of the biggest challenges of *Bright Lights* from the very beginning was the massive amount of material Fisher and Lexi had to somehow study, screen, and either set aside or organize into something useful. I had two people working forty or fifty hours a week on a lifetime worth of archives; and other than a general idea of the concept, we really weren't even sure where this documentary was headed. I would love to take a nice big bow for the end result, but that credit goes to Fisher and Lexi. Rather than try to steer, manipulate, and stage it into some preconceived structure, they let it take on a life of its own. They gave it its shape and its direction as it went along, with footage from literally thousands of hours of archived film, interspersed with footage of more than a year of our current, ongoing, abnormal-normal lives.

And so, with the *Bright Lights* cameras rolling . . .

Mom went on the road, to play the Mohegan Sun Casino in Connecticut. The only staged scene in the documentary, just to give Mom and Carrie something to do while they talked, was when Carrie went next door to Mom's house to help her pack for that trip, with Mom's dog Dwight and Carrie's dog Gary there to supervise. The truth is, Carrie never in her life helped Mom pack. Mom, in the meantime, kept asking, "Where are my marks?" and, "What do you want me to say?" as if we were making a semi-scripted movie. She seems a little confused in that first scene, not because she was coached to be but because she was.

Carrie and I were very torn about Mom's trip to Connecticut. On one hand, she was frail, and logically she should have been home, taking it easy and enjoying the luxury of not having to work anymore. On the other hand, performing for the fans she loved nourished her soul. She wasn't just living when she performed, she was alive, and the days of exhaustion that followed when she left the stage were a small price to pay as far as she was concerned. There was no stopping her, so what else could we do but cheer her on?

We held the third Profiles in History auction on May 18, 2014, at the Debbie Reynolds Studios in North Hollywood. Cat and I drove down in the RV well ahead of time, with her "emotional therapy chicken" Nugget and my "service dog" Yippi, to set up for what we knew would be Mom's final auction. Mom hid her heartbreak at the previews as always; and at this particular event she was also hiding the fact that a couple of weeks before the auction, she fainted in her bathroom and literally fell on her face. She was very badly bruised and shaken, but there was never even a passing mention of postponing the auction. She, Carrie, Cat, Nugget, Yippi, and I posed on the red carpet for the press with big, happy smiles on our faces as if everything was going exactly as planned, because Mom would have killed us if we hadn't.

The third auction included Elvis Presley's grand piano; Harpo Marx's signature top hat and wig; and Mom's cherished Rat Pack suits, given to her by the Rat Pack themselves—Frank Sinatra, Dean Martin, Peter Lawford, Joey Bishop, and Sammy Davis Jr. At Mom's insistence, the five of them even tossed in their socks and underwear.

That auction pulled in a total of $2.6 million. Grand total for all three auctions: right around $30 million. I'll always believe that if she could have afforded it, Mom would have bought back every piece we sold.

Carrie (and her dog Gary, of course) headed off to London to start rehearsals for *Star Wars: The Force Awakens*. She was working out, getting in shape to bring Princess Leia back to life. She was even doing something she'd avoided for years: attending what she always referred to as "celebrity lap dances"—huge autograph conventions where thousands of fans would line up with photos, posters, books, T-shirts, hats, you name it, to be signed by their favorite stars. (The fans paid cash in exchange for the autographs, hence Carrie's lap-dance analogy.) She was also trying to keep herself and her medications balanced, sometimes successfully, sometimes not so much.

Mom was booked to play the South Point Hotel, Casino, and Spa in Las Vegas on November 11, 2014. She'd been performing there for the last few years; but by now she was really struggling health-wise, so she adjusted accordingly. No, she didn't cancel. Ever. She simply recruited Carrie, Billie, and me to perform with her, because "the show must go on."

I played guitar for Mom's country medley. We ran a great montage of film clips and home movies, and we chatted as if we were at home in our living room. And then Carrie, who'd orchestrated the whole show, walked onstage singing "I'll Never Say No" from *The Unsinkable Molly Brown*, not to the audience, but to Mom. Of course, since she was Carrie, she had to toss a couple of ad libs into the lyrics. "I'll weep if you want me sad" became "I'll weep 'cause I'm bi-polar," and she transformed "Today is tomorrow if you

want it so" into "Today is tomorrow if you've had too much blow."
Billie and Carrie did a sweet, beautiful duet of "How I Love My
Little Baby" from the Debbie Reynolds/Eddie Fisher film *Bundle
of Joy*; and the four of us closed the show with a rousing rendition
of "There's No Business Like Show Business."

There was one more surprise for the audience that night: Mom
announced that this would be her last performance in show business. There were a lot of protests from the audience, and a lot of
laughs as well from her die-hard fans who didn't believe it for a
second. Carrie and I, standing behind her onstage, were caught
completely off guard and exchanged a silent "Yeah, right." But as
it turned out, she was right—it really was her last performance.
She'd always believed in a great entrance and a great exit. She saw
to a great exit that night at the South Point, giving her audience
everything she still had in her and sharing the spotlight with her
children and granddaughter, because she wouldn't have had it any
other way.

And then, on January 25, 2015, the Screen Actors Guild held its
annual awards gala, at which Carrie would be presenting Mom with
the prestigious Life Achievement Award. It was a huge, nationally
televised honor; and, as Carrie pointed out, it's not as if the industry had exactly lavished Mom with awards for her amazing career.
She'd been nominated for one Oscar, five Golden Globes, and two
Emmys; and in 1998 she and Carrie and I won the American Film
Institute Platinum Circle Award, given to "families whose creative
contributions have significantly enhanced the entertainment community." It seemed as if everyone else on the planet had gone out
of their way to thank Mom for all she'd done for them, and she was
grateful for every single award she was given. But that her peers,
the fellow actors she loved and respected so much, were finally celebrating her with their highest distinction after sixty-seven years
in show business took our breath away.

Now all we had to do was get Mom to the gala and get her
through it. The chronic pain that had plagued her for years was

Carrie onstage at the South Point Casino during
Mom's last performance in show business.

getting worse, mystifying every highly recommended specialist from Beverly Hills to the Mayo Clinic; and Darvon, the one
medication that seemed to help, had been taken off the market. So
between her pain and the variety of new meds and ever-changing
doses she was on, she was in no shape, mentally or physically, for a
long, celebrity-filled press frenzy at the Shrine Auditorium, award
or no award.

Carrie wasn't faring too well either, as the SAG Awards drew
closer. She was at the rehearsal the night before, when we faced
a couple of realities together on the phone. At best, Mom would
never make it through an entire evening sitting at a table in the auditorium with the rest of the stars and nominees. We'd get her into
her seat at the table shortly before her award was announced, Carrie would introduce her, and then Mom would come up on stage
to accept it, with Carrie right there with her for support. (Mom's
edict to all of us when we were out in public: "Go ahead and put

your arm around me, but never let it look as if you're holding me up.") At worst, Mom wouldn't even be able to get out of bed, in which case Carrie would accept the award on her behalf.

Carrie broke down after we hung up the phone. There were times for her, and for me too, when it hit us like a ton of bricks that we had a new "normal" to adjust to when it came to our mother. It wasn't as if Mom was going to wake up one morning and be the strong, razor-sharp, energetic force of nature we'd always known again. So, hard and heartbreaking as it was, she was the mom we had now, and whatever happened, we'd love her and take care of her right through it, whatever it took.

Mom made it to the Shrine Auditorium that night. On the way there, she was disoriented and very weak. She couldn't stand on her own for more than a few seconds at a time, and obviously they wanted her onstage when she was presented with the award. So, thanks to some last-minute arrangements with the stage manager, I carried her up the steps to the stage and held her there while her film clips ran, with Carrie waiting for her beside the podium several feet away.

Then, the moment the film clips ended and the spotlight hit her, Debbie Reynolds stood up and walked to that podium on her own. She looked beautiful. There were only brief glimpses of her frailty and she glowed sharing the stage with Carrie. She basked in the lengthy standing ovation she received from her peers, and she cherished that SAG Life Achievement Award for the rest of her life, more than she could have ever expressed.

That night at the SAG Awards was the last sequence shot in *Bright Lights*. Mom had tried to shut down the project more than once, afraid it was turning into the puff piece she never wanted to do. Carrie was busy with *Star Wars* and had started to lose interest. But Fisher and Lexi were champions and kept it moving to the very end, and finally it was time to start the gargantuan job of shaping and editing it into the family love story it turned out to be.

The timing of making *Bright Lights* will always amaze me. It was and is a great lesson in diligence and not giving in to the bad habit of procrastination. As it turned out, if we'd waited just a few more months, it would have been too late.

It was August 14, 2015. Carrie was in London. Cat was back east, touring with her stage hypnosis show. Mom and I were at the Las Vegas house, relaxing in the pool after the daily thirty-minute swim we did together to try to rehab her, talking about how much she loved Vegas and discussing the possibility of spending even more time with us there. She'd been seeing my back doctor, Aury Nagy, a brilliant neurosurgeon who specialized in chronic back and neck pain; and while the cause of Mom's pain was still a mystery, she had faith in him and was feeling as if he might be the man to solve it.

That night, at about 1:00 A.M., Mom fell in her bathroom. Her pain escalated dramatically, particularly in the area of her gallbladder, and she was writhing by the time the ambulance got her to the hospital. I was in the ambulance with her, holding her hand, trying to stay calm through my fear, reassuring her as best I could as she barked out last-minute requests like "You'll take [her dog] Dwight, right?" She clearly thought it was the end for her, and I wasn't sure she was wrong.

She was given an MRI within minutes after we got to the emergency room. Dr. Nagy studied the results and discovered that not only had she cracked a rib, but she also had a cyst on her spine, a previously undetected cyst that could easily have been the root of the pain she'd been suffering for all these years.

He wanted to operate immediately. She was eighty-three, so there were obvious risks. But she was hearing glimmers of hope that maybe, finally, someone might be on the verge of curing her pain instead of just treating it, and her response to consenting to surgery wasn't yes, it was hell, yes.

The operation on her back was a success. Her recovery was slow, but not even postsurgical pain and medication could stand in the way of her being Debbie Reynolds. She was lying in her hospital bed, groggy and only half awake, when a call came in from Cheryl Boone Isaacs, president of the Academy of Motion

Picture Arts and Sciences. Ms. Isaacs was calling to announce that the Academy had chosen Mom to be the recipient of their distinguished Jean Hersholt Humanitarian Award, honoring "an individual in the motion picture industry whose humanitarian efforts have brought credit to the industry." I was ecstatic when I put the phone to Mom's ear and asked Ms. Isaacs to repeat what she'd just told me. I recorded their conversation and played it at the 2016 Academy Awards Governors Ball when Billie proudly accepted the Jean Hersholt Humanitarian Award on Mom's behalf and Carrie and I beamed from the Governors table.

It was about three weeks after surgery when we discovered that Mom's "slow recovery" was actually a stroke that had probably happened either during or immediately after the operation. Her ability to communicate came and went, but there was one thing she was adamant about—she wanted to go home. And no doubt about it, we wanted her there. We set up a fully equipped hospital room in her house on our compound in Las Vegas, hired a staff of round-the-clock nurses, and bought and customized a Mercedes SUV so she'd have a bed to lie in when we transported her from one place to another and made the daily Baskin-Robbins run she insisted on. Then we settled in to take the hard ride of loving and caring for the victim of a significant stroke.

If you've been there, you know how hard it is. Part of you prays they'll pull out of it and be themselves again. Part of you tries to make peace with the fact that it may never happen, no matter how unsinkable they are. And whichever way it goes, it's part of your new reality to get used to the idea of not knowing from one day or one hour to the next who they'll be when you come walking into their room.

For a few weeks Mom didn't speak or move.

There were good days, and there were bad days, with several trips to the hospital in between.

Mom loved to watch TV, and one night we put on Leonardo DiCaprio's *The Aviator* for her. The instant she realized it was about Howard Hughes, her eyes lit up and she said, "You know,

Mr. Hughes gave me my very first job." She then proceeded to tell the long, fascinating, incredibly detailed story of her history with Howard Hughes as if it she'd just finished writing about it in her *My Life* memoir a few hours earlier.

The next morning, she and Cat were lying in bed watching TV when Mom reached over, took Cat's hand, and asked, "Dear, how are we related?" Cat explained that she was my wife, her daughter-in-law, to which Mom replied, "I'm so glad, you're a wonderful girl." Cat always made a point of tucking Mom's feet under the covers, and Mom would say, as if it was occurring to her for the first time, "No one ever tucked me in in my whole life." She never said good-bye to Cat without a farewell "You're such a good girl," the exact words she said after their first dinner together.

Then she went through a phase when, out of nowhere, something seemed to take over her mind and she'd be mean, lashing out, even biting and hitting the nurses, with no memory of it when the episode passed. One particularly scary day, Mom had absolutely no idea who she was, no connection at all to her own identity. Without batting an eye, Cat announced, "Boy, do I have good news for you!" and happily filled her in, explaining that she was Debbie Reynolds, loved by millions of people all over the world, that she sang and she danced and she lived to entertain people. Mom listened and nodded, but it didn't seem to be ringing any bells. So we spent the day with her and threw her her own Debbie Reynolds film festival, starting with *The Unsinkable Molly Brown*, and sometime during that magical marathon a lightbulb clicked on again. Who she was came back to her while she watched herself on the screen, and Cat was right, she took it as very good news.

And then came a time when she spoke only one word: "Go." Sometimes she'd say it urgently. Sometimes she'd say it quietly. Sometimes she'd say it angrily, and then again pleasantly, within minutes. We couldn't figure out what she meant by it, if she was trying to tell us she wanted us to take her somewhere or if she was trying to tell us to leave.

Cat was alone with her one morning when, after days of nothing but "Go," Mom said, clear as a bell, "I have something to say." She repeated it emphatically, while Cat gaped at her and yelled for me.

I ran in from the next room. Mom looked right at me, and she couldn't have been less equivocal and more matter-of-fact.

"I don't want to do this anymore," she told me. "I don't want to be here. I don't want to live like this. I don't want to struggle like this. No more 'rah-rah' [pep talks]. Just let me go." And with that, her eyes began to roll back, and she actually started to fade out and "leave the building."

Next thing I knew I was on the bed, practically on top of my mother, one arm behind her shoulders to lift them, the other hand on the back of her head to hold her face an inch from mine.

"No, Mom. You're not going anywhere. You have things to do here, we need you here, you want to be here. You're just going through a really hard time healing, and you're tired of it. You have every right to be, but that's all that's happening. You're not leaving us. You're staying right here."

When Cat and I were alone again, she told me it was like watching someone on the verge of flatlining being resuscitated with words and love. It was a long, hard fight, but from that moment on, Mom started working her way back to us. A few months later, when she was lucid again, she confirmed that she'd heard every word I said and thanked us, not just for keeping her alive but for making her live.

20

FULL CIRCLE

Together on stage at Lincoln Center— Carrie,
Gary, me, and Mom via cell phone.

Mom's stroke devastated Carrie. She made the trips from
London and L.A. to Las Vegas as often as she possibly
could, and it was comforting and stressful for both of
them. It always comforted them to be together. But it was stressful for Carrie to keep trying to find her mom through the haze
the stroke had left behind, and stressful for Mom to keep trying to
fight through that haze and be the mom her daughter knew.

When Carrie decided she wanted to take Mom back to L.A.,
back to Mom's other house right next door, it worried me for both

of them, but I wasn't about to argue. It went without saying that even though she still had a lot of *Star Wars* traveling left to do, Carrie would make sure Mom had everything she needed, twenty-four hours a day. Mom would be in a home she loved; Carrie and Mom would be neighbors again, together, where they belonged; and Cat and I wouldn't exactly be disappearing either.

Once all the arrangements had been made, we transported Mom to Los Angeles in her van, into her house, into her bed. She settled back against the pillows and looked around her bedroom, the bedroom she'd taken such joy in decorating over the years. It was good to see her face relax into a contented smile.

"Carrie's house is so nice." She sighed.

"This isn't Carrie's house, Mom, it's yours, don't you remember?" I asked her.

She shook her head. It was news to her.

I wasn't about to push her, but I wanted to see if I could get her to connect to something. I pointed to the stained-glass windows.

"Christi made those for you, remember?"

Her eyes lit right up. "Of course, dear," she said, as if it was the dumbest question she'd heard all day.

Every glimmer of proof that she was still in there made me smile, but God, I missed my mom.

With Mom just steps away again, Carrie became territorial of her, as if she could protect Mom and herself from her terror of losing her by taking charge of everything and everyone around her. She'd kick the nurses out of Mom's room when she was there so that she and Mom could be alone together, and she kept Mom fairly sequestered. Mom, who'd been trained by the studios as a teenager to never, ever be seen by anyone looking less than movie star gorgeous, had shockingly stopped caring about her hair and makeup, and Carrie wasn't about to let her be seen looking less than perfect. It was a fascinating evolution of their relationship, not one either of them would have chosen, but in a way something that drew them even closer to each other. Mom got the incredibly attentive, tender,

Mom's Coldwater Canyon house, just steps away from Carrie's.

loving daughter she'd always wanted; and Carrie got the mother she didn't have to compete with or risk disappointing anymore, the mother who just adored her and needed her, the parent she could deeply connect with by parenting, like she'd experienced parenting Eddie five years earlier.

Cat and I were dividing our time between Las Vegas, the ranch, and L.A. Carrie's *Star Wars* obligations still demanded a lot of trips back and forth to London, and Cat started scheduling her visits to Mom's based on whether or not Carrie would be there. Mom noticed and asked Cat about it.

Cat explained gently that she and Carrie had never really bonded and that she didn't feel welcome or comfortable at Mom's when Carrie was around. "But please don't worry about this," she added. "It's not your problem. I'll talk to Carrie about it one of these days."

Mom took Cat's hand and said, "Oh no, dear, don't do that. It will make Carrie cry."

Privately, Cat didn't really believe that anything she could do or say would make Carrie cry, but she kept her promise to Mom and didn't have that talk with Carrie.

Apparently Mom did. Several days later Federal Express

delivered a package in Las Vegas from Carrie to Cat. Cat's jaw hit the floor when she opened it to find a huge gorgeous glass rooster, in honor of Nugget.

She immediately sent Carrie a long thank-you email. Carrie wrote back within minutes, several thoughtful paragraphs that were essentially an apology. In part it read, "I guess you're a lot like me—you probably wouldn't know this, but I'm very sensitive, and I always jump to the worst thought first." It was important to her that Cat know she had no idea she'd been making her feel unliked and uncomfortable. By the time the email exchange between them ended, they'd made a pact that they were going to get to know each other, and that they were both looking forward to it.

From then on, Carrie never came back from London without bringing a present for Cat, from more giant roosters to clothes to a rooster apron. Cat kept trying to reciprocate, but one of the countless interesting facts about Carrie is that she loved giving gifts exactly as much as she hated receiving them.

Carrie and Cat never really did have a chance to get to know each other, but there was a very sweet kindness between them for that next year, and no unfinished business, which is the gift Cat cherishes most of all.

And speaking of unfinished business, I made a promise to myself that I intend to keep.

Mom and Cat were lying in Mom's bed one day having one of their talks when Mom excitedly told Cat that RJ, aka Robert Wagner, was coming over the next day.

"I can't wait to see him," Mom said, and then, after a pause, added, "Do you think I should tell him how I feel?"

Cat asked her what she meant.

"I want him to know that I'm in love with him. I went out with him before I met Eddie, remember? I've held this in my whole life, and it's high time I say something, don't you think?"

"I'm not sure that's a good idea, Mom," Cat told her. "You know he's married, right?"

Mom smiled at that. "I don't want him to leave his wife and be with me, dear. I just believe people should know how you feel."

Cat simply nodded, and they left it at that.

The next evening Cat called Josephine Bouchard, Mom's amazing, indispensable nurse, to ask how the visit with Robert Wagner went. Josephine didn't know what she was talking about. Robert Wagner hadn't come for a visit, nor was he ever planning to come for a visit. It was simply one of the post-stroke fantasies Mom had from time to time, very real to her when she talked about them but not so real that she was disappointed when they didn't happen.

So there you go, RJ. Debbie Reynolds loved you all her life. She never got the chance to tell you, but "people should know how you feel."

And there you go, Mom. Message delivered.

There was one high point as the year drew to a close—Carrie called and asked if I would escort her and Billie to the Hollywood premiere of *Star Wars: The Force Awakens*. She got an immediate "I'd love to."

It was December 14, 2015. Half a mile of Hollywood Boulevard was closed off. Masses of fans started camping out two weeks ahead of time in anticipation of the long-awaited *Star Wars* rebirth; and crowds of fans and the press swarmed the entrances of the Dolby, the Chinese, and the El Capitan, the three theaters where the movie was being debuted that night.

A loud roar of cheers greeted Carrie as she and Billie and I emerged from the limo and walked the red carpet and the gauntlet of media together. We finally settled into our seats in the beautiful Dolby Theatre, and when Carrie reached over to hold my hand I instantly flashed back to 1977. Suddenly my sister and I were at that first *Star Wars* screening on the 20th Century Fox lot, nervously holding hands, praying to God this sci-fi movie we were about to watch wouldn't be embarrassing, and this Princess Leia character wouldn't destroy Carrie's career. Now here we sat, thirty-eight years later, looking forward to the latest edition of one of the most successful franchises in film history. Princess Leia had become iconic, and as Carrie said on the way home that night, with nothing short of amazement, "Remember when I'd never been Princess Leia before? Now I'm going to be her forever."

It was an unforgettable evening. Literally. I was so proud of my girls—my sister and my gorgeous niece, who had a cameo role in *The Force Awakens*. I can't count the number of times it flashed through my mind how I would have traded places in a heartbeat with the girl who deserved to be there most of all, the one without whom Carrie and Billie and I wouldn't even have existed, the one who was home in bed in Coldwater Canyon, struggling like hell to be Debbie Reynolds again.

In the spring of 2016 I showed Mom the final cut of *Bright Lights*, before its world premiere at the Cannes Film Festival on May 14.

She didn't really understand what she was looking at. She was delighted by some of the archive footage—home movies from when Carrie and I were little children, Carrie and I spending Christmas at the Great Wall of China, our family trip to Europe with Harry, Carrie onstage at age thirteen (beautifully) singing "Bridge Over Troubled Waters," things like that. But then there Mom would be on-screen, present tense, talking into the camera, or there I'd be, showing some of her memorabilia, and it thoroughly confused her. And she didn't appreciate one bit that there was Carrie, on film, singing about being bipolar and having a manic episode in a scene with her manicurists.

"What's that doing in there?" she demanded, accompanied by *the look*.

I reminded her that it was reassuring for a lot of people with the same mental illness Carrie had that she was so open about it and let audiences see it in action, rather than hiding it as if it were something to be ashamed of. "Helping people" was one of Mom's most easily accessible buttons to push, particularly after her decades with the Thalians, so that reminder calmed her down.

In the end, *Bright Lights* was okay with her . . . whatever the hell that strange, unscripted format was.

Carrie, on the other hand, was given one rough cut of *Bright*

Lights after another. She already had a notoriously limited attention span. Now she was also so scattered, between *Star Wars* and travel and the upcoming release of her book *The Princess Diarist* and taking care of Mom, that she kept not getting around to watching the whole thing. Fisher and Lexi talked to her about it any time she wanted, and she looked at segments of it here and there, in no particular order. But then some shiny object would come along and distract her until it crossed her mind again. Oh, well. Not my problem. We were taking *Bright Lights* to the Telluride Film Festival in September, she'd see it then.

Wrong again. She missed the screenings but made it to two of the three Q&As. At first I was told she was suffering from a case of altitude sickness. Later, when there was an emergency drama about having her meds flown in because she'd run out of them, I found out that her assistant Freddie had brought exactly the right amount of medication she'd need for the several days we'd be there, but Carrie had blasted through them in the first couple of days. I didn't confront her about it. Been there, done that, got the *What's the Point?* T-shirt. And I wasn't going to start any drama between us when we were taking a special trip together before we left Telluride.

There's a small, beautiful town in Colorado called Ouray, about fifty miles from Telluride, that's hallowed ground to our family.

When Carrie and I were very little, Mom shot a movie called *How the West Was Won*, in the hills around and above Ouray. A couple of years later *The Unsinkable Molly Brown* was shot in the same area. We were among the few lucky children of movie stars whose moms loved taking them on location, and Grandma was there to keep an eye on us when Mom was busy filming.

Mom and Grandma fell so in love with that part of Colorado that they bought some land between Ridgway and Ouray, and Grandpaw built a house there. The family spent the Fourth of July and a lot of other happy, magical holidays at that house with Grandpaw and Grandma; and when I was seventeen I bought my first piece of property right down the street from the Ouray house, property I still own and still treasure. Rene and I went there together. Christi and I spent time there, and at her request, some of her ashes were spread on that land. Cat and I have taken many trips to Ouray and will take many more.

But being there with Carrie in September of 2016, walking those streets together that we'd walked with Mom and our grandparents when we were tiny and life was perfect, was incredibly golden for both of us, a day I'll never forget.

We had one more stop to make before we headed back to Telluride. It's a place called Deb's Meadow, in Mom's honor, at a marked turnout above Ridgway, just below the summit of Chimney Rock, and its name is displayed on a wooden sign on a tree. Mom and Robert Preston shot a romantic scene there in *How the West Was Won*. Harve Presnell sang "I'll Never Say No" to Mom in that meadow in *The Unsinkable Molly Brown*. (I stood in that exact spot and sang "I'll Never Say No" to Cat on our first trip there.) John Wayne famously rode across Deb's Meadow, his horse's reins in his teeth, a Colt Peacemaker in each hand, taking on four outlaws in the classic 1969 Western *True Grit*. Carrie and I never went to Ouray or Telluride or anywhere else within striking distance without a special visit to Deb's Meadow.

I'd just shifted the four-wheel-drive Range Rover into park at the Meadow's entrance when my cell phone rang. I answered it to hear, "Hi, dear. It's your mother. Debbie."

It was such uncanny timing that I almost dropped the phone. So did Mom, when I told her where we were. It wasn't a long conversation, but it was long enough for both Carrie and me to say, "Thank you for bringing us here," and tell her how much it meant to us that, even when she had the massive responsibility of starring in a major motion picture, she never left any doubt in anyone's minds, including ours, that we came first, that we were her best pals and her favorite sidekicks. Whatever she was part of, we were part of, the most important people in the vast universe of Debbie Reynolds, no matter what. Like countless other locations, Deb's Meadow wasn't where Carrie and I watched Mom make movies. It was another beautiful place where Mom and Carrie and I were together while

Mom and Harve Presnell filming
The Unsinkable Molly Brown in Deb's Meadow.

Mom made movies, and I'll always believe that somehow, with a mom's internal GPS, she knew where we were that day and had no intention of letting us take a trip to Deb's Meadow without her.

I still think of that phone call at that exact moment, and it still gives me chills.

Carrie finally saw *Bright Lights*. Or at least part of it.

It was October 10, 2016, at the New York Film Festival at

Lincoln Center. Carrie flew in for the occasion, as did one of the film's executive producers, the extraordinary Sheila Nevins of HBO. Sheila and Carrie had formed their own mutual admiration society when Sheila executive-produced Carrie's *Wishful Drinking* documentary for HBO, and we were proud and grateful to have her on board when *Bright Lights* got under way.

The theater was filled with an upbeat, enthusiastic crowd that night. Carrie and Sheila and I were excited when they settled into their seats behind me, the lights dimmed, and the screening started. It was rolling along beautifully until Carrie found herself watching, for the first time, the scene between her and Eddie.

In 2010, three months before Eddie died, when Carrie was in Berkeley helping to take care of him, she decided she wanted to shoot a completely unscripted, spontaneous conversation between the two of them. Eddie was in bed, on oxygen, heavily medicated and only marginally coherent, and Carrie was beside his bed, adoring him, baring her soul to him. Her walls were down, and all her defenses were gone. It was right there on-screen for everyone to see that Eddie was Carrie's kryptonite. She told him, without a trace of blame or resentment, that she'd believed as a child that if she was funny enough and engaging enough, he wouldn't leave. She confessed that she'd always wanted to be his best girl, but the competition was pretty tough—"although I'm funnier than Elizabeth Taylor." She asked him, almost begged him, to tell her he loved her. "I'm crazy about you," he said, and it was almost as heart-wrenching to watch as it had been for her to go through it six years earlier.

It was too much for Carrie. She was out of her seat and out of the theater before the scene was over. Sheila and I were right behind her and comforted her backstage, and she managed to pull herself together by the time the film ended and the post-screening Q&A session started. No way was I going to say, "Why the hell didn't you screen the rough cuts when you had the chance so you wouldn't have been ambushed like this?" It was so beside the point. I just hated seeing her so torn up by it that night.

Mom, of course, was three thousand miles away when we

screened *Bright Lights* at Lincoln Center, and it killed her not to be there, especially when she was having a fairly good day. So during the Q&A session, someone asked, "How's your mom?" and I said, "I'm afraid no one but Mom could answer that . . . so let's ask her," and I grabbed my cell phone and called her. Carrie looked at me, panic-stricken—there was no way of knowing how coherent Mom would be at any given moment. But when she answered, and I held the phone up to the mike and told her where Carrie and I were and what we were doing, she didn't just rise to the occasion, she blew the room away by bursting into a happy, spontaneous, a cappella rendition of "I've Got You Under My Skin." The audience went wild, Carrie and I exchanged "holy shit!" grins and Mom had a fantastic time answering questions and interacting with the crowd for a few more minutes. It meant so much to the audience, and to Mom, that it gave me an idea for the next *Bright Lights* event at the San Francisco Film Festival on November 3, 2016.

We'd already set up a 60-inch TV for Mom in her bedroom in L.A., with a camera on top of it so that we could Skype with her (once our great old friend and IT guy Mark Shepherd was there to set it up for her—she was unapologetically low-tech) when we were at the ranch or in Vegas or on the road. So that night in San Francisco, during the Q&A session, I replied to a question by saying, "That's something only Mom could answer, and un-fortunately, she's not here. . . . Oh, wait, she is here!" And with that, Debbie Reynolds appeared on the screen, live and beaming, hair and makeup by Uncle Bill for the occasion, the ever-present Dwight in her lap, ready to interact with and be nourished by a theater full of the fans she loved, and one more massive, joyful standing ovation for an unsinkable woman who, right to the end, never took them for granted.

Just as there was "no such word as *can't* in our family," there was also no such thing as an understated holiday or birthday in our fam-ily if Mom had anything to say about it. She pulled out all the stops, and then some, for every special occasion, whether we wanted her to or not; and if you'll recall from earlier in this book, I've got photos of the hired Santa Claus, and Eddie and me in matching velour pullovers on our way to a puppet show, to prove it. And if we thought a little inconvenience like a stroke was going to stand in her way, we couldn't have been more mistaken.

October 21, 2016, was Carrie's sixtieth birthday. Not just any birthday, obviously, and it wouldn't surprise me to learn that Mom was trying behind our backs to have it declared a national holiday. Carrie was on overload with *Star Wars* and *Princess Diarist* commitments, I was on overload with *Bright Lights* and other commitments, and there wasn't a chance that an appropriate bash could be held on the actual day. So schedules were checked and double-checked and coordinated, and it was finally decided that Carrie's sixtieth birthday party would be held at Carrie's house on November 19, 2016.

It was going to be huge. Gigantic. Monumental. Ice sculptures? Hell, yes. Bubble machines? Bring 'em. If it was spectacular and belonged at a party, book it. And Mom set about inviting everybody. By everybody, I mean everybody, including Carrie's childhood Girl Scout troop. Mom was so excited, not just to be orchestrating something very important for Carrie but also to be doing something productive, to be waking up every morning with a purpose for the first time since her stroke. The fact that planning this party was stressful and tiring, even with all of us pitching in to help with what few details Mom would delegate, paled in comparison to the light it put back in her eyes.

Carrie, in the meantime, wanted absolutely no part of it. She was busy in London filming *Star Wars: The Last Jedi*, on top of which her book *The Princess Diarist* was being released on November 22. She was scheduled for a full lineup of appearances and book signings when she wasn't on the *Star Wars* set, and there was no way she was going to squeeze in a quick round-trip from London to L.A. for a birthday party she hadn't asked for in the first place.

She was dug in about it, and so was I. I was on Mom's side, and on Mom's end, watching the extraordinary efforts she was making to give her daughter the best party ever. I knew it would devastate her if Carrie refused to be there, and Mom was too frail for us to take the age-old "she'll get over it" position anymore. I didn't give a rat's ass how inconvenient it was, how much rescheduling it took, or whether or not Carrie felt like it. After all our mother had done for us all our lives, Carrie could damn well get her ass on a plane and give her the pleasure of throwing her a damned birthday party—period, end of discussion, buh-bye.

Carrie came back at me, just as hard and just as furious. Typical Todd, doing Mom's bidding, and to hell with what anyone else wants or feels. The whole stupid thing couldn't have been happening at a worse time, considering her schedule. The last thing she needed was being surrounded in her own house by a bazillion people, some of whom she hadn't seen since she was about twelve years old; and furthermore, she wasn't coming—leave me alone, fuck you, etc.

I finally had to break the news to Mom that Carrie wasn't one bit happy about this party and that she was threatening not to come. Mom called Carrie. I didn't hear their conversation, but by the time they hung up, Carrie had done a complete 180-degree turn and decided to come after all. She was still pissed off at me and told me I'd have to be in charge of everyone at the party she didn't know, including the Girl Scouts. Whatever, fine with me, as long as she wasn't going to disappoint Mom I would have agreed to just about anything.

The bottom line: It was a fantastic party. Crowded, absolutely, but really fantastic. Carrie stayed in her bedroom for the most part and held court, occasionally wandering through the house to say hello to the guests and then heading straight back to her bedroom again. Mom was in great form, all things considered, holding court in the living room, enchanting everyone with story after story and relishing every second of finding herself in World Class Hostess mode again on behalf of her cherished daughter. She knew it would exhaust her and take her days to recover. She didn't care. It was more than worth it as far as she was concerned.

The party didn't end until the wee hours of the morning. Cat had taken Mom home, tucked her into bed, and stayed with her while she fell asleep. The guests had all left. Finally it was just Carrie and me, alone in the house, after an evening of paying little or no attention to each other.

Carrie came up behind me. I turned around to look at her and was surprised to see that she was in tears.

"I can't do this," she said. "I can't have this tension between us. I can't have you and me being mad at each other."

She went on to talk about the fact that a day would come, we had no way of knowing how soon, when Mom would be gone, when it would be just the two of us, and we were going to need each other more than we ever had in our lives.

"I need you to know that I'm not mad at you anymore, and I need to know that you're not mad at me anymore either. I need to know that we're good. Please? We're good, right?"

Of course we were. We always had been. We always would be, not just to honor Mom's memory someday but because the childhood tenderness between us was our beautiful, indestructible default. Carrie was my girl, and no matter how much we fought or how pissed off we might get at each other, nothing would or could ever change that.

"We're good," I said. I didn't need to say the rest of it out loud. She already knew it all by heart.

It was the last face-to-face conversation my sister and I ever had.

The next time Mom and I saw Carrie, she was on life support.

21

GOOD-BYE, DEAR

"What a glorious feeling. I'm happy again."

Artist Ricky LaChance's touching illustration of Mom and Carrie.
(illustration courtesy of Ricky LaChance, etsy.com/market/ricky_lachance)

O n Friday, December 23, 2016, Cat and I had just arrived at the Niner winery in Paso Robles for lunch when my cell phone rang. It was Carrie's assistant Corby McCoin. I stepped outside to take the call. Corby was so frantic it was hard to follow what she was saying, but I got enough. Carrie had suffered some kind of major episode and lost consciousness on the plane home from London, and they couldn't resuscitate her. Corby was following the ambulance from LAX to Cedars-Sinai, and I needed to get there ASAP.

I raced back into the restaurant, told Cat what was happening, and ran to my Range Rover. I made the three-hour drive to L.A. in just under two hours, while my cell phone rang nonstop with reporters trying to reach me. I answered a couple of times, if only for a break in the noise, and explained that I was on my way to the hospital and didn't know anything beyond the fact that Carrie was in intensive care and I assumed they were trying to stabilize her. Within minutes, thanks to typical creative editing on the part of the press, I was being widely quoted as saying that Carrie was in "stable condition." What?

Bryan and Billie were already there, distraught, when I got to the ICU at Cedars. Carrie's bed was in a semi-inclined position. They'd restarted her heart, her body temperature had been dropped to protect her brain, and she was on life support. It shocked me to see her, not because she looked terrible, but because she didn't. She looked perfect. Somehow, except for the tubes that were keeping her alive, she looked as if she might open her eyes at any moment, jump out of bed, and ask me to sneak her out of there and floor it to the nearest Baskin-Robbins.

Mom arrived a few minutes after I got there. Another shock—she was sharp as a tack, by far the most lucid I'd seen her since her stroke, and she was totally composed as she sat by Carrie's bed and held her hand. I stood nearby and watched the two of them, trying to wrap my head around what was happening, and the fact that, impossibly, Mom had seen it coming.

Everyone who was very close to Mom knew about an unusual gift, or burden, of hers: she had prophetic dreams. They weren't always 100 percent accurate, but they came true often enough that when she'd announce she'd had a dream, we'd silently pray, "Dear God, please let it be a good one."

When Carrie and her assistant took off for London on business that December, it was part of Carrie's plan to take a side trip to Belgium for a vacation before heading back to London for a *Princess Diarist* book signing. Mom couldn't remember specifics of the dream she'd had about that side trip, she just knew it sent her into a panic. She tried desperately for a week to reach Carrie to beg her not to go to Belgium, to simply stay in London and then fly straight home after the book signing so she'd be in L.A. with us for Christmas; but sometimes when Carrie was away from us, she'd detach and not want to talk to us until it was her idea.

Finally Mom's assistant Donald Light was able to connect the two of them. Mom didn't want to scare Carrie by telling her about her ominous dream, so she simply tried to discourage her from the Belgium idea by emphasizing how much she wanted her home, that we were all waiting for her, fun, fun, fun, holidays, holidays, holidays, and, and, and. But Carrie had it in her mind that she was taking a vacation in Belgium, and off Carrie went for a vacation in Belgium. Period.

Another of Mom's dreams in that same time frame was more specific. She dreamed that Carrie's plane went down on her flight back to Los Angeles, and Carrie didn't survive. She wasn't sure of the specifics, she was just sure Carrie was in grave danger on that plane. She was terrified the whole time Carrie was gone and praying nonstop when she was finally on her way home. And now here she was, the daughter Mom loved more than life itself, comatose in the ICU, machines keeping her alive, after collapsing on a plane from London as it made its descent into LAX.

It was bizarre, almost eerie, to try to imagine that Mom had been given some otherworldly warning of what was coming for Carrie. Then again, considering the otherworldly connection between my girls, I didn't doubt it.

We got back to Mom's and Carrie's side-by-side houses to find a massive crush of reporters, photographers, and fans blocking Coldwater Canyon and the gate to the property, all of them yelling questions and pushing and shoving for position. Thankfully, Bryan had already put in an urgent call to Gavin de Becker, an old, fiercely loyal friend of Carrie's, Mom's, and mine. Gavin's a re-nowned security specialist, the best of the best, and he and his team were already on their way for twenty-four-hour-a-day patrol, both at home and at the hospital, for as long as we needed them.

I can't begin to count the number of times we went back and forth to Cedars-Sinai, or the relentless number of phone calls that were flooding in. Carrie's closest friends, who'd been given a pass-word to get into the trauma center where she was, started showing up and holding vigil. Cat arrived from the ranch and held down the fort at Carrie's house, deliberately staying away from the hos-pital to leave space in the crowded waiting room and hallway for those who'd been in Carrie's life for decades. We were all on auto-matic pilot, in too much shock to let ourselves process the reality of what was going on.

And then there was Mom, still lucid, still composed, insisting that we go ahead with our traditional Christmas Eve dinner at home the next night, exactly as planned. There was no point in arguing with her, no reason to remind her that Carrie had only collapsed and been put on life support the day before—she hadn't slipped into denial or stroke-induced amnesia about it, she was very well aware of it, and we were having a proper Christmas Eve dinner, period. So she and Cat and Uncle Bill and I went through the motions of a somber, quiet meal together, Mom even wearing a pair of silly moose antlers at the table. The only conversation I remember was Mom's wanting to be reassured that yes, Carrie's Christmas present was wrapped and waiting for her in Mom's bed-room.

Mom agonized every year over what to get Carrie for Christ-mas, and that year I'd had a brainstorm about a gift from both of us. Carrie collected what she called "paintings of ugly children." Her walls were covered with gilt-framed portraits of past-century, velvet-costumed, somber-looking boys dressed in girls' cloth-ing, and she delighted in pointing out their resemblance to Shia LaBeouf as an underage Dutch prostitute, Richard Dreyfuss as a young girl holding a rose, Ross Perot in a red gown, etc. I happened to find a high-end "painting of an ugly child" at an auction a few weeks earlier that Mom and I knew she'd love, and it was to be our mutual present to her for Christmas 2016.

Mom was exhausted by the time we finished dinner, so Cat took her home, tucked her into bed, and then sat there beside her, quietly marveling at her. Finally she couldn't resist asking the obvious question: "Mom, how are you doing this? How are you managing to hold it together like this, with everything that's going on?"

If there had been any doubt about Mom's clarity before that moment, it vanished with her answer.

"You see, dear," she said, "I can't allow my emotions to take over. This situation is so sad and so dire that if I give in to my emotions, it will kill me, and then I won't be here for her. If she comes out of this, she's going to need months of physical and emotional therapy because of her brain being without oxygen for so long, and I'm going to be here for every minute of it."

Cat took Mom's hand while Mom added, "You know I talk to God every single night. And now I'm asking Him if I could please have a little more time with Carrie, not when she's in a coma but when she's herself, even if it's just for a day or two."

We said the same prayer when we sank into bed that night, not for ourselves but for Mom. She said many times, for as long as I could remember, that her greatest fear was outliving her children. It wasn't just her daughter clinging to life in a hospital room, it was an essential part of herself, and the thought of my mom's greatest fear coming true was unbearable.

We wandered through Christmas Day and the day after. Round trips between the ever-present crowds on Coldwater Canyon and the ever-present crowds at Cedars-Sinai became our new normal, and every hour that passed without that dreaded phone call from Carrie's doctors was giving me more and more hope. Yes, she was still on life support, but I really believed she'd pull out of this, because she was Carrie, because she was my girl. She always pulled out of these things. I'd seen her do it with my own eyes, how many times? Why should this time be any different?

Billie, Bryan, and I were in the private family room on Monday when one of her doctors brought us Carrie's toxicology report and started to explain it to us. He wasn't even two sentences into it when the three of us held up our hands to stop him, silently gesturing "We don't need to hear this. We already know." There were a whole lot of drugs in her system, and sadly, it didn't surprise me. Days earlier, I'd found the coat Carrie was wearing on the plane. I absently picked it up, reached into one of the pockets, and found a small piece of paper, folded over and over into a tiny square. I'd seen Carrie with those before. Sure enough, when I discreetly unfolded it, there were the traces of fine white powder I expected to find there. I didn't say a word to anyone about it. I just folded it up again and slipped it back into Carrie's coat pocket.

It was no secret among us that Carrie had never really stopped self-medicating. Even Mom knew that, she just chose not to discuss it. The only thing I hadn't been sure of, until she disappeared for two days at Telluride, was whether or not she was letting it get out of control. Given what I found in her coat pocket and what little remained of it, one could be left with the conclusion that maybe Carrie had finally pushed the envelope too far one too many times.

Bryan sprang into action when we saw the toxicology report, engaging an attorney to make sure everything possible was done to protect its contents. We'll never know how or who, but there seems to be someone at every hospital in Los Angeles who's willing, for a fee, to leak confidential patient information to someone in the press. Despite Bryan's best efforts, the word was out, and the tabloids had their usual field day.

I spent some private time with Carrie in her room before I left. I'd been talking to her nonstop whenever we were alone together, whether she heard me or not. Mom had remembered every word I said to her when she seemed so out of it after her stroke, and she'd thanked me later for "bringing her back." If it worked on Mom, why wouldn't it work on Carrie?

"Don't you leave me here alone," I told her that night, half expecting her to open her eyes for her little brother. When she didn't, I leaned over, put my lips next to her ear, and whispered those words from our childhood with Mrs. Yang, words that meant nothing to anyone else and a lifetime of memories to us: "I love-ally you, bay-bay."

It was very early the next morning, Tuesday, December 27, 2016, when I got an urgent call from the hospital: For the first time since the previous Friday on the plane, Carrie had gone into cardiac arrest. Mom was sound asleep, and I slipped out without disturbing her.

Billie and Bryan were already there when I walked into the family room. About twenty doctors were there as well, and one of them was explaining that they'd been raising Carrie's body temperature when her heart stopped, but they were able to bring her back. He left the room, and we exhaled, until he reappeared a handful of minutes later, to tell us she'd had another cardiac arrest, but they were working on her and she seemed stable again. The same thing happened a third time, and then a fourth, an absolute roller-coaster ride from hell in less than an hour.

The doctors were amazing, incredibly compassionate and invested in getting Carrie and us through this as best they could. They'd given Carrie fairly good chances over the past few days. But that morning, after that last cardiac arrest, one of them walked into the room again, and it was apparent from the look on his face that he hated what he had to tell us.

"I've got to give you the facts here," he said. "Every time her heart fails, and every time we bring her back, it's hard to calculate the damage it's doing to her brain. It's a diminishing return, and you have a right to know that the odds of her coming back fully are significantly reduced."

He never said the words "You should think about letting her go." He never needed to. He managed to communicate it gently with his tone and his manner. We got the message, and there was nothing more to say.

I'll always hate it that it was up to Billie to make the decision.

It's an awful burden I wouldn't wish on my worst enemy, let alone my beautiful young niece, who'd already been through more than she should have. She was brave enough and loved her mother enough to do the most unselfish, most loving thing. By the time I walked into Carrie's room several minutes later, she was surrounded by what seemed like half the hospital personnel, the machines had been turned off, and my sister had silently slipped away.

It was still early morning, and Mom was in bed. All I remember about the drive home from the hospital was the urgency of it—it was unthinkable that she would hear on the news, or from anyone else but me, that Carrie was gone.

She was awake when I walked into her room. She anxiously watched me take every step, already anticipating what I was going to say.

I knelt beside her bed and simply said, "We lost her."

She was silent for a second. Then I put my head on her chest and she quietly replied, "I really hoped that we'd have more time with her."

She didn't cry. I did.

We sat together for the rest of the day. She was razor-sharp, as sharp as I'd seen her in years, and she had a lot on her mind, about her last wishes.

Mom had been planning her own death for fifty years. She had the most detailed, exhaustive, specific will her attorneys had ever seen; and she regularly refined it and adjusted it to keep it current. It was a long-running joke between me and Carrie that if you were walking through Mom's house and your eyes happened to land on something for more than about two seconds, Mom would say, "Oh, do you like that, dear? I'll leave it for you in my will," and put a sticker on it for you. Her will even included the words "When I go, don't put on some big event. Don't make a big deal out of it."

She'd also specified that she wanted to be cremated and have her ashes buried with Grandpaw and Grandma at the small Valhalla

Memorial Park Cemetery in North Hollywood. She and I had argued about it more than once. She never really understood how widely loved and admired she was, and she'd protest every time I suggested we buy a larger plot, somewhere more accessible, where her friends and fans could easily come pay their respects.

Not once while she was making those plans did it occur to her that Carrie might go first, and that awful reality inspired her to change her mind.

"You were right," she told me. "You should buy a nicer plot for Carrie, or maybe a crypt, where people can visit her, and someday I'll be there too. And I don't want to be cremated after all."

Part of the reason Mom had originally wanted to be cremated was that she never wanted her body to be left alone when she died, or run the risk of someone somehow getting a hold of it. When she changed her mind about being cremated, I promised I would personally see to it that there was someone with her every second until she was safely buried—which led to her going into a panic about where Carrie's body was and who had it.

She was completely undone by the news that Carrie's body had been taken directly from Cedars-Sinai to the coroner's office.

"What are they doing to her? Who gave them permission to do that?" she demanded.

The answer was, none of us. We'd all fought it. We didn't need or want an autopsy. To this day I still don't understand it. An autopsy for what, exactly? To figure out that Carrie died of drugs and "sleep apnea"? As if we needed it confirmed that drugs were involved? And if we didn't need to know that, who the hell did?

The thought of Carrie's body being alone, lying on a steel table somewhere and dissected by some stranger, was abhorrent to Mom. She wanted her daughter back.

"I miss her," she said. "I really love her." Then she looked up at me, suddenly anxious, and added, "That's not to say I don't love you, dear." I pointed out something that had always been a core fact of my life—Mom and I had been crystal clear on how we felt about each other since the day I was born. It didn't just go without saying, it transcended words.

She was still stressed out about where Carrie's body was, and still asking questions about it every few minutes, as she drifted into other subjects, including Christi's dad, Larry Zabel. Larry had passed away in 2012, four years after Christi, and Mom had always agreed with me that he was a great, very special man. "Why couldn't I have fallen for a guy like him?" she asked rhetorically, and we both smiled a little.

Whatever she needed to do to process the unimaginable reality of Carrie's death was fine with me, and focusing on helping Mom through this was easier than focusing on the grief that was trying to interject itself and drop me to my knees. Finally Mom closed her eyes and dozed off, and I slowly walked next door, back to Carrie's house, past the huge, growing crowd of reporters, fans, security and *Star Wars* laser swords, Princess Leia dolls, and other tributes to Carrie people were bringing in her memory.

I couldn't help but think what an unfair time it was for Carrie to leave. What a waste. She was at the top of her game, acting, writing, singing, more comfortable in her own skin than I'd seen her in many, many years, maybe ever. She should have had a chance to stay longer and enjoy it. . . . Or was the top of her game exactly the right launching pad for her to just take off and keep on going? Or did it even matter, when in the end, all the answers to all the questions I could possibly come up with led back to the same bottom line: Carrie was gone. The big sister who held my hand when I took my first baby steps because Mom was too busy memorializing the event on film. My favorite playmate; the confidante who shared my deepest childhood secrets; my hilarious, brilliant, occasionally impossible best friend, roommate, and travel buddy; my princess, now everyone's Princess; my girl was gone, and there wasn't a damned thing I could do about it.

Cat and I stayed in Billie's room off Carrie's kitchen, close to Mom and her nurse, Josephine, on that first long, sleepless night.

The next morning Cat headed back to the ranch to round up some clothes and toiletries for both of us. We'd driven down separately on Friday the twenty-third, the day of Carrie's collapse, without pausing to grab more than a few basic necessities. It was now Wednesday the twenty-eighth, and God only knew how long we'd be in L.A., taking care of Mom and taking care of business in the surreal, overwhelming wake of losing Carrie. Between friends, reporters, and talk-show producers, the phone was ringing off the hook, and I kept having to remind myself that falling apart wasn't an option. I'd have to do that some other time. For now, I had to hold it together, if only to try to keep Mom as calm as possible.

It was almost 11:00 A.M. before she woke up, later than usual, but Josephine and I were glad she'd been able to sleep at all. When she did wake up, she was groggy but completely lucid and aware of what was going on.

"I want to be with Carrie," she said into my eyes.

I sat beside her on the bed. "We're people of faith, Mom. This would be unbearable if we weren't. But we're blessed to know that we'll be with Carrie again, we'll all be together again."

I was talking about someday. I had no idea she was talking about now, that she was planning her departure.

She settled back onto her pillows as if she were going to take a nap.

Within moments, she was snoring. I'd never heard her snore before.

Then, a moment later, I noticed a slight droop in her lip and called in the nurse.

Mom's vital signs were normal, but I didn't buy it. Something wasn't right, and I yelled to her assistant Donald to call Mom's doctor, Dr. Kattan, and tell him we needed him ASAP. By the time he got to the house, I'd opened Mom's eyelids and shined a flashlight into her eyes. Her pupils were fixed and dilated and didn't respond to the light.

Josephine reviewed Mom's vital signs with Dr. Kattan as soon as he got there. Despite how normal they were, he agreed that Mom was in trouble and we needed an ambulance. I texted Billie and Cat that we were on our way to Cedars, with Mom this time.

The scene out front was insane. Carrie had been gone for only twenty-four hours. Now here was an ambulance inching its way to the gate while Gavin's security team cleared a path through the surging mass of people and *Star Wars* mementos. A few photographers managed to snap shots of the paramedics loading Mom into the back of the emergency vehicle, and me climbing in right behind her.

The EMTs checked her vital signs one more time. Normal. It made no sense. No one seemed to have any idea what was going on.

Next thing I knew we were swallowed up by the organized frenzy of the emergency room entrance. Mom was immediately put on limited life support and wheeled off for an MRI. By the time a female neurologist came to escort me into a consultation room, Mom's cardiologist Dr. Karpman was with me.

The neurologist closed the door, turned to me, and said, "Your mother has had a massive hemorrhage at the base of her brain." It was that moment that Bryan and Billie joined us.

Dr. Karpman nodded and took a stab at optimism with something like "Well, obviously it won't be a quick, easy recovery, but . . ."

The neurologist cut him off. "I'm sorry, Dr. Karpman, but you haven't seen the MRI. I have. I'm afraid there's no coming back from this."

The only words I could manage were "How long?"

"Your mother may breathe for a while on life support, but her system is shutting down." She paused before adding a simple, straightforward "Maybe an hour."

I made an urgent handful of calls to the people who were closest to Mom, and we spent that hour at Mom's bedside in her hospital room. Billie and Bryan were there, of course, as well as Uncle Bill, Donald, and Mom's cherished friend Margie Duncan.

By the time Cat got there, after setting a land speed record from the ranch to Cedars-Sinai, Mom was gone.

I knew it wasn't Mom lying so still in that bed. It wasn't Mom who'd been rushed to the hospital a couple of hours earlier. It was just the vessel she'd traveled in on this earth for eighty-four amazing years. The mom I loved, the mom I would grieve and miss for the rest of my life, had left while I was sitting beside her on her own bed, in the home she loved, right next to Carrie's, and she'd given me the privilege of seeing her leave.

Needless to say, the news that Debbie Reynolds had died just a day after her daughter Carrie Fisher passed on hit the international press like a nuclear bomb. It was a huge story, no doubt about it. I don't have the words to describe how overwhelming it was for the family while we were reeling from the shock and the loss of the two most powerful, definitive women in our lives.

The common theory about Mom's passing was that, after losing Carrie, Debbie Reynolds died of a broken heart. Take it from the son who was there, who knew her better than anyone else on earth—that's simply not true. Debbie Reynolds willed herself right off this planet to personally see to it that Carrie would never be alone. That had been her driving force all of Carrie's life, including having me so that Carrie wouldn't be an only child, and it continued to be her driving force when Carrie left.

And I became laser-focused on keeping my promise to Mom and doing the same for her.

Between Gavin de Becker's Marine Corps security guards and me, Mom's body was never alone from the moment she took her last breath. I called a variety of mortuaries until I found one that approved both of my demands: round-the-clock security for Mom, and Cat being allowed to do her makeup, as she'd done a thousand times before when she and Mom were in Mom's bedroom doing the "girl stuff" that delighted them. No way would Mom have rested in peace knowing that the last time her loved ones saw her, she had no eyebrows. (The MGM Studios makeup department shaved her eyebrows when she was a teenage starlet, and they never grew back.) By the time Cat was finished, Mom didn't look like a wax figure of her former self. She looked beautiful, glowing, and healthy, like Debbie Reynolds getting some well-deserved sleep. That was a great comfort to everyone who asked to see her before her casket was closed and she took her final journey.

Billie and I had looked for an urn for Carrie's ashes, but we couldn't find anything we thought she would have chosen. Then a brainstorm hit. One of Carrie's most prized possessions was a giant porcelain Prozac capsule she'd come across somewhere,

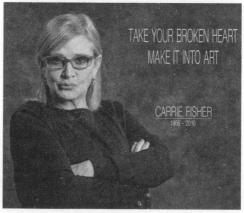

Remembering My Girls.

an antique marketing display prop from the 1950s. She'd moved that giant pill from one house to another over the years, and she even had it duplicated in tile as part of the kitchen floor design of her Coldwater Canyon house. Not only would it make a perfect urn for her ashes, with some delicate modifications by my old friend Fred Walecki, but Billie and I also knew that Carrie would probably have chosen it herself if she'd known what was coming.

Carrie's Prozac urn sat beside Mom's casket at the funeral service. Then, in private, after the service, we placed it inside Mom's casket where it belonged. Mom and Carrie are together on earth in a beautiful spot at Forest Lawn, and they're together for eternity on the Other Side. I don't just believe that, I know that; and while I'll always have to do it through tears sometimes, I celebrate that fact, and them, every day of my life.

And on my behalf and theirs, thank you for the joy, appreciation, and love you so generously showed them, that inspired and propelled my girls throughout their lives. I can tell you first-hand, from the bottom of my heart, they felt exactly the same way about you.

EPILOGUE

As I write this, it's been a year since Mom left to be with Carrie on the Other Side. The holidays were tough, but we were determined to celebrate—Mom would have been furious if we'd spent Christmas, her favorite holiday, giving in to grief.

Cat and I invited family and friends to our house in Las Vegas. We brought Mom's year-round, fully decorated Christmas tree from her living room to ours for the occasion, and Uncle Bill was able to make the trip from North Hollywood. As our reluctant patriarch, he took his place at the head of a table set with Mom's best china, flatware, crystal, and decorations for the first Christmas dinner he'd eaten in eighty-five years without his little sister.

We were lucky and grateful to have him. On New Year's Eve of 2016, four days after Carrie passed on and three days after Mom joined her, I got an urgent call that Uncle Bill was in the emergency room at St. Joseph's in Burbank, suffering from congestive heart failure. I raced over in the middle of the night and found him lying there swollen and hooked up to machines that had become far too familiar to me in the past couple of weeks. I couldn't imagine losing him and having to get through one more death in the family when the reality of the first two hadn't begun to sink in yet. But he pulled through, thank God, and he's now alive and well in the La Maida house he shared with Mom, the house she made sure will be his for the rest of his life, being cared for by Mom's amazing nurse, Josephine.

Looking back, it's been one hell of a year.

On January 5, 2017, Billie and Bryan and I hosted a private

gathering at Carrie's house. There were lots of tears and hilarious stories and memories among guests like Meryl Streep, George Lucas, Penny Marshall, Gwyneth Paltrow, Jamie Lee Curtis, Gavin de Becker, Meg Ryan, Richard Dreyfuss, and Paul Allen. Gavin gave a great speech about his decades of friendship with Mom and Carrie, and Meryl sang one of Carrie's trademark songs, "Happy Days Are Here Again." The next day about a hundred of us gathered at Forest Lawn for final good-byes, including an insightfully beautiful speech by Richard Dreyfuss, before Mom's casket, with Carrie's Prozac urn nestled inside next to Mom, was sealed into its tomb.

On January 10 Meryl was presented with the Cecil B. DeMille Award at the Golden Globes. She ended her powerful acceptance speech with a sweet, tender "As my friend, the dear departed Princess Leia, said to me once, 'Take your broken heart, make it into art.'"

It was January 19 when I got a shocking call that Carrie's and my old friend Miguel Ferrer had died of throat cancer. Miguel and I grew up together. I loved him. We'd played golf together not long before and had a great time laughing and reminiscing, and we'd put in a lot of phone time when Mom and Carrie "left the building." I knew he was sick, but he was such an optimistic, positive guy that he never even hinted that he might be on his way out. I wish I had a do-over with Miguel—our lives were so busy that we didn't get to see each other nearly as often as I'd have liked in those last few years, as if I needed yet another reminder to never take it for granted that there will be a "next time."

In late January there were women's marches around the world protesting the incoming Trump administration, and we were so touched, in fact blown away, by the fact that Princess Leia, aka Carrie Fisher, became an icon of those marches. Carrie would have been thrilled, having less to do with politics in general than with the fact that her mission as a fierce, funny, outspoken champion of women was being so passionately carried on. As I told a *Vanity Fair* columnist, "What an enormous influence she's had on women. Women around the world, women who are struggling for their identity, for their position, for equality. . . . We started to see how many people idolized her." Thanks, all of you. "A woman's place is in the resistance" indeed.

On March 25 we held a public memorial for Mom and Carrie in the Hall of Liberty at Forest Lawn. To appease Mom's dislike of that kind of thing, or of any kind of big deal being made over her, we called it a "show," for the twelve hundred people who attended and the worldwide audience who watched the live-stream of it. Everyone involved in putting it together—Cat, Dusty, Henry, Ryan Hathaway, Jon Haas, and countless others—worked so hard and so joyfully, basing every decision on the answer to the question "Would the girls like this?" A Marine Color Guard was there, honoring Mom's devotion to war veterans dating as far back as her entertaining the troops in Korea. Dancers and teachers from the Debbie Reynolds Studios performed. The Gay Men's Chorus of Los Angeles brought down the house with a spectacular rendition of "True Colors." There were film clips and home movies galore. John Williams, who composed the stunning "Leia's Theme," not only gave us permission to use his music for the service but told me that if we were having an orchestra, he'd be happy to conduct. Dan Aykroyd, Gavin de Becker, Mom's cherished Thalians friend Ruta Lee, and so many others spoke and sang and danced.

As it turned out, one of the most touching moments was kind of an accident. With a giant photo of Princess Leia looking down on the stage from the overhead screen, R2-D2 made his entrance from the wings, making sad R2-D2 noises as he searched for her. Finally he stopped to stare at her picture, and I ended up spontaneously joining him, sitting on the floor beside him with my arm around him. What no one realized was that actually he was stuck, and what looked like my moving to hug him was really my moving to get him unstuck. But it worked all over the place, and even choked me up, as did the whole perfect afternoon, and we all came away knowing that "the girls" wouldn't have changed a thing.

Bright Lights was honored with a wealth of award nominations, from the Emmys to the Cannes Golden Eye Awards to the Critics' Choice Documentary Awards. Fisher and Alexis most deservedly won the Best Documentary Feature Audience Award at the prestigious Hot Springs Documentary Film Festival; and I'll always be indebted to the extraordinary Sheila Nevins, our HBO executive producer, for being an all-too-rare combination of "suit" and caring, compassionate human being. Thank you again, Sheila, and Fisher and Lexi, and everyone else involved in *Bright Lights* from the bottom of my heart. Needless to say, when we were filming that complex ninety-five-minute family love story, we had no way of knowing we were actually shooting a posthumous tribute to Carrie Fisher and Debbie Reynolds. All things considered, the timing still amazes me.

By far the most monumental, emotionally, and physically exhausting challenge of 2017 was going through each and every item owned by two women who were born collectors and deciding what to keep, what to give to special friends that hadn't already been designated, what to donate to the various charities and schools that were close to Mom's and Carrie's hearts, and what to sell at the Profiles in History auction we'd scheduled for September. I don't know how many times Billie and I walked through both of their houses and came away too overwhelmed to decide much of anything. One notable exception was the day we passed the Tesla Carrie had ordered while we were in Telluride just a few months earlier. I reminded Billie that it belonged to her now, to which Billie, as generous as her mother, replied, "I think she would like you to have it."

For a while we talked about re-creating Carrie's writing room and Mom's sitting room at DR Studios. Then we were hit with a painful slap of reality: Sentiment or no sentiment, the tax laws made it impossible for us to keep DR Studios, and we had to sell it. So much for how much that place meant to Mom and so many other people, and so much for our idea of housing a mini-Carrie-and-Debbie museum there. Now, in addition to relocating those rooms, we were facing a whole new Herculean task: Every spare corner, nook, cranny, and cubbyhole of the 19,000-square-foot building that housed DR Studios was filled with still more treasures of Mom's, and every one of those treasures had to be cleared out by the time escrow closed. Since there's "no such word as *can't*," my crew and I got it done—I'm still not sure just how.

The good news about DR Studios is that the buyer leased it back to a couple of wonderful young choreographers/teachers; and the studio will be open and operating for at least the next year, with additional plans under way for a possible franchise.

The three-day Profiles in History auction in September went well, with 1,500 lots sold—maybe about 10 percent of the treasures in Mom's and Carrie's collections. The other 90 percent of them are safe and sound in giant warehouses, one in Las Vegas and one at the ranch. It's safe to say there will be more auctions.

And speaking of the ranch, we put it on the market at the same time the auction was held, and we're still looking for the very special buyer it will take to truly appreciate it. Christi and I were around thirty years old when I bought the ranch, so we didn't bat an eye at how much work it was. I'm in my late fifties now; and as much as I will always love that ranch, Cat and I are determined to downsize and simplify our lives rather than find as many ways as possible to wear ourselves out. Our house in Las Vegas is a perfect home base for us and our animals. Sadly, both Yippi and Nugget have gone on to hang out with Debbie and Carrie and the rest of the family, but we have enough chickens, doves, pigeons, and a neighborhood Cooper's hawk to keep us on our toes. And Mom's little house on the compound, where Uncle Bill and other special guests stay when they come to visit, is so her, so magically filled with her most treasured things, that you almost get the feeling she could come bursting through the door at any moment.

Carrie's and Mom's houses on Coldwater Canyon belong to Billie, as Debbie and Carrie wanted, and Carrie's house is currently being remodeled. Every square inch was eclectically, definitively Carrie's, like living inside her head. Now that Carrie's moved on, it's getting ready for a new identity.

Cat's joyfully busy turbo-charging Cat Cosmetics and working on a new stage show for her upcoming 2018 tour. She's also pursuing going into private hypnotherapy practice in Las Vegas and Los Angeles.

In addition to a year's worth of sorting, hauling, storing, donating, auctioning, and cherishing the treasures Mom and Carrie left behind, I've been writing this book, building a family website, and continuing with a project Carrie and I were working on together—the bible for an only slightly fictional "coming of age" television series called *813 Greenway Drive*. So stay tuned.

Last but certainly not least, on December 14, 2017, I attended the Grauman's Chinese Theatre premiere of *The Last Jedi*. I marveled to myself and to the press how amazing it was to remember standing there forty years earlier, having no idea what *Star Wars* was going to become, for the world and for Carrie. And now there I was, forty years later, literally in my mom's footprints in the cement of that historic forecourt, cutting the ribbon on a plaque that read: *Carrie Fisher, Beloved by Fans Worldwide, December 14, 2017. Dedicated to Carrie by the TCL Chinese Theatre, Her* Star Wars *Home Since 1977. "We love you, Carrie."*

Carrie and Billie both knocked it out of the park with their performances, and I got a huge kick out of seeing Carrie's dog Gary in his brief cameo role. Everyone involved outdid themselves in *The Last Jedi*, and God bless those fans who camped out a week ahead of time to be first in line to see it.

Of course, neither George Lucas nor anyone else knew what was coming in real life when they made that movie and put Princess Leia in a coma on life support. It was excruciating for me to see art imitating life so closely, less than a year after sitting by my sister's hospital bed watching her in exactly that same condition trying to survive. Oddly, it was a memory of Mom and a movie called *Charlotte's Web* that got me through those scenes in *The Last Jedi*.

I was in my teens, in our projection room on Greenway Drive, watching the animated feature *Charlotte's Web* with Mom, who was the voice of Charlotte the Spider in that movie. I was loving it until the point came in the film when Charlotte was dying. Some combination of the story itself and the fact that it was my mom's voice talking about the cycle of life and the natural inevitability of death, and leaving her babies behind to carry on with lives of their own broke my heart, and suddenly I was crying inconsolably. Mom put her arms around me to comfort me and reminded me that what was going on on-screen was storytelling, it wasn't real life, and I should always remember to keep those two things separate when I was watching a movie.

It was literally a flashback to that moment with Mom, and that movie, that helped me through that sequence in *The Last Jedi*—it was Princess Leia, not Carrie, in a coma up there on that screen, Princess Leia, not Carrie, on life support, a spectacular character in a spectacular fictional story, nothing more, nothing less. In real life, Carrie was already happy and thriving and at peace with Mom, not in a galaxy far, far away, but very nearby, on the Other Side, cheering us on as our real lives continue to evolve into 2018 and beyond.

And however you choose to define it, may the Force be with you.

ACKNOWLEDGMENTS

It's an understatement to say that properly acknowledging the important people in the sixtieth year of my journey is a challenge. I'm resisting the temptation to leave it at a simple, "See previous four hundred pages." My life has been extraordinary not only because of my mother and sister but also because of so many others who've helped shape me into the man I am and am still becoming. Most of you will find yourselves in the pages of *My Girls*. To those of you who didn't make it into the final edit, you may not be in this book, but you are in my heart, and I thank you.

To Cat: My love, my wife, my girl, my partner, the best friend I have in this world. You were meant for me, and I was meant for you. You've made me believe in soulmates, sent by the angels just for me. Your childlike wonder and enthusiasm brightens and inspires me every single day. May our life journey together continue to be the great love story it's been since the night Henry saw to it that we officially met. As Mom summed it up so perfectly, more times than either of us can count, "You're a good girl."

To Uncle Bill: Thank you for not making me the oldest surviving member of the family. Your sister Debbie always described you as "quiet, steady and reliable"—quiet by necessity, because who could get a word in with this group; steady, which was one hell of a feat considering the rollercoaster ride of a life we've had; and reliable, yes, in fact the greatest brother and uncle there ever was or ever will be.

To Bryan Lourd: It is said that crisis doesn't build character, it reveals it, and you've been revealed to be a man Cat calls the father we all wish we'd had. For one of the busiest men on earth you've been a rock and a stable life raft for Billie, and that is a gift to me. You make your daughter, my niece, your priority. Imagine that in Hollywood. Thank you for being exactly who you were and are every step of the way.

To Billie Lourd: It's been my joy to watch you grow from a tiny baby to a smart, gifted, beautiful woman who, from the very beginning, has always possessed her own distinct, remarkable identity. I want to share something important I've learned in this lifetime: That shadow of celebrity in which we both grew up really isn't a shadow at all, it's just a part of who we are, a part that makes us stronger, and you're the strongest of us all. You're the reason we had Carrie for so many extra innings. I love you, and I'm more than proud of you.

To John Courtney and Major Brunk: You were my wingmen before we even knew what that word meant. We made some of the best movies ever produced by eleven-year-olds, and you had a hand in lighting the flame of my lifelong passion for filmmaking.

To Richard Landers: You've been an important part of my life and my creativity since I was a teenager, and like a second son to my mother. Thank you for taking such great care of her sound throughout her career. I never had to worry, because you were there, and I'll always be grateful to you for being such a good, loving son to her to the very end.

To Joey Singer, Mom's music director and conductor: Thank you for always letting her know she was supported, before, during and after her shows. She loved you, as we do, as a part of our family.

To Bob Lange: Best. Entertainment Attorney. Ever. My eternal gratitude, Bob, for taking such excellent care of my family for all these years. You are truly a rare breed in your animal kingdom.

To my mother's long-time assistant and companion Donald Light: I know it's not easy to devote your life to taking care of someone, but you did it, and you did it so well. Mom called you "her soldier." You stepped into countless situations that would have crumbled a lesser man and pulled her through them without so much as a change of expression. Thank you for so much, including your care of the memorial site that makes Debbie Reynolds's and Carrie Fisher's fans feel their presence when they come to visit. I'm glad Mom didn't let you quit after the first auction. I hope you are too.

To Miguel Ferrer: I miss you, and I always will. Your graduation to Heaven was a shock to me, and I'm still processing it. What a ride we had together, and being the archivist I am, I've got the photos to prove it. I know you'll take good care of Mom and Carrie and my grandparents until I get there.

To Henry Cutrona, my "brother by another mother": You haven't just been by my side for decades of pain and glory, you helped jar my memory and bring back so much of it during the writing of this book. There really are not enough words.

To Fred Walecki: What a man you are, the real deal, my spiritual champion and my loyal friend. You're the man who says, "I'm on my way," before a crisis even hits the news, getting things done when everyone else is saying nothing can be done. You and Henry are two honorable lifelong friends I can always count on. If my worth is measured by friendship, I'm a rich man because of you both.

To Dori Hanaway: Thank you for being my mother's loyal, treasured friend for so many years. You and Mom laid a lot of the groundwork for *My Girls* when you wrote *Unsinkable* together, and she adored you.

To Jon Nappa, my longtime friend and writing buddy: We wrote the 813 Greenway Drive screenplay together and, in the process, brought the early chapters of this book into such clear, technicolor focus for me that they were that much easier to write. My thanks, always.

And speaking of this book—

To my intrepid literary agent Jennifer DeChiara, who guided

me safely into the expert hands of Lisa Sharkey and her A-team, Matt Harper and Elissa Cohen, at HarperCollins: Thank you all for making *My Girls* a daunting, joyful reality.

And to Lindsay Harrison, the best writing partner I could have hoped for: There is no chapter of my life I didn't open up to you without a moment of hesitation and editing, and for me, that took an enormous amount of trust. Thank you for conveying my stories, my life and my love for my girls so beautifully, and for keeping me and this book moving and on track. I couldn't have done *My Girls* with anyone else, and it was a pleasure sharing a foxhole with such an outstanding writer and woman.

And to Vanessa, Brandon and James Rivers, Jon Haas, Mark Sheppard, Dusty Ebsen, Fred Pierson, Art Kelm, Margie Duncan, Ruta Lee, Armando Garbada, Gavin de Becker, Dan Aykroyd, Bootie Bell Chewning, David Rudich, David De Salvo, Kevin Sasaki, Connie Freiberg, Ken Copeland, George Lucas, Warren Buffett, Steve Wynn, Sheila Nevins, Joe Maddalena, Nancy Seltzer, Fisher Stevens, Alexis Bloom, Barbara Strong, Emmett Alston, Pinky Babajian, Penny Worth, Michael Gonzales, Art Petrie, Dennis King, Josephine Bouchard . . . and several others I'll think of right after this book has gone to print and it's too late to add you . . .

Each of you knows why I'm grateful to you, I just hope you know how much.

JUN - - 2018

YEADON PUBLIC LIBRARY
809 LONGACRE BLVD.
YEADON, PA 19050
(610) 623-4090